NOTRE DAME COLLEGE OF EDUCATION
MOUNT PLEASANT
LIVERPOOL L3 5SP

HISTORY.

Sig. Head of Dept. J. N. McGurk

FROM THEODORIC TO CHARLEMAGNE

ART OF THE WORLD

A Series of Regional Histories of the Visual Arts

FROM THEODORIC TO CHARLEMAGNE

A HISTORY OF THE DARK AGES IN THE WEST

BY

PAOLO VERZONE

Translated by Pamela Waley

METHUEN — LONDON

Title-page:

Apse mosaic. S. Apollinare in Classe, Ravenna.
6th century. Cf. p. 75

CONTENTS

5

LIST OF COLOUR PLATES

LIST OF FIGURES

ACKNOWLEDGEMENTS

The undermentioned kindly allowed reproduction of the plates on the following pages:

Cambridge, The Master and Fellows of Corpus Christi College	169	Paris, Bibliothèque Nationale	141, 166, 167, 187, 195, 199, 200
Chur, Domschatz	218	Paris, Musée de Cluny	152, 153
Dublin, National Museum of Ireland	235	Stockholm, Royal Library	243
Dublin, Trinity College	225, 227, 231	Trier, Domschatz	206
Florence, Biblioteca Laurenziana	164	Vatican City, Biblioteca Apostolica	102, 147, 148
Florence, San Marco	172		
Kremsmünster, Stift	216	Vienna, Österreichische Nationalbibliothek	210
London, British Museum	162, 237, 238, 242		
Monza, Tesoro del Duomo	131, 133, 134	Würzburg, Universitätsbibliothek	203, 204

The plates on the following pages were kindly supplied by:

	Page
E. Böhm, Mainz	183
Leif Geiges, Freiburg	232
The Green Studio, Dublin	158, 225, 227, 231
Atelier Niko Haas, Trier	206
Hans H. Hofstätter, Baden-Baden	181
R. Kammel, Rastatt	57
A. Luisa, Brescia	89, 97, 125, 126, 131, 133, 134, 179
J. Remmer, Munich	222, 223

	Page
Foto Scala, Florence	30, 119, 164, 172, 175
Sears & Sons, Cambridge	169
M. Seidel, Mittelwald	152, 153
J. Skeel, Pluckley	162
P. Verzone, Turin	3, 41, 55, 76
Theo Vonow, Chur	218

The remaining plates were kindly provided by the museums and institutions concerned.

PREFACE

In earlier studies that I have published on European art between the late Roman period and the year 1000 the problem of the relationship between Byzantium and the West received only superficial treatment. I cannot today regret this prudence, since at that time my knowledge of Near Eastern art was almost entirely derived from books. Since then circumstances have permitted me to spend some years in the ancient capital of the Byzantine Empire, to travel widely in Anatolia and to participate in several seasons of excavation at Hierapolis in Phrygia. This has enabled me to become well acquainted with the monuments of early Christian art in Constantinople and Asia Minor as well as with those of the Classical period, and to gain familiarity with the finest examples, in which Hellenistic elegance, in some form or another, is always evident.

I can now undertake a survey of the buildings and works of art of the 'Dark Ages' in the West from a particular standpoint, studying them, that is, not only in themselves, as representing stages of an evolution, but also as they are affected by the Byzantine world.

The result of these researches provides the substance of this study, in which the phases of the enduring influence of the Eastern empire, from 425 to 800, are examined and explained. During this period of unremitting struggle Byzantium fought energetically to defend step by step its European possessions, at first against the encroaching Germanic tribes and later, when these had merged with the local populations, against the new nations of Europe. We shall see how in the course of this tenacious defence the furthest provinces – Gaul and Spain – were the first to be abandoned, and how the focus of the struggle then shifted and the fulcrum of defence became Italy, vital because of its economic resources and, above all, its geographical position. History records that, after the sudden and triumphant progress of Islam in the eastern basin of the Mediterranean, the Empire was reduced to dire straits and was forced to abandon the defence even of the Italian peninsula, maintaining only a few footholds which were finally eliminated by Charlemagne and the Papacy.

The object of the pages which follow is to show that the cultural influence of Byzantium always accompanied the actions of its soldiers, sailors and statesmen, and that it continued to spread for some time, even in the lost territories, through religion and through works of art which were acknowledged models of luxury and beauty, eagerly sought after by the great. This supremacy, however, declined in the eighth century, when new forces and ideas, first asserted in the British Isles, in Germany and in Gaul, extended their influence as far as the Mediterranean basin, overthrowing aesthetic and cultural principles whose norm of formal refinement was rooted in Mediterranean traditions. The stages of the struggle between the young nations of the centre and north of Europe with the over-cultured and over-subtle heirs of Greece and Rome occupy the last pages of this volume, and I hope that they will suffice to illustrate the profound transformation of western thought and taste whose outcome was the birth – on Christmas night, 800 – of a new and revolutionary political organism, the Carolingian Empire, and the emancipation of European art from Byzantium and the classical heritage.

I. THE WESTERN EMPIRE UNDER THE EFFECTIVE TUTELAGE OF THE THEODOSIAN EMPERORS OF CONSTANTINOPLE (425–455)

During the third century A.D., as a consequence of civil wars, the Roman Empire underwent profound social as well as political changes. In the disturbed state of affairs prevailing after these struggles, many families succeeded in greatly enlarging their holdings of land at the expense of the unprotected elements in society, and became an all-powerful oligarchy. These *potentiores* resembled a little the great feudatories of the Middle Ages. They came into possession of civil and religious offices as well as of the most productive land. Though they had been pagan by tradition and culture and were only gradually converted to Christianity, once they had become Christians they often occupied the leading positions in the Church.

The art of the late imperial period mirrors faithfully this refined society, to whose characteristics buildings, marbles, mosaics and paintings all bear witness. Although the so-called 'villa' at Piazza Armerina lies outside our subject, its sumptuousness provides a good instance of that found in aristocratic residences of the period. The religious art of the time, however, is directly connected with our theme and requires treatment here, for there is no substantial change in the direction of artistic development until later, in the eighth century.

As well as living in luxury, the *potentiores* tried to imitate the splendour of the court itself, not only because the imperial Palatium was the last word in this respect but also because their local prestige was dependent on this imitation. At the court everything had to be sublime, both to impress the beholder and to affirm the quasi-divine nature of the Emperor himself. The imperial insignia and diadems, the pavements, throne, canopies, even the sarcophagus in which the corpse of the Emperor Constantine lay in state, were all of gold. So too were the private furnishings: when the Empress Eudoxia, the wife of Arcadius, received Bishop Porphyrius in audience, she did so seated on a golden bed. The same taste for luxury is to be found in building. In the assembly rooms of civic and private palaces and in the principal churches, walls and floors were adorned with marble and porphyry and furnishings and doors with silver and ivory. This fondness for ostentation and costly materials was accompanied by a decline in the respect for formal classical values. The laws of proportion were observed with increasing laxity, then finally abandoned altogether.

There was no longer any interest in the portrayal of personality by physical features, attitude and the expression of a particular emotion: instead of individuals, the essence, the life of the spirit was sought. According to Plotinus, 'a body is beautiful only if it is illumined by the soul.' In consequence the eye, the mirror of the soul, became the most important feature of the human figure. The people portrayed in fourth-, fifth- and sixth-century miniatures, mosaics and frescoes seem to have a special vivacity in their gaze. This derives from a white spot within the eye which serves to accentuate and enliven it, and it is this apparent flashing of the eye which gives such figures an air of interior exaltation.

Philosophy of art

The presentation of abstract, spiritual values was an essential element in scenes of ceremonial, sacrifices, imperial donations and heavenly consistories. In such ritual compositions, which were fully in harmony with a rigidly hieratical society, every personage portrayed had a position which defined his rank, and supremacy was indicated by dimensions larger than life. High spiritual status was portrayed by means of a gaze that was both upward- and forward-looking, to suggest communication with the world of ideas and with those celestial beings beyond the mere reality of the senses, which was considered an inferior form of existence.

In processions the Emperor had always to be motionless, to indicate the impassivity of a superhuman character. Ammianus Marcellinus tells us (XVI, 10, 9) that when Constantius II first entered Rome 'he was greeted by joyful acclamation, but he himself was motionless, as he was when he appeared in his provinces, seeming rather a likeness of a man than a human.' The saints, too, practised this impassivity which typified higher natures: Gregory Nazianzen relates admiringly of St. Basil that in circumstances which might have caused him to show emotion, 'in his body, his eyes and his thoughts he was without movement . . . as upright as a stele erected to the honour of God.' (*Eulogy of St. Basil*, 52, 2.)

In a world dominated by notions of this sort it was natural that symbols which were best calculated to express abstract ideas should gain a firm hold and should come to replace traditional realistic representation.

Christian architecture

The new religion triumphed with the Theodosian edicts of 391 prohibiting any manifestation of paganism. Throughout every province of the Empire countless buildings were raised dedicated to the Christian

14

rite. Each town had a bishop. In the West his see normally comprised two churches (one for the bishop and the other for the usual religious services) and a baptistery. In the different quarters of the city were minor churches, and outside the walls other cemetery churches (sometimes dedicated to the Apostles) and *martyria*.

The cult of the martyrs was already beginning in the late fourth century. The buildings which contained the bodies and relics of these witnesses to the faith were like large tombs. Originally, it appears, special services involving processions and panegyrics were held within them, but not the Eucharistic synopsis. They were visited constantly by devout pilgrims, both local inhabitants and strangers, particularly at anniversaries, and rooms or porticoes had to be provided to accommodate the large numbers of these visitors. Much light is thrown on the functions, iconography and Christian symbolism of these martyria by the works of Paulinus of Nola. Paulinus was born of a family of *potentiores* in Aquitaine. After a magnificent early life he moved at the age of forty (in 396) to Cimitile, near Nola, where he possessed a large estate, and devoted himself to the cult of St. Felix, an eastern priest, who was venerated locally.

Through his acquaintance with aristocratic *milieux* in Spain, Aquitaine, Rome and Campania, we may look on Paulinus as a representative of the cultivated society of the whole Mediterranean world. In the years 401 to 404 he built a church in honour of St. Felix. Describing this church in a letter (*Epistola* 32) he says that the exterior had two colonnades and that four rooms *(cubiculi)* were arranged laterally to the nave 'for those who prayed secretly or meditated on the law of God and also for the burial of the religious and of members of the household'. Paulinus gives the text of the metrical inscriptions which were to be found throughout the building, including one in the apse which is particularly interesting because it concerns the Mystery of the Trinity: excavation has revealed that the main apse of Cimitile was trilobate, consisting of two small apses within the curve of the larger one. He also mentions that Christ was portrayed as a Lamb on a rock from which flowed four springs (the 'living streams of the Evangelists'), together with the dove of the Holy Ghost. Within a shining globe was a cross and around it a garland of twelve doves, the Apostles. More information can be gained from Paulinus' *Carmen* 27, which states that in front of the church was an atrium, where St. Felix' tomb was apparently situated; here gathered 'dense crowds', who were accommodated in cells *(habitacula)*, from the windows of which could be seen relics of the Apostles and the tomb of Felix.

Martyria

Cimitile

15

Paulinus had adorned the new church with paintings of scenes from the Old Testament. 'It is an uncommon custom to paint churches,' he tells us, 'but in this particular case, the faithful being for the most part illiterate peasants, wont to honour the gods with the stomach, the paintings serve as a distraction, so that they pass the time deciphering and admiring them instead of excessive drinking.'

Eliminating the elements of rhetoric and poetry, as well as the affected disdain of the nobleman for the ignorance of his rustic worshippers, we may deduce the following:

1) in the porticoed atrium of the martyrium was the hospice for the pilgrims, who passed the night eating and drinking in honour of the saint;

2) there were four lateral rooms within the cemetery church, for contemplation and burial;

3) there were paintings of Old Testament scenes in the nave;

4) in the apse was a Cross in a circle of light surrounded by twelve doves, the Apostles; and the Lamb, the ancient symbol of the Divine Sacrifice, was portrayed on a rock whence flowed four rivers, the Evangelists.

Role of the Court The more important churches and martyria were often built with the aid of gifts from the Emperor. This assistance usually took the form of marble columns (many marble quarries being state property) but occasionally the Emperor might also provide the plans for the building, drawn up by his court architects. Marcus Diaconus tells us that in Arcadius' time Bishop Porphyrius, thanks to the intercession of Eudoxia, succeeded in getting an imperial order that the hated Marneion, a pagan sanctuary at Gaza, should be demolished, and that later the Empress sent the bishop, by boat, the columns for the church that was to be erected on the site of the Marneion, together with plans for the building, which was put up under the direction of a local architect.

The concentration of wealth and power in the hands of a few may have given rise to an elegant culture and the production of an élite art, but it had unfortunate consequences as far as the Empire was *Popular resentment* concerned. The poverty and insecurity of the great majority of the population naturally led to mistrust and resentment not only among the poorer elements but even within the aristocracy. Men who had turned to Christianity often took up the cause of the disinherited classes. Around 440 Salvianus, a priest of Marseilles who had been born of a noble family, wrote a bitter invective against the corruption and arbitrary arrogance of officials. Not a few Romans, he said, 'preferred to live poor but free in the lands of the barbarians rather than as slaves in their own'.

This feeling of pessimism and discontent played its part in increasing the pressure of the 'barbarians' in both east and west. These so-called 'barbarians' were of Germanic descent: an eastern group of peoples comprised the Goths, Vandals, Burgundians, Gepids and Lombards; another, the western Germans, included Franks, Saxons, Frisians and Thuringians. The Scandinavians made up a third group: for a long time they remained in their original area of habitation and it was only in the seventh century that they made their appearance on the western European scene. *'Barbarians'*

The Goths settled from the third century onwards in the lands around the Danube. They consisted of two distinct federations, the Ostrogoths in the Crimea and the area of the Don, the Visigoths between the Dniester and the Danube. A pastoral people, their inescapable poverty condemned them to restlessness. In the third century the Huns drove them further towards the imperial provinces, which they invaded. The Emperors attempted to tame these hungry peoples by settling them on the land and by offering them employment in the army, but this policy did not solve the problem and the admission of Goths into the army proved to have its dangers. *Goths*

When the Visigoths at last moved westwards as an army, under Alaric, they removed the threat to Constantinople only to imperil the Western Empire. The first invasions of Italian territory, which occurred in 400 and 402, were unsuccessful, Stilicho overcoming the invaders at Pollenza. Nevertheless the gathering of troops in order to defend the peninsula meant that the Rhine military frontier had to be dismantled, and Franks, Vandals, Burgundians, Suevi and Alans were able to cross freely into Gaul, where they raided and devastated a very wide area. *Visigoths in Italy*

After the execution of Stilicho (408), the way was open for Alaric to enter Italy, and in 410 he sacked the city of Rome; but this dramatic victory did nothing to solve the real problems of the Visigoths, who needed food, not works of art. The Byzantine fleet had effectively blockaded the coast so that they were unable to establish a foothold in central or southern Italy, and they had to move further south in the hope of passing on to Sicily and thence to the wealth of North Africa. But this proved impossible to achieve, and after Alaric's death in Calabria the Visigoths retraced their steps under the leadership of Athaulf. Since Illyria was now occupied by other barbarians even poorer than they, they forced their way into Provence and Aquitaine,

17

settling there with the consent of Honorius. Athaulf had captured Honorius' sister Galla Placidia at Rome, and he now married her at Narbonne (414), with Roman pomp and a rich display of jewellery. His aim was to set his rule on a legitimate basis and, in time, to instal his people within the realm of Roman civilization.

Orosius reports a significant speech made by Athaulf at the time of his marriage. 'He had once thought of substituting a Gothic state for the Roman one and himself for the Emperor, but he had come to realize that it would be impossible to create a state based on Gothic power alone. His aim was therefore to restore the Roman Empire to its former greatness with the aid of the Goths.'

Arians and Catholics

Unfortunately the fusion of Goths and Romans was to take a long time, owing to a contrast in religion. Though the Visigoths were Christians, they were Arians, convinced adherents of their religious belief; they had their own clergy, and remained isolated from, or even in conflict with, the local Catholic population.

Devastation of Rhenish provinces

Although the Rhenish provinces were not yet under permanent barbarian occupation in the early years of the fifth century, they were much devastated and their productive capacity was badly affected. Excavations have revealed that Roman villas in the Rhineland at Mungersdorf, at Braunsfeld near Cologne, at Nennig, at Oetrange near Trier and at Mayen, all became ruins in the early fifth century, some as the result of fire, others simply because their owners had abandoned them.

Byzantine influence in Italy

After the death of the Emperor Honorius the whole Mediterranean basin was for the last time under the sway of a single ruler, but this only lasted a few months. Soon (in 423) the *primicerius notariorum* John was nominated Emperor in the West. Galla Placidia fled from Ravenna to the shelter of Constantinople, where she begged for help. Theodosius II reacted promptly and effectively, sending two armies from the East, one of which, under Aspar, moved from Dalmatia to Aquileia and then on to capture Ravenna. John was despatched to Aquileia and ignominiously put to death (425). After this victory the court of Constantinople set Valentinian III on the throne with the support of his mother, the energetic and commanding Galla Placidia. For some thirty years, up to 455, the Western Empire was in a position of real subordination to Constantinople, and this was for Europe and for Italy in particular a time in which a certain equilibrium and a relatively stable way of life prevailed.

MAIN BASILICAS IN ITALY
Ravenna

From the time of Honorius the official residence of the court was Ravenna, a port on the Adriatic coast which could be defended and

provisioned by the Byzantine fleet and which was the key both to the
'Gothic line' and to the routes in the Po valley. When this small town
became a capital it gained an episcopal see (transferred from Classe)
as well as churches and public buildings. Of those dating from the
time of the Empress and her son there have survived the church of
S. Giovanni Evangelista and the so-called mausoleum of Galla Placidia.
During the same period other larger buildings were constructed at
Milan and Rome. They too were paid for by the Theodosian dynasty
and all of them, except in Rome, reveal some Byzantine influence.
There can be no doubt that Galla Placidia was in frequent contact
with her nephew Theodosius II. She must often have resided at Constantinople, where according to the *Notitia Urbis Constantinopolitanae*
she had two palaces, one in the first region, the area of the Imperial
See (the *domus Placidiae Augustae*) and the other in the tenth region,
which had formerly been a suburb. The storm endured by the imperial
family which led to the building of S. Giovanni at Ravenna is also
evidence of sea journeys between that city and Constantinople.

APPX. PL. II

*Ravenna,
S. Giovanni
Evangelista*
FIG. I

This church was built to proclaim the devotion of the Theodosian
house to the venerated Apostle, the glory of religion in Asia Minor.
St. John's martyrium had been built at the end of the fourth century
on the hill-side at Ephesus. Dominating the major pagan sanctuary
in Asia Minor, that of Artemis, it stood as a challenge and an affirmation
of the victory of Christianity.

The devotion of the Theodosian family to St. John the Theologian
was manifested in the mosaics. In the apse, Bishop St. Peter Chrysologos,
the consecrator of the basilica, occupied the centre, on the right were
Theodosius II and Athenais-Eudocia, on the left Arcadius and Eudoxia.
The scene consequently represented a glorification of the imperial
family of the East; honour was paid to the western court on the
triumphal arch, where Christ was represented in the centre, in the
act of handing the Gospel to St. John, and on either side were Galla
Placidia, Justa Grata Honoria and Valentinian III led by St. John.

The building is three-aisled, and the equidistant columns of grey
marble are joined by wide arches so that the nave gives an impression
of spaciousness. The Corinthian capitals are spoils and vary in type
but they are surmounted by slender pulvins carved with foliage and
crosses, made for this building, and the original effect, when the floor
was much lower than it is now, must have been very noble. The
presbytery area, with a polygonal apse flanked by two external
rectangular chambers, and the well-lit tribune, similar to the church
of the Acheiropoeitos, Salonika, indicates eastern influence. On the

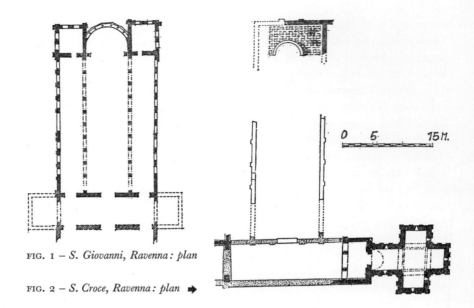

FIG. 1 – *S. Giovanni, Ravenna: plan*

FIG. 2 – *S. Croce, Ravenna: plan* ➡

other hand, the blind arcading on the walls of the aisles, the absence of women's galleries, and the probability that the apse had a flat ceiling (as in some Milanese churches) are typical western features. The church was probably preceded by a narthex, separated from the nave and aisles by a wall with three doors, which were found in the excavations of 1949; this narthex apparently had two projecting lateral chambers. Traces of the double communicating arches can be seen at the entrance to the church.

Ravenna, S. Croce

FIG. 2
Galla Placidia's other foundation at Ravenna was S. Croce, thought to have been built *circa* 425. This church was of a type similar to churches in Milan and in the West in general: a single nave with two lateral arms ending in straight walls. Of this original cross-plan, however, only traces of the presbytery remain, with a rich marble pavement and a synthronos which was excavated in 1926. Recent drillings have revealed a three-aisled plan without columns, similar to that of the church of the SS. Apostoli at Como, but of the original structure there survives only one of the lateral chapels of the narthex, the so-called mausoleum of Galla Placidia, which, as the mosaic makes clear, was really a martyr's chapel dedicated to St. Lawrence.

*Ravenna,
Chapel of S. Lorenzo*
The structure of this building is well known: a Roman cross plan with a high dome covered by a hipped roof. The exterior is of rough brick in accordance with western taste and technique (like the blind

arcading of the basilica at Trier and Milanese churches of the late fourth century); the cornices are flat corbel tables, still classical in style. The interior, however, with a high centre bay carrying a pendentive dome, derives from the small cruciform churches of the Sassanian, Roman and Byzantine East. The interior is very lavishly decorated: mosaic with gold tesserae covers the walls and vaults, with marble revetments beneath, and the effect of the whole is the most refined and suggestive that early Christianity has bequeathed to us.

The original baptistery of Ravenna cathedral was built when the see *Ravenna I* was transferred from Classe to Ravenna, when the city became a capital at the beginning of the fifth century, in the time of Bishop Ursus. Of this building there remain only the octagonal perimeter wall with niches and the intarsia work of marble and porphyry, which is now badly cut into by the overhanging arches. Later, in the time of Bishop Neon (*fl.* 459), were added the two wall arcades carried on *Ravenna II* free-standing marble columns and imposts, the vault constructed of hollow clay tubes fitted one inside the other (a technique common in Italy from the fourth to the sixth century), the mosaics and the stucco ornament – in other words, the whole decorative inner shell. It seems probable that the building was surrounded by an ambulatory or at least had annexed rooms. In 1864, Lanciani found pavements between the cathedral and the baptistery and signs of communicating doors in the walls, and also the bases of the eight columns of the bottom row, much thicker and more irregular than the present ones, at a level of about 3.5 metres below the present floor. There is also documentary evidence for the existence of a portico joining it with the cathedral. The mosaic decoration will be discussed later. Each of the arches of the upper zone is decorated with triple stucco arcades with rinceaux above them, of which a large part was destroyed by restorations in the last century. Each of the triple arcades contains a window in the centre, and on either side an aedicule in perspective containing figures of saints; decorating the gable are little symbolic scenes, such as two deer with Christ trampling upon the dragon, or handing the scroll of the Law to Peter.

The baptistery of S. Giovanni in Laterano is preceded by a pincer- *Rome II* shaped atrium and has a simple octagonal plan with a two-storeyed hypostyle structure with a porphyry font in the centre: this was erected by Sixtus III (432) to replace an existing one with circular plan. The *Liber Pontificalis* (ed. Duchesne, 1, p. 174), describing this font, gives an idea of the sumptuous gold decoration which adorned this type of building. The porphyry basin had both interior and exterior covered with silver weighing over 3000 lbs. In the centre of the font four porphyry columns supported a golden vase weighing fifty-two pounds, in which on Easter Day incense was burned. At the edge of the basin, on the right of a lamb from whose mouth flowed a jet of water, was an almost life-size statue of the Saviour in silver, and on the left was another silver statue, of St. John the Baptist. Water flowed into the basin from seven silver deer, and a censer of solid gold adorned with forty-nine precious stones added to the richness of the chapel.

Rome, S. Pietro in Vincoli Another legacy of the munificence of the Theodosian family is the church of S. Pietro in Vincoli in Rome. Some inscriptions, now lost but preserved for us by copyists, attribute the reconstruction of this church to Eudoxia, the wife of Valentinian III (*c.* 440), the work being executed at the expense of Theodosius II and his wife Eudocia. The building, which was altered substantially in the Baroque period, retains the skeleton of the primitive building, a nave and two aisles with arches on Doric columns of spoils, without pulvins. The presbytery area, which preceded the semicircular apse, was separated from it by a triumphal arch on cross-piers, decorated on the nave side by a pair of columns, probably not part of the original plan, and had a space on either side of it. This tripartite transept has a strongly marked rectangular plan which makes the presence of a dome unlikely. Recent investigations (by Matthiae) have brought into question the antiquity of much of the present structure and suggest that there was an earlier apsed hall, in part open to the outside.

Rome, S. Sabina

APPX. PL. 6 Another church of the same period, but this time due to the liberality of a private citizen, is S. Sabina on the Aventine, which was built, according to a mosaic inscription of the time of Celestine I (422–32), by a priest from Illyria, one Peter, and completed, according to the *Liber Pontificalis*, under his successor Sixtus III (432–40), when Peter had become a bishop. It is of particular interest because part of the original marble revetments are still to be seen in the nave. The central nave, divided from the two aisles by arches and columns, is spacious and considerably higher than the aisles, which are decorated externally with blind arcading, like S. Giovanni Evangelista at Ravenna. The arches are supported directly by Corinthian capitals on well-matched fluted columns. The general impression made by the interior of the basilica is not however the same as in S. Giovanni Evangelista. S. Sabina, with its noble columns, uniform even as to the capitals, closely spaced and without pulvins, is Roman and not eastern: the Urbs in the fifth century was still attached to its past, whereas Ravenna was drawing upon the new strength which flowed from Constantinople. The *opus sectile* revetments of the arcades are of cipolin with horizontal bands of isodomic masonry, but above the columns are panels of green serpentine inlaid with porphyry discs or scrolls on pedestals, and an upper band with squares of cipolin, porphyry and serpentine accentuates the design below. Of the mosaics there remains only the monumental inscription over the door, in gold on a blue ground with flanking figures on a gold ground (the two elements of the church, the *ecclesia ex circumcisione* and the *ecclesia ex gentibus*); but Ciampini (*Vet. Mon.* i, Plates 47, 48) has left us a record of other mosaic revetments. At either side of the inscription were St. Peter and St. Paul, and in the arches above the symbols of the four Evangelists. Around the triumphal arch there were clipei (medallions) with the heads of Christ and of saints (fourteen of them and two others which were defaced), and at the sides symbolic representations of Paradise, Jerusalem and Bethlehem, with jewelled walls as in S. Maria Maggiore. The iconography of the medallions, similar to the front of the chapel of S. Zeno in S. Prassede, seems to belong to the ninth rather than to the fifth century.

The largest church in Rome remaining from the second quarter of the fifth century is S. Maria Maggiore, also built at the time of Sixtus iii, soon after the Council of Ephesus (431), according to an inscription in the building. It is a large hypostyle edifice with marble Ionic columns and architraves (which are constructed internally of brick platbands) and originally terminated in a semicircular apse, but at a later date the presbytery was prolonged and a transept formed. Apparently the front of the church opened to a narthex. The nave, with its majestic rows of closely-spaced epistyle columns, is still Classical Roman in style.

Rome, S. Maria Maggiore

In spite of two succeeding reconstructions, the noblest and purest Byzantine taste is still evident in the great martyrium of S. Lorenzo in Milan, which we probably owe to the munificence of Galla Placidia. The erection in the Lombard capital of a sumptuous memorial to the deacon of the Roman church had considerable religious and political significance in the second quarter of the fifth century. The cult of the Roman saint existed alongside that of local martyrs (such as St. Nazarius and St. Celsus) and of eastern martyrs (St. Babylas) and this act of homage, rendered in a metropolis that had been a political capital and enjoyed considerable prestige in north Italy and in Gaul as a religious centre, was symptomatic of the relations between the Empress and the Pope. Besides the central building dedicated to St. Lawrence

Milan, S. Lorenzo
FIGS. 3, 4

23

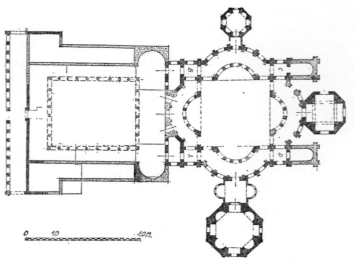

FIG. 3 – *S. Lorenzo, Milan: plan*

there were in fact two chapels within the sanctuary of Milan dedicated to the canonized Pope Sixtus II and to St. Hippolytus, both Romans and associated with the titular saint. A third chapel, even more sumptuous, dedicated to St. Aquilinus and probably built to house the tombs of the Imperial family, gave additional importance to the sanctuary.

S. Lorenzo is dated by some to the end of the fourth century, but the attribution to Galla Placidia is more likely. The edifice was undoubtedly erected at imperial expense. It was built outside the city walls and its foundations are blocks of stone remaining from a public building, the amphitheatre. This was still in use in 396, since in that year there took place the episode related by Paulinus (*Vita S. Ambrosii*, 34), the escape of a criminal, Cresconius, who had been thrown to the wild beasts, and thus S. Lorenzo cannot have been built by Valentinian II (*ob.* 392). The attribution to Galla Placidia is traditional: the biographer of St. Veranius, Bishop of Cavaillon, says 'Galla Placidia. . . in honore eiusdem martyris domum mirificam costruxit. . .' (*Acta Sanctorum*, Sept. VIII p. 468) and Benzone in the tenth century writes 'Galla quidem/Romanorum nobilis patricia/condidit Mediolani celsa aedifica/ ubi est nostri levitae celebris noticia . . .' (Pertz, *Rer. Germ. Hist. Script.* XI, 680). The original plan of S. Lorenzo was of very noble conception: an inner shell formed by two-storey ambulatories following the perimeter

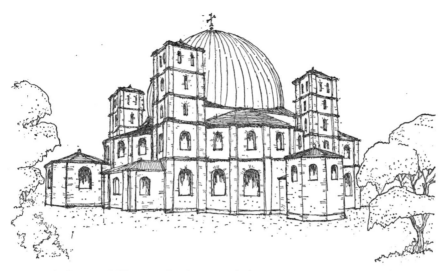

FIG. 4 – *S. Lorenzo, Milan: exterior (reconstruction)*

of the quatrefoil. At the four corners rose four towers whose mass balanced the effect of the large arches. The central space was twenty-four metres square and must have had a dome of timber framing covered with lead, and decorated with mosaic ('de super tegens universa musyvum', according to Arnulf in Pertz, *RGHS* VIII, 24–25), which was destroyed in a fire which raged in the district on 17 March 1071. The main hall was preceded by a narthex which has now disappeared, and by a porticoed courtyard which was apparently flanked by two rows of rooms for pilgrims, following a practice which has already been mentioned, and of which evidence can be seen at Antioch (St. Babylas), Hierapolis (St. Philip), Ephesus (the early St. John) and elsewhere. On the street was an imposing propylaeum, the 'sixteen columns' of S. Lorenzo.

The architectural composition of the building is predominantly Byzantine in taste and it is probable that the plans were prepared by court architects in Constantinople, following a practice which has already been mentioned. The Panagia in Athens has an almost identical plan; it was built in the middle of the so-called Stoa of Hadrian, probably a quadriporticus with rooms for worship for the royal family, and on a site belonging to the imperial treasury. The columned propylaeum preceding the sanctuary was also a Byzantine arrangement which is found, for example, at Alahan Manastir in

Cilicia. The masonry technique and the decorative corbels of the cornices are manifestations of Milanese workmanship and belong to local tradition; the columns both of the propylaeum and of the interior appear to be spoils.

Milan, chapels As we have said, three chapels lie on the principal axes of the church: S. Sisto, octagonal in plan, with niches, S. Ippolito (which may have been built before the great martyrium), cruciform with a central crossing, and the last and largest, S. Aquilino, also a niched octagon, but two-storeyed and with galleries above the niches and a pincer-shaped narthex. It seems probable that S. Ippolito and S. Aquilino were mausolea of persons connected with the imperial family. (There is nothing to show that the Palatium of Milan was not inhabited in the first half of the fifth century. It was still habitable at the time of Attila's invasion.) The monumental mausoleum of S. Aquilino, which was known as 'the Queen's chapel', is particularly interesting for the mosaics of the narthex which still exist. There is nothing to indicate that it also served as a baptistery. The stone channel which runs below the pavement across its foundations was, as I have shown elsewhere, a drain to discharge the rainwater which converged into a recess close by. Indirect evidence that the S. Lorenzo complex of buildings served as a place of burial for members of the Theodosian family is provided by the fact that only after the dynasty had come to an end (457) did the bishops of Milan seek burial there, beginning with Eusebius, in about 464, in the chapel of S. Sisto which he himself added to the building, and Theodorus (c. 489), in S. Ippolito itself.

Ravenna, 'oriental' sarcophagi Byzantine influence can also be seen in some of the sarcophagi in Ravenna which date from the first half of the fifth century and which show symbolic figures and scenes, or figured scenes with symbolic elements. These are among the first traces of the intrusion of the taste for the abstract into the figurative tradition.

One group shows single figures framed in niches decorated with scallop shells on spirally-twisted or fluted columns. They obviously derive from those of 'Asiatic' style, combining figures with architectural elements, which are characteristic of the workshops of Asia Minor, an old example of which, outstanding for its size and expressiveness, is to be found in the Istanbul Museum (Sidamara). The Ravenna sarcophagi (most of them were probably executed on commission in the East and then shipped to the Adriatic metropolis) are of a simpler and later type with regular intercolumnation, squatter in shape and with more space around the figures.

The two sarcophagi in S. Francesco are of this type, that of Liberius and that in the left aisle. They are similar in style and the first has been attributed to Liberius III (*c.* 380). On the front of each is depicted the *traditio legis*, and the Apostles are represented in the arches. In a third sarcophagus with figured niches, that of St. Barbatianus, figures are mixed with symbols. On the front are Christ, St. Peter and St. Paul, presented frontally, with a great vase at either side; on the ends are pairs of lighted candles in candlesticks, with a large cross and a Chi-Rho monogram. The decorative elements almost dominate the composition: the ornamental band round the top of the trough and the edges of the cover bear large rinceaux of leaves, the crosses on the cover are carved with jewels, the Chi-Rho is enclosed within a wreath with flowerlets. This sarcophagus can be dated to 440–50, and to this period probably belong two other famous sarcophagi, those of Isaccius and of the Pignatta family, since the scenes connected with the Marian cult which they show can hardly belong to a date before the Council of Ephesus (431).

The sarcophagus of Isaccius shows the Virgin enthroned and the Magi on the front; on the short sides are Daniel in the lions' den and the resurrection of Lazarus. The figures are in very free positions and in high relief, so that an earlier date (the beginning of the fifth century) has been suggested. The Pignatta sarcophagus has two episodes relating to the Virgin, the Annunciation and the Visitation, on the ends, while on the front is Christ enthroned between Peter and Paul. The craftsmanship of these two sarcophagi is exquisite; the relief on the first has great plasticity, that of the second is fluid and soft, but both styles seem to belong to the refined school of the Byzantine capital.

Isaccius

Other marble tombs show traditional Christian scenes such as Christ alone or surrounded by Apostles in the act of handing the scroll of the Law to St. Peter as the sign of the authority conferred on him. This appears on the sarcophagus of the Twelve Apostles in S. Apollinare in Classe, with expressive plastic figures. On that of Archbishop Rinaldus is Christ in majesty between Peter and Paul who offer wreaths with veiled hands. Here the mystic symbolism of the stylized landscape, with a palm-tree on either side and clouds in the sky converging upon the figure of Christ, is accentuated by the four rivers flowing from the throne.

Beside these marble tombs carved with figures there are others, more numerous, with symbolic decoration only. The two most famous of these are in the mausoleum of Galla Placidia. One is known as that of Constantius III and shows three lambs between two palm-trees, with the four rivers flowing beneath the centre lamb, which stands rather

FIG. 5

FIG. 5 – *Sarcophagus. Mausoleum of Galla Placidia, Ravenna*

higher than the others. On the other, known as the sarcophagus of Honorius, the Holy Lamb with a cross stands within a gabled aedicule, with a scallop-arched aedicule on either side containing a cross. The impression of spaciousness and the noble execution of the figures make it clear that these impressive works were produced in Constantinople. Other symbolic carvings are outstanding for their elegance, including the posterior faces of the best figured sarcophagi. The back of the sarcophagus of Isaccius has two elegant peacocks and two well-spaced palm-trees on either side of a simple disc with the sacred monogram, and that of the Pignatta sarcophagus has two well-carved deer drinking from a large cantharus. Other symbolic scenes (the posterior faces of the Rinaldus sarcophagus and of that of Ranchio, at Cesena) show besides the pair of confronted peacocks a stylized tree with volutes ending in a large flower. A sarcophagus in Ferrara cathedral has a Chi-Rho between matching pairs of peacocks beneath the same stylized tree with two volutes only, while the principal face copies that of the Twelve Apostles at Ravenna and the ends have roughly carved figures. This poses again the problem of provenance: it cannot be assumed that the elegant sarcophagi are the work of Byzantine artists and the cruder work that of local craftsmen. The source of the Ravenna school of sarcophagi is, however, generally acknowledged to have been

Constantinople (Bayet, Kollwitz, Hanfmann) or Asia Minor (Wulff, Dalton, Morey): recently De Francovich appears to suggest that some sarcophagi may have originated in Ravenna itself.

This fine work, believed to be contemporary with the church (*c.* 430), had on the front twenty-eight panels (now eighteen) in alternating pairs of larger and smaller size, with borders of elaborate cymation in low relief, and vine leaves and grapes similar to those of the ambo from Salonika (*c.* 500) now in the Istanbul Museum. The smaller panels bear scenes of the Passion and of the Theophany after the Resurrection, while the larger ones, being higher, allow more complex scenes; they are divided into several horizontal zones showing episodes from the Old and New Testaments which were perhaps originally arranged to point analogies. One unpaired scene is a realistic representation of the Crucifixion. The style contains elements of both eastern and western taste, as is natural in a work executed in Rome at a time when the unity of the Empire had not yet broken up. The iconography is somewhat obscure: some scenes are not easy to identify, such as that in the lower centre which is variously interpreted as 'Imperial address to the senate and people' or 'The annunciation to Zacharias'. It is considered probable that at least two sculptors were responsible for the carving. The reverse of the panels shows delicate foliation with figure-of-eight knots and more frequently geometric ornament: interlacing circles and polygons with overlapping discs at the interstices. The same geometric motifs, which belong to popular art and are typical of the fifth century, are found in pavement mosaics. Some of the large polygons contain a decorative rosette or projecting boss in the centre.

Rome, doors of S. Sabina

The mosaics of the first half of the fifth century at Ravenna are clearly marked by Byzantine taste. In the mausoleum of Galla Placidia the lunette in the presbytery shows St. Lawrence, bearing a jewelled cross on his right shoulder, beside a flaming gridiron (the triumph of martyrdom in imitation of Christ); over the door is a young Christ seated in an airy landscape among the Apostles as lambs, holding the *Crux invicta*. In the barrel-vaults is a decoration of delicate rosettes on a blue ground like a textile pattern, and in the lunettes of the transept arms are symmetrically arranged pairs of deer drinking from a central spring in a pattern of gold acanthus scrolls which emerge from the spring and twine around the deer in delicate tracery against the deep blue sky. In the centre of the cupola, or rather the sail vault of the tower is the *Crux celestis* among hundreds of concentrically-arranged gold stars. On the pendentives are the symbols of the Evangelists, typical of eastern taste. On each of the four walls of the drum (beneath

Ravenna, mosaics Mausoleum of Galla Placidia

PLATE P. 30

a scallop canopy), are pairs of Apostles in the act of acclamation, and two doves with a cantharus. The composition as a whole makes an overwhelming impression – the luminous, mystical atmosphere evoked by the blue and gold contrasts with the idyllic and naturalistic picture of Christ caressing a lamb, and with the dynamic scene of the lunette opposite; and the composition is crowned by the sky of the dome, with the cross implying the divine presence.

The other mosaic which expresses its sacred theme with both animated figures and the abstract calm of symbols is that of the dome of the Orthodox Baptistery. The centre shows the Baptism of Christ in the Jordan, and upon this scene converge the Apostles arranged in a ring in two symmetrical files, led respectively by St. Peter and St. Paul. The Apostles are separated from each other by a delicate acanthus design which rises to the decorative band above, almost as a frail support for it, like the slender columns of fantastic architecture in the frescoes of painters of the Classical period; the trailing coloured veils of the figures emphasize the gracefulness of the composition. The Apostles have slender bodies clothed in flowing robes which swing out behind them, accentuating the animation of their attitude.

*Ravenna,
Orthodox Baptistery*

In the outer ring are eight identical canopies with small columns and lattice-work, curving at the centre into an exedra: these are occupied alternately by four Gospel-books and four jewelled thrones with a jewelled cross upon a silk cushion (the *etimasia*).

The composition thus displays an abstract and centralized view of three zones: the earthly zone, containing the symbols of the triumph of Christ and the testimony of the Prophets; the heavenly zone, with the chosen disciples of the Saviour, and the supernal zone, with the scene of the first Baptism, that of the Son of God Himself.

The lavish use of gold, as background to the Baptism, in the robes of the Apostles, in the acanthus stems and in the architectural elements of the base, make the dome seem a casket of shining jewels. The eastern nature of the composition is clearly shown in the band containing typical fantastic architecture, in the Hellenistic grace of the decorative elements, and in the stately gait of the Apostles, who seem to move forward as lightly as if they had no weight.

In contrast to the magnificent basilicas built with imperial aid and encouragement in Ravenna, Milan and Rome are the buildings erected in traditional local style to supply practical needs.

Dome mosaic. Mausoleum of Galla Placidia, Ravenna. *Cf. p. 29.*

In northern Italy during the fifth century the episcopal centres were generally very simple, as has already been said, and important buildings were often merely rectangular halls. Such are the cathedrals of Brescia (beneath the Romanesque rotonda) and Pula. Here there is no distinctive arrangement for the presbytery except a free-standing semicircular stepped bench for the clergy, the synthronos.

Parenzo II

Other churches, still rectangular in plan and with no terminal apse, had two rows of columns; a good example is the cathedral of Parenzo (Poreč) in its second stage. One of the churches there occupied more or less the present site and in fact part of the walls and of the façade was used in the time of Bishop Euphrasius for the building which we see today. The altar was raised on a podium about one metre high, standing in the nave within the curve of the semicircular masonry clergy bench. The church also retains the mosaic floor: in the aisles it is divided into rectangular sections with repeated predominantly geometric designs of interlacing octagons, frets, reticulation, discs, crosses and so on, which indicate the second half of the fifth century. The free-standing podium had a rinceau pattern on the top surface and as a decorative border. The wall of the synthronos was decorated with frescoes imitating marble and bands of red.

Parallel to the church with columns lay a second hall to the north, long and without columns, but again having a synthronos. At the east end some mosaics have been found, some 35 centimetres above the level of the entrance door. It is possible that the room was divided by a transverse wall.

Aquileia II

FIG. 7

Of greater importance but with the same rectangular apseless plan were the two churches of the second phase of the cathedral at Aquileia: the north church, part of which lies beneath the present campanile, was very spacious (73 metres by 31 metres) with the nave more than 18 metres wide. The mosaic pavement, with a simple geometric pattern of the early fifth century, has a rectangular bay for the altar, and a solea between the presbytery enclosure and the ambo already in the centre of the church. In front of the façade there was probably a long narthex common to both this church and the south church. Only traces of pavement mosaic have been found of this, which must have occupied roughly the same site as the Romanesque building, but it too must have terminated at the east in a straight wall. In front of this church (which was certainly the bishop's church) stands the

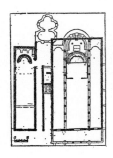

FIG. 6 – *Cathedral, Parenzo: plan of phase II*

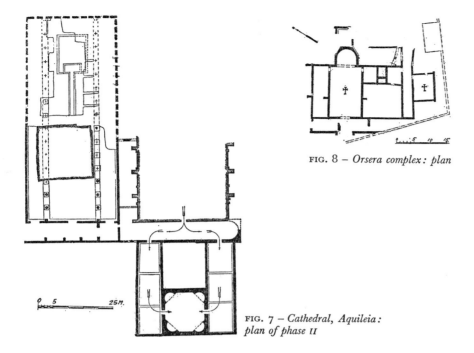

FIG. 8 – *Orsera complex: plan*

FIG. 7 – *Cathedral, Aquileia:
plan of phase II*

baptistery, octagonal with four niches, which was joined to the narthex by two corridors (annexes for instruction and for undressing). The mosaics here are mid-fifth-century in style, whereas those of the first church are rather older.

Besides these important cathedrals there are other, more modest, complexes of three buildings – a hall for worship, a second, smaller hall and a baptistery – together with dwellings for the episcopal household, found generally in Istria. The principal example is that of Nesactium, which was excavated before the first World War. The two halls are rectangular and united by a large narthex, and there are several annexes adjoining the smaller church. At Orsera there is a less important example, where a polygonal apse was added to the principal hall at a second stage, and a large narthex ran across the front: the lesser hall was to one side of the group of buildings.

Smaller cathedrals

FIG. 8

We have said elsewhere that in the West a cathedral consisted of two churches and a baptistery. These baptisteries generally had a central plan, like a tomb, and the analogy was offered by the liturgy of the rite of baptism with its reference to death and resurrection. Suitable areas for instruction and for undressing also formed part of the building.

BAPTISTERIES

33

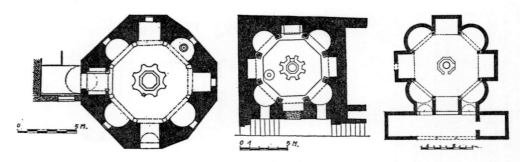

FIGS. 9, 10, 11 *(from left to right) – Baptisteries of Albenga, Fréjus and Novara: plans*

Albenga

FIG. 9

Among the baptisteries of north Italy and Provence is a group of three very similar buildings. The most important, at Albenga, still has the mosaics of its east niche. Standing beside the present cathedral, it is an octagon with eight niches, alternately rectangular and horse-shoe shaped, like S. Aquilino in the S. Lorenzo complex in Milan, but with columns in the corners between the niches. These columns support the sustaining arches of the drum, on large corbels embedded in the wall masonry. On the outside, the niches are masked by a decagonal wall. The central core was covered by a dome up to the last century, when it was demolished, although it was constructed of Roman spoils and supported by earthenware pots. Some holes in the impost, thought to be grooves for the roof timbers, must have contained wooden tie-beams. The drum has sixteen blind arches containing windows; there were supporting earthenware pots in the sides of the niches. Access to the baptistery seems to have been originally by two doors in the sides of the presbytery niche.

The decoration of the interior is Classical in style but extremely simple. The projecting entablature above the columns consists of plain blocks which replace both architrave and frieze; the cornice is a continuous moulding which also serves as window impost. In the centre of the core is the eight-sided font with a wide star-shaped edge and two steps leading down into it; it had eight columns at the corners which supported a ciborium, and could serve for both adult and infant baptism.

According to a well-known inscription, important building work was carried out in 'Albingaunum' by Constantius, the general of Honorius, but the mosaic inscription in the baptistery mentions relics of St.

34

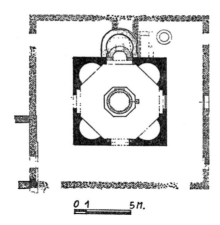

FIG. 12 – *Riva, S. Vitale:*
plan of baptistery

0 1   5 ʍ.

Stephen, whose body was found in 415, of St. John the Evangelist
(which indicates influence of the Theodosian family), of St. Lawrence
and four Ambrosian saints. This suggests not only a date later than 415,
but the time of Galla Placidia.

The baptistery at Fréjus is almost identical with that at Albenga:
internally a niched octagon with corner columns. The cathedral is
built on the same axis to the east; it is now a single nave with Romanesque vaulting, probably built at least in part on the earlier
foundations. In the centre of the baptistery is the font, also octagonal,
with projections to carry a ciborium, and there are doors in the sides
of the east niche, as at Albenga. In the lower part of the present cupola
there are traces of the earlier brick dome.

Externally the building is square in plan and not polygonal, and the
drum, which has been rebuilt very high, is cylindrical. The masonry
of the arches is polychrome, with alternate courses of stone and brick.
The classical flavour of the interior is less marked than at Albenga:
instead of the entablature there are roughly shaped impost corbels.

The baptistery at Novara is also a niched octagon with two doors in
the sides of the east niche, corner columns of spoils on high bases, and
windows in the drum. The perimeter wall is, however, different: it is
not solid masonry with niches recessed into it but a brick wall of
constant thickness. There are stone corbels roughly carved and arches
which in part are supported irregularly. Recent excavations have
brought to light fragments of the font and of mosaic paving in black
and white blocks arranged geometrically, and precious traces of mosaic
in the soffits of two lower windows.

The present cupola and the cornices of the barrel-vaults are Ro-

Fréjus
FIG. 10

Novara
FIG. 11

35

manesque, as are the frescoes of the drum; the original cupola was probably a light structure, a timber frame clad with strips of lead and dome of cane and stucco.

The close similarities between these three buildings suggest a common plan provided for all three by the court, and this supposition is strengthened by their likeness to the niched octagon of the chapel of S. Aquilino.

Earliest baptisteries in Switzerland Riva S. Vitale FIG. 12

In the area of Lombard occupation, at Riva S. Vitale in Swiss territory, there is a small octagonal baptistery almost contemporary with the Albenga group. The octagon has a span of about seven metres, the rectangular niches are atrophied to no more than blind arcading and there are no corner columns. The cupola must have been a light one with a timber frame – the present one is Romanesque. Excavations within have brought to light the font, which is octagonal with steps leading down, and the remains of a black and white tile floor of interlacing decagons, hexagons and triangles. Outside, the foundations of a square enclosure have been discovered; evidently there was a square ambulatory around the octagonal core, used for the instruction of catechumens and for undressing.

St. Maurice d'Agaune

A similar arrangement, but with a simpler, square chamber and an ambulatory, has been excavated at St. Maurice d'Agaune in the Valais. It has been attributed to the sixth century, but the shape of the round basin, with a stair leading down, of the earliest type, and suitable for adult baptism, indicates a rather earlier date. A similar one exists in the original cathedral at Aquileia (early fourth century) and many examples are found in the East and in North Africa, where they remained the usual form for a long time.

CEMETERY CHURCHES

Apart from cathedrals, urban churches and martyria, fifth-century towns had also cemetery churches. Strictly speaking, the martyria were also cemetery churches, that is, they were built outside the walls, among tombs; but, as we have said, they were constructed not as halls for worship but as venerated sepulchres. The other funerary churches of north Italy and Provence were halls, but they often had rooms projecting laterally near the presbytery.

Similar halls already existed at the end of the fourth century; at Milan, for example, there were those of S. Nazaro (dedicated to the Apostles) and S. Simpliciano. S. Lorenzo itself has a central area with ancillary chambers. Paulinus of Nola gives us an explanation of the purpose of these rooms – meditation and burial. The chamber which was the church proper was sacred, and dedicated to the martyrs and their relics alone; and those persons who wished to be near the venerated remains of the saints sought to have their sarcophagi placed in these lateral rooms, separated from but close to the central chamber.

A church with a single nave, semicircular apse and two projecting rooms was excavated at Como, beneath the present S. Abbondio. This building had also long lateral areas, like aisles, separated from the nave by a wall pierced by an arcade. The first church was erected on the site, according to tradition, in the first half of the fifth century by the bishop, St. Amanthius, who brought there relics of the Apostles and was himself buried in the church. Certainly St. Abbondius (*c.* 450) and other fifth-century bishops had tombs there, and thus the dating to the second quarter of the fifth century seems justified. It is further supported by the discovery of small marble tiles in *opus sectile* belonging to the early pavement, similar to others in Lombardy of that period. During the excavations, tombs with late fifth-century and early sixth-century inscriptions were found beneath floor level; the oldest were of 485, 486 and 490, which proves that at this time the prohibition against burial within churches was relaxed.

Como, SS. Apostoli FIG. 13

The monastic church ('fondo Ritter') which has recently been excavated at Aquileia is of great interest for the development of the basilica church. Originally (in the second half of the fourth century) it was a large rectangular hall (16.85 by 68.25 metres) with a geometrically patterned floor of polychrome mosaic in large irregular sections. At a second stage (about the middle of the fifth century) it was divided into three aisles by two lines of small marble pillars and an apse was added, semicircular internally and polygonal externally. The pavement in the eastern area was raised by about 40 centimetres. A narthex was also added to the building, with two projecting lateral chambers.

Aquileia, monastic church

A Christian cemetery complex has recently come to light between Aquileia and Altino. It was dominated by a large church, a simple rectangle in plan (19.2 by 40 metres), three-aisled and hypostyle. Fragments of a geometrically patterned floor provide evidence for dating: they show simple designs in black on a white ground, similar to those of the more elaborate fourth-century floors at Aquileia. The church is thus probably of the late fourth or early fifth century, a date which is suggested also by the dedication to the Apostles typical of that time (Milan, Ravenna, Como and elsewhere). The dedication appears on a tombstone: 'Jacet ante limina Domnorum Apostolorum e . . . Sanctus Maurentius presbiter.' To the south of this church and adjoining it was a *cella trichora*, a little martyrium. In the centre, beneath the altar, is a small cruciform recess lined with marble, of a

Concordia Sagittaria FIG. 14

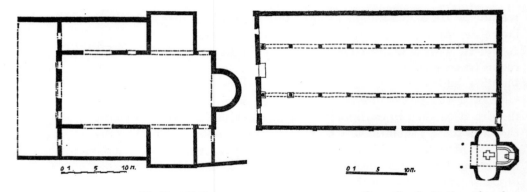

FIG. 13 – *SS. Apostoli, Como: plan*

FIG. 14 – *Concordia Sagittaria: plan from phase I*

type found in fifth-century buildings in the East (St. John Studios, Constantinople; St. John, Ephesus; St. Demetrios, Salonika). This Byzantine cruciform burial place is explained by the presence in Concordia Sagittaria of a Syrian colony; inscriptions found in the cemetery refer to soldiers from the neighbourhood of Apamea in Coele-Syria, one of which is dated 409–10.

It is possible that the martyrium was open-fronted and that the faithful could see through a screen the venerated body of the saint who was buried there. At a later stage the little building was lengthened and became a three-aisled basilica, preceded by a narthex and a long narrow atrium with three porticoed sides and a fountain in the centre. In this atrium has been found an inscription relating to a child, Aurelius, son of an ἔχατρος who (like two other soldiers, one of whose inscriptions is dated 409) was from Secla, in Coele-Syria. Laterally to the narthex there was an enclosure full of sarcophagi, and there were others in the narthex itself.

Pilaster strips at the corners of the church and in the sarcophagus enclosure are the only sign of decoration, and there are intermediate pilaster-strips also where the trichora was lengthened into three aisles. Two of the apses were polygonal externally.

SCULPTURE At the beginning of the fifth century there was a flourishing school of marble sculpture and ivory carving in Provence, connected with the Mediterranean world and with north Italy, but less influenced by Byzantine taste than the great Italian centres. Work of great artistic merit produced by local craftsmen between 420 and 470 can be seen in Marseilles. In the Musée Borély are some sarcophagi, two of which show the *traditio legis* with Christ and the Apostles framed individually

38

within trabeated colonnades or arches. On the front of one cover, symbolic motifs (a Chi-Rho in the centre and two deer drinking from the four rivers) contrast with the miracle of Cana and the spies returning from Canaan. A third tomb has predominantly symbolic motifs: the two deer drinking from the four rivers, and two scenes from the miracle of Cana, and on the cover the Chi-Rho between six converging lambs, the last of which are emerging from a door.

Characteristic of this school are some altar-tables which show along the edge the Chi-Rho with twelve doves representing the Apostles (six at St. Marcel de Crussol) converging upon it. In the finest and most noble of these, from the Abbey of St. Victor, the Holy Lamb is shown with twelve other lambs amidst splendid rinceaux with grapes and foliage.

The mosaics of Milan, and still more those of Rome, show clearly their derivation from Roman art. Many compositions are entirely within this tradition, and have groups of human figures very similar to scenes in mural paintings and in illustrated manuscripts. MOSAICS

In fact very little of the Milanese mosaics remains. One niche in the chapel of S. Aquilino, in S. Lorenzo, has the subject, so dear to Christian art, of Christ among the Apostles, and a pastoral scene with figures lying among the rocks of an airy landscape. Fragments of other mosaics, figures of saints on a blue ground, came to light in the small narthex during restorations in 1941. *Milan, S. Aquilino*

The scenes relating to the Virgin and the Old Testament which can still be seen in S. Maria Maggiore at Rome seem to belong to the time of Sixtus III. They are of exceptional importance for their Marian iconography, having been executed immediately after the Council of Ephesus (431). At the crown of the arch, below St. Peter and St. Paul and the emblems of the four Evangelists, is a circle containing the *etimasia:* a jewelled throne with the royal insignia (a crown and a purple robe) surmounted by a jewelled cross, denoting the triumph of sacrifice. On the footstool is the Book with the Seven Seals of the Apocalypse. On the sides of the arch are displayed episodes from the life of Mary, in three registers. These are not the human episodes which were to spread from Byzantium in the sixth century, but scenes exalting the Mother of God with regal ceremony and court dress, and with angels forming a royal bodyguard. *Rome, S. Maria Maggiore*

On the left is the Annunciation: the message is given by four angels to the Virgin, who wears royal dress and is seated in great dignity, while a fifth angel hovers above with the dove of the Holy Ghost; this is followed by the angel warning Joseph. (A recent interpretation seeks to identify these respectively as the three angels with Sarah and with Abraham.) In the register below is the Adoration of the Magi, portrayed in an unusual way: the Infant Christ is seated on a throne with four angels as bodyguard; on the left is the Madonna, again royally clad, on the other side a female figure (St. Anne, or perhaps the Church) and two Magi coming from Jerusalem, which can be seen in the distance. In the top register on the other side is the Presentation in the Temple, with the nimbed Infant, Simeon, Anna and a retinue of old men. The other episodes are less important iconographically: the angel appearing to Joseph, the Holy Family approaching Aphrodosius, the Massacre of the Innocents, the Magi before Herod. (Brodsky thinks this ruler is Valentinian III.) The scenes are crowded with figures and are framed in narrow borders, almost touching one another. The walls of the nave, between the windows and the architrave, are covered with small square panels (twenty-seven remain of the original forty-two). With four exceptions these each contain two scenes, one above the other, showing episodes from the Pentateuch. The scenes are very lively and again crowded with figures; the groupings, animation, well-balanced attitudes, architectural elements to suggest perspective, and the hint of landscape with hills outlined against a glowing sky, all derive from classical experience, but Roman rather than Hellenistic. The figures are compact and their dress is of heavy material. Those of the arch are richly clad in jewelled garments suggestive of late Roman taste, and their strange flashing gaze is characteristic of the fifth century.

Albenga

PLATE P. 41

Another mosaic in Liguria of the same period (425–50), on the other hand, has only abstract symbols: this is the mosaic revetment of the presbytery in the baptistery at Albenga. On the end wall are two lambs facing a cross, and in the barrel-vault above is a composition which corresponds with that described by Paulinus of Nola: a mantle of stars on a blue ground, in the centre of which is represented the celestial sphere, the dwelling of God, with three concentric discs of shaded colours occupied by a triple Chi-Rho (perhaps representing the Trinity). Around this are twelve doves, the Apostles. The ornamental borders are of narrow stylized leaves on a white ground, but at the front, where there is a list of relics, is a wide garland of laurel between two bands of gems.

GAUL IN
THEODOSIAN
PERIOD

Between 418 and 460 the whole of Gaul, even the north, except for the region under the control of Visigothic *foederati*, remained subject to the Empire. The *Notitia Dignitatum* of the period of Honorius (395–423) shows that it then consisted of seventeen provinces. The northern

Apse mosaic. Baptistery, Albenga. *Cf. p. 40.*

ones lacked ethnic unity, and the withdrawal of many garrisons from Stilicho's time onwards had the effect of intensifying civil disorder in these distant regions.

The transfer of the imperial residence from Trier to Arles at the beginning of the fifth century marked the start of the abandonment of the Roman bases in northern Gaul. This coincided with large-scale inroads by eastern Germanic peoples, the Alans and Vandals, of whom the latter passed from Gaul into Spain and thence to Africa, where they were able to find that abundance of provisions which they had sought in vain in Europe. Except in those towns which had been devastated by raiders and in certain Rhineland frontier zones which were now occupied by barbarian peasantry, life in Gaul still retained a certain degree of civilization in the second quarter of the fifth century. In the cities some trade continued, while descendants of the Gallo-Roman aristocracy still lived in luxury on their estates, providing office-holders for courts, municipal administration (in the *civitates*) and bishoprics.

Burgundians Barbarian pressure was increasing, however. When the Burgundians, who had first been admitted to imperial territory in 408 around Mainz and Worms, arose in revolt in 436 they were severely repressed by the imperial troops of Aetius. Later they were transferred to the area of Geneva, but from here they spread into what is now Burgundy (which derives its name from them), and there they settled, first as Roman *foederati* and later as an independent people. Though Arians at first, they were subsequently converted to Catholicism without great difficulty.

Franks The Franks, however, constituted the greatest danger to Rome, because of the distance from the Mediterranean and also because of the nature of the frontier. The Salian Franks – to use the name given them by the Emperor Julian – were those nearest to the North Sea. They first spread within Belgium, then towards 435 they settled around Cambrai. Aetius concluded a treaty with them, to be valid until about 470, which recognized their possession of the area they had conquered and accepted them as *foederati*. The Ripuarian Franks crossed the Rhine at the beginning of the fifth century and installed themselves at Cologne and other cities on the left bank of the river. The Roman cities deteriorated greatly; many buildings were destroyed and the walls dismantled. The situation grew continually worse because the new inhabitants settled in their own separate encampments rather than within the cities. This was partly for their safety, but partly also because of their indifference towards an entirely alien civilization.

The bishops alone were able to make some defence of the old institutions and urban organization within the frontiers of their possessions, but as the Frankish occupation proceeded the appearance of the towns gradually changed. With conditions so hostile to the development of art and architecture, there was little ecclesiastical building of any importance. Almost nothing remains of any churches of the mid-fifth century in northern and central France.

Perhaps the only basilica which still exists is the Basse-Oeuvre at Beauvais. It is a small church joined slightly to one side of the great Gothic transept of St. Pierre, which dominates it. It is three-aisled, divided by masonry piers, with a timber roof. A large horse-shoe arch leads from the central nave to the Gothic cathedral. Well known to French scholars, it was attributed to the eighth or ninth century, but is now generally thought to be of the tenth, a dating suggested by documents which refer to building carried out by Bishop Herveus (987–98), or by the fact that some foundations for the cathedral were laid in 949; but the uncertainty of the documents, which mention the work only in passing, and the fact that early cathedrals consisted of more than one building, cause the question of the chronology of the edifice still to be left open.

Churches Beauvais, Basse-Oeuvre

APPX. PL. 10

The suspicion that the church may be attributed to a date as early as the fifth century is aroused by the construction of the walls: the base is of large blocks of stone with reddish-coloured mortar, laid in regular courses (three courses can still be distinguished); the facing is of smaller limestone blocks, regularly cut and laid in courses with a pinkish mortar of lime and crushed potsherds'; and at intervals there are bands of brickwork consisting of roof-tiles in pairs. This masonry technique can be seen almost intact in the north wall, but in the south walls large areas have been restored.

Buildings in small blocks of stone *(petit appareil)* are common in the imperial period in Gaul, and they continued also into the late Roman period. The systematic preparation of these evenly-cut blocks involved a widespread organization which could not have arisen at any later date, and still less in the tenth century, a time of great disturbance in the quarrying industry, and in which masonry work was usually crude.

The use of courses of brick in masonry of stone cut in little bits was common throughout the imperial and late Roman periods in Gaul (amphitheatre at Bordeaux, thermae at Arles, baptistery at Fréjus) and is found also in north Italian buildings (S. Stefano, Verona, mid-fifth century).

Mortar comprising crushed terracotta, although still used sporadically in the Middle Ages (and some use is made of it in the Gothic cathedral at Beauvais) was employed most frequently in the late Roman period (S. Croce, Ravenna; S. Stefano, Verona), and also in the East, where its use has continued from antiquity to the present day and it is known as *khorosan*.

The polychrome archivolts of the windows of the Basse-Oeuvre are found again in the Fréjus baptistery and, less well preserved, in the amphitheatre at Bordeaux, and in any case they are common in Byzantine buildings: in St. Eirene, Istanbul there are frescoes, in St. Demetrios, Salonika, strips of marble; in the Albenga baptistery and in S. Stefano, Verona, there is also a band of brickwork at the window imposts, a sign of the continuance of classical taste. The width of the lights of the windows – the splay must have been altered later – is also characteristic of fifth-century buildings. In order to settle the question, however, it would be necessary to excavate down to the Roman level. No dating can be successfully defended unless it is based on archaeological evidence and clear analogies are lacking because unfortunately very little fifth-century building survives in northern France.

The façade, on the other hand, must be considered medieval, and may be attributed to Bishop Herveus. An obvious break separates it from the original nave, and a facing of re-used small blocks contains early Romanesque ornaments. Blocks from the early masonry can be seen in other buildings round the cloisters. Some well-known French churches, recently re-examined by Dr. Lesueur, have facing walls, or stretches of wall, in *petit appareil*. Some of these (Cravant) are perhaps very old either wholly or in part, others are Romanesque but use old stone blocks from other buildings in their walls, and yet others have facing walls which use stone blocks, contemporary with their construction, inserted for decorative effects. The blind triangular arches between the windows and the flat corbel table cornices (Cravant, St. Généreux) are also fifth-century ornamental devices.

Metz, St. Pierre
FIG. 15

Another church possibly of the fifth century is the wide-apsed hall outside the walls of Metz, beneath St. Pierre de la Citadelle. The nave (34 by 18.5 metres) had no internal pillars and the apse was curved internally and polygonal externally, an arrangement that suggests a date rather later than the beginning of the fifth century, to which it is usually attributed because of the stamps on the bricks and because of the difficult conditions of life in Metz after the invasion of 408.

The church must have had a hypocaust: the subterranean chamber of a hypocaust has been brought to light together with channels through the walls. The principal entrance, perhaps a triple door, was 5.10 metres wide, and access was also through two doorways near the apse, in the north and south walls. The walls, less than one metre thick, bear no

FIG. 15 – *St. Pierre de la Citadelle, Metz : plan*

FIG. 16 – *Churches, Hemmaberg : plans*

trace of plaster and it has been suggested that the building may not have been completed. There is some doubt as to whether it may not have been intended as a basilica for secular rather than for religious purposes.

Christianity reached Noricum and Rhaetia in the fifth century, and excavations have revealed several buildings of an ecclesiastical nature whose features correspond to the modest provincialism of the centres of habitation of those countries. The churches are as a rule simple rectangular buildings with a semicircular or semi-oval clergy bench. The church at Aguntum is of this type, 100 Roman feet in length, with a paved presbytery and surrounded by graves. So is that at Hemmaberg, a site visited by pilgrims for the grotto of St. Rosalia, who gave protection against the plague. The church at Hemmaberg was built at the top of a hill, together with a smaller church and an octagonal baptistery – a small cathedral complex. The main church had a floor mosaic which ran around the clergy bench; the second church had a projecting curved apse with a mosaic pavement, and an iconostasis with four columns which preceded the synthronos. The simple octagonal baptistery had a hexagonal font with a large ciborium on four columns. The style of the mosaics suggests a fifth-century dating.

Noricum, Rhaetia

FIG. 16

45

II. THE FIRST ECLIPSE OF BYZANTINE INFLUENCE IN THE WEST (455–527)

HISTORY
*End of
Theodosian dynasty*

In 455 Valentinian III, having aroused the enmity of the army and the court, was assassinated. Marcian, the husband of Pulcheria, the intriguing and devout sister of Theodosius II, and the last of the Theodosian emperors, died two years later. The end of this prestigious dynasty, which had controlled the destinies of East and West for over half a century, was accompanied by the collapse of Roman authority in Europe. Between 457 and 476 the last Emperors of the West, lacking adequate support from Byzantium, had only the appearance of power; they were elected and deposed in conditions of disorder and bloodshed, as they had been in the third century, and moreover with the security of the frontiers in a critical state.

Gaul

From 455 onwards, the Germanic peoples in lands adjacent to the Empire or actually settled in imperial territory rebelled more or less openly, assuming power in the region they occupied and spreading into the neighbouring territories. In Aquitaine the Visigoths, who in 455 had confirmed their loyalty to Rome and had supported the nomination as emperor of Avitus, a member of a noble Auvergnat family, in 466 rebelled under their king, Henricus, and spread into the centre of France. The moribund government in Ravenna accepted the situation in 475 *de iure*, recognizing as theirs central and southern Gaul, with the exception of Provence. In the same year of 455, the Ripuarian Franks occupied Trier and set up a kingdom on the left bank of the Rhine, while the Salian Franks founded another kingdom further west around Cambrai and Tournai. In the same period 455–470 the Alemans invaded Alsace, the Palatinate and Bavaria.

Vandals

In Rome the imperial forces, consisting to a large extent of barbarian mercenaries, expended their military energies in quarrelling among themselves and were incapable of preventing the Vandals settled in North Africa and Sicily from landing at Ostia and sacking Rome. Imperial insignia and rich furnishings were seized as booty and carried off to Carthage.

Odoacer

Finally in 476 the leaders of the Germanic troops in Italy rebelled against the imperial power and nominated as 'king' one of themselves, the Hun Odoacer, an Arian who had entered the service of the Empire as a young man in Noricum, and had attained the highest rank of

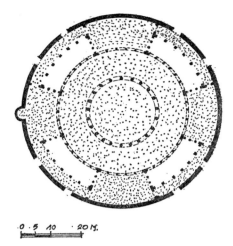

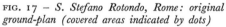

FIG. 17 – *S. Stefano Rotondo, Rome: original ground-plan (covered areas indicated by dots)*

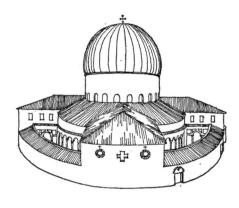

FIG. 18 – *S. Stefano Rotondo, Rome: exterior (reconstruction)*

military authority. He deposed Romulus Augustulus, took the government into his own hands and requested recognition from Constantinople. Zeno, without making an open break with him or opposing him overtly, denied him this and nominated as Emperor another general, the Dalmatian Julius Nepos.

Odoacer, who in many ways is an enigmatic figure, was unable to assert himself in these conditions, although he sought a *modus vivendi* with both Romans and Catholics, and tried to avoid a definite clash with the Emperors in Constantinople. Zeno on his side encouraged his future conqueror to act against him.

During the reigns of the last Emperors and that of the tolerant Odoacer the Catholics continued to erect important churches.

An important building of the third quarter of the fifth century is the martyrium of S. Stefano Rotondo, on the Coelian hill, which was consecrated by Pope Simplicius (468–483) shortly before the arrival of the Ostrogoths in Italy. The discovery of the relics of St. Stephen was the work of a priest, Lucianus, in 415, but this probably did not result in the immediate spread of the cult of the protomartyr in the West. The structure of the martyrium is not yet quite clear. The central core is circular in plan with two annular ambulatories. The central space was probably covered by a dome with a timber frame clad in lead. The inner ring around this space is still covered by a roof and a ceiling and has columns all round it, as the central core has. The outer ring,

CHURCH ARCHITECTURE IN ITALY, 450–488
Rome,
S. Stefano Rotondo,
FIGS. 17, 18, 19

47

FIG. 19 – *S. Stefano Rotondo, Rome: original interior (reconstruction)*

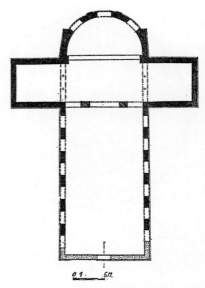

FIG. 20 – *S. Stefano, Verona: plan. The three arches between nave and presbytery are later, probably 7th century*

on the other hand, was intersected by eight radial walls, each one pierced by a triple opening and by a door. These walls enclosed four similar radial chapels arranged as a cross, and the spaces between these chapels communicate with the first ring by six arches on columns. Investigations have suggested the existence of four small unroofed courtyards within the perimeter wall with arcaded porticoes against the outside wall. In other words, the building may have been enclosed by a wall only along the external perimeter with all the other walls open to circulation by means of colonnades. Thus it would be possible for pilgrims beneath the various porticoes to have a view of the centre of the building, now occupied by a towered wooden structure with a small cupola, where it is reasonable to suppose that the relics of the protomartyr were kept.

The construction and decoration of S. Stefano seem to have been the work of local craftsmen who used materials from older buildings: the shafts of the columns differ in shape and dimensions, but the capitals and architraves of the central colonnade (the other colonnades support arches), which were made for the building, are rather crudely worked, with leaves and volutes different in style from Byzantine ones.

Perhaps at a later date vaults were constructed over the four open

FIG. 21 – *S. Stefano, Verona: exterior (reconstruction)*

courtyards: this seems to be the implication of fragmentary remains of clay-tube structures.

Another important church was built at the same time, also in honour of St. Stephen, at Verona, which was not a martyrium but a basilica church typical of a traditional north Italian style. The building was completely altered in the tenth century, and the façade again in the twelfth, but the fifth-century core is still recognizable. It was a single wide nave (*c.* 12.5 by 40 metres) terminating in a curved apse; the existing outer walls in stone with courses of brick are the original ones, except for the façade. Two wings project from the presbytery area, probably two funerary chapels, which were perhaps separated from the nave by arcades and columns. The apse was not vaulted but had a flat ceiling, and was preceded by a large arch, perhaps adorned with two flanking columns. The windows are rather wide and joined by an impost moulding. The capitals, spoils re-used again in the fifth-century building, are Corinthian, crudely carved with thin, flat caulicoles and similar to those found in the cathedral at Verona, but of rougher workmanship. The cathedral capitals can be dated by the style of the pavements to the first half of the fifth century.

The attribution of this Veronese church to 450–470 (which corresponds

Verona,
S. Stefano

FIGS. 20, 21

49

to the dating of the Rome martyrium) is on the whole acceptable. In any case, the building was in use in 520, the year in which Theodoric, to punish the Catholics who were in conflict with the Jews as well as with the Arians, ordered that the altar should be destroyed.

Ostrogoths in Italy In 454 the Ostrogoths, who had been subject to the Huns, rose against Attila's sons and defeated them. The Byzantine Empire offered this warrior people the opportunity of settling as *foederati* in Noricum and Pannonia. A little later, the court received for a few years a youth of Amal descent as a guest in the palace at Constantinople: this was Theodoric, who was subsequently to show himself a soldier of excep-

Theodoric tional courage and ability. Theodoric's career as a military commander began in 459; soon the Emperor Zeno made him *patricius* and even adopted him as a son, and later he rose to become *magister utriusque militiae* (commander-in-chief) and consul (484). He was further honoured with a triumph and a statue erected in front of the palace. By 487 his authority was such as to cause serious concern to the Byzantines, and yet at the same time his ability and achievements had won him a great reputation. Zeno suggested that he should move into Italy with his people, the Ostrogoths: by this means he hoped both to regain control in Italy (which had been lost since 472) and to avoid the dangers implicit in the presence of a war-like people within the frontiers of the Empire.

In the following year (488) Theodoric left for Italy accompanied by the 'countless throng' *(innumerae catervae)* of his people. The conquest of Italy was accomplished in a few years. Odoacer, if we are to accept the traditional story, was murdered with his entourage in the Palatium of Ravenna after the fall of that city (15 March 494) and in 498 Anastasius recognized Theodoric as ruler in Italy. The Eastern Emperors sent him the imperial insignia *(ornamenta palatii)* formerly presented to them by the unfortunate Odoacer in recognition of his respect and submission, and imperial support gained for Theodoric the sympathies of the Italian aristocracy.

After the conquest of Italy Theodoric sought to fit his people – who still lived in encampments, separate from the Roman cities – into the fabric of local culture and imperial law and administration. In attempting this he was no different from the other barbarian leaders, but he did differ in that he stood a greater chance of success; although more or less illiterate himself, he had become acquainted with the refinements of civilization through his residence at the court of Constantinople. Moreover he gained the collaboration of Cassiodorus, a senator of real sensitivity and culture, who went so far as to provide

Theodoric with an aristocratic family tree. From Cassiodorus' letters we can learn of Theodoric's attempts to preserve the monuments of Rome. When he visited the city in 500, he not only promised the population that he would observe former imperial conventions but also distributed gifts and offered entertainments, and after conquering Provence he announced its restoration to Roman sovereignty.

In his dealings with the Eastern Empire Theodoric was ostentatiously faithful and loyal. He erected a statue in his 'palace' at Ravenna to the Emperor who had sent him to conquer Italy, and he maintained a formal subordination to Constantinople, entitling himself merely *Dominus* or *Victor ac triumphator semper Augustus*, promulgating edicts instead of laws, and so on. It was only in his last years that his attitude to the Romans changed and his hostility towards the Catholics increased. This change was due to the anti-Arian measures promulgated in Constantinople by Justin I, measures against which he had intervened unsuccessfully, hoping to secure their virtual revocation.

It was in fact the religious question which brought about the downfall of the Ostrogoths. The sectarian difference between their Arianism and Catholicism kept the two peoples irrevocably apart. Their long residence in civilized areas had given the Ostrogoths a certain degree of culture, and settling as a conquering minority, they might well have fused with the Roman population or perhaps have been absorbed by the wealthier and milder majority among which they were living. But this did not occur. Their religious attachment was so strong that they virtually forbade the building of new Catholic churches throughout the period of their rule, and such an attitude naturally caused embittered feelings. We have no explicit documentary evidence concerning the differences between the observances of Orthodox and Arian in the fifth and sixth centuries, but there can be no doubt that the points of disagreement must have become gradually emphasized or created by the clergy of each sect. Like the Visigoths and Vandals, the Ostrogoths, when they came as conquerors, maintained themselves as independent religious communities with their own churches, bishops and clergy. New churches came into being as the pugnacious centres of a faith against which the priests of the Orthodox successfully incited the hatred of the local population, while the Arians reacted in turn by forming an alliance with another religious minority, the Jews.

As far as the architecture of Arian ecclesiastical buildings in Italy is concerned, the only ones erected in this period, as has been said, do not differ from the traditional Catholic buildings. The churches are halls or hypostyle basilicas and the cathedrals were complexes of

Arianism

ARCHITECTURE
OF ARIAN
CHURCHES

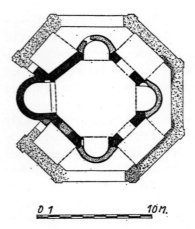

FIG. 22 – *Arian Baptistery, Ravenna: plan*

0 1   *10 M.*

church, baptistery and episcopal dwelling, but on a smaller scale than orthodox Catholic ones, since they served smaller communities.

Rome, Arian church (later S. Agata)   The oldest Arian church, S. Agata, originally consecrated to Christ and the Apostles, had already been founded in Rome by Ricimer, the conquering Vandal general, who left his name in an inscription in the mosaic. The building, which has been altered by restoration, retains its primitive structure beneath the Baroque decoration: a nave and two aisles with marble columns, arches and a semicircular apse. The central nave is wide, twice the width of the aisles, and the triumphal arch bears a mosaic which will be discussed later; the columns have granite shafts, of spoils, with Ionic capitals.

Ravenna, Arian Cathedral   The buildings of the Arian Cathedral at Ravenna are also preserved. The church was the present Spirito Santo, formerly dedicated to the Resurrection *(Anastasis)*; of moderate size, it is three-aisled, with columns of grey marble, terminating in an apse. The external decoration, as usual in fifth-century Milan and Ravenna, has blind arcading containing large windows and a posterior portico takes the place of a narthex.

Ravenna, Arian Baptistery FIG. 22   The baptistery in front of the cathedral is a modest imitation of the Orthodox Baptistery. The central space is octagonal with four apses, with an important difference in that the presbytery apse is markedly deeper than the others. A narrow ambulatory surrounded the central chamber in which the font stood, covered by vaulting. The small dimensions of this ancillary building show that at the end of the fifth century adult baptism must have been rare among the Goths and therefore large buildings for this purpose were not necessary. Here, too, there was around the walls a double row of small columns and arches, but of painted stucco, not marble.

The most important religious building erected by Theodoric, however, is S. Martino 'in coelo aureo' (referring to the gilded wood of the ceiling), later S. Apollinare Nuovo. The change of title to that of the patron saint of the Catholic Franks was made at the time of the reconciliation of the church to orthodox Catholicism, with obvious reference to that event.

Ravenna, S. Apollinare Nuovo

This spacious church is three-aisled, with twenty-four columns of Proconnesian marble, and ends in an apse. The shafts, capitals and pulvins seem to have been worked by Byzantine hands in the quarries of Marmara and were certainly a gift from one of the Eastern Emperors. Work of this kind is often found in Istanbul in museums and in cisterns, fortuitous relics of the innumerable hypostyle buildings of the fifth century. The design is distinctive: they are Corinthian capitals with flat, thorny leaves and at the top of each face is a projection carved with more acanthus leaves; above this is a narrow strip which indicates the abacus and ends in small volutes. Some Greek letters included in the carving confirm the eastern provenance of this work. The masonry of the building, however, has nothing oriental about it; there are no women's galleries, and the blind arcading outside is common at Milan as well as Ravenna. The apse has been rebuilt and so has the colonnaded atrium.

As architecture shows uniformity between Orthodox and Arian churches of the late fifth century, so too do the mosaics, from a stylistic point of view. The iconography of some Gothic mosaics, however, shows interesting differences. The mosaic in S. Agata dei Goti, which was destroyed at the end of the sixteenth century, showed the Saviour with an open book seated on the celestial globe and surrounded by the Twelve Apostles in various attitudes, with St. Peter turning towards him holding with veiled hands the keys of the heavenly kingdom (Ciampini, *Vet. Mon.*, Plate 77). It is possible, however, that this detail, with its reference to the Roman pontiff, was the result of later alterations made after the reconciliation of this church to Catholicism.

MOSAICS IN ARIAN CHURCHES

Rome, S. Agata

The mosaic of the dome of the Arian Baptistery at Ravenna is a rather crude imitation of that in Bishop Neon's baptistery, but without the outside circle of architectural elements and symbols. The Apostles, on a gold ground, are separated by palm-trees with a few leaves at the base and at the top of each. In two groups of six, they converge upon an *etimasia*, the throne with a cross. The twelve figures do not move through space with any vigour, their motion is hardly perceptible,

Ravenna, Arian Baptistery

53

confined by the palm-trees and the border of jewels at the base of the mosaic and around the central disc. The Apostles are differentiated slightly in face, clothing, attitude, but the gesture of the hands is identical in all, holding crowns with one hand veiled, the other bare. Only St. Peter carries his keys with both hands veiled, but this is perhaps a later alteration. At the apex of the dome, the Baptism of Christ contains larger figures, not very graceful, in a rather confined space. The composition as a whole, with rather solid, cramped figures, suggests that the work is that of local craftsmen following Roman tradition. The variety and elegance of the many-coloured garments, gleaming with gold, is lacking here, and so too is the air of spirituality which emanates from the Apostles in the other baptistery, the work of a master craftsman from the East.

Ravenna,
S. Apollinare Nuovo

PLATE P. 55

The Arian mosaics of S. Apollinare Nuovo are only partially preserved on the two walls of the nave. The two processions of martyrs, with the groups of the Virgin and of Christ, are the result of alterations made after the reconciliation, and of these two bands of mosaic only one end, with schematic representations of Classe and of the Palatium of Ravenna, belong to the time of Theodoric. Traces of figures, smaller than those of the saints of the present mosaic, with arms open in the act of acclamation, can be seen in the colonnades of the Palatium, and it is evident that the original scenes had figures proportionate to the buildings. It is possible that they showed processions emerging from the palace and from Classe, with the Visigoth king among the crowd of the faithful and the courtiers, but this is purely hypothesis. Of greater importance are the thirty-two nimbed figures between the windows of the nave, who probably represent prophets or the authors of books of the Bible, holding in their hands sealed volumes or open or closed scrolls instead of the wreaths and symbols of martyrdom. No name is given by which to identify them. They stand in a variety of attitudes, some declamatory, some at rest with their arms concealed within the folds of their robes, so that each has an individuality, standing out against the gold background which merges into a small trapezoid of earth at his feet, which in some cases suggests the shadow thrown by the figure, a touch of classical realism. Above each of these large figures, and beyond a decorative border, a conch-canopy surmounted by a small cross flanked by two doves and with a pendant cross beneath it stands on a blue ground.

S. Apollinare Nuovo, Ravenna, showing wall mosaic in nave. First and second half of 6th century. *Cf. above and p. 92.*

In the tympanum over each window is a chalice between a pair of birds (pheasants, partridges, quails), and above these, in the uppermost band of mosaic and level with the conch-canopies, are twenty-six panels representing episodes in the life of Christ. The thirteen panels on the north side show miracles and parables, those on the south show scenes from the Passion. Since the pictures are relatively small, the scenes are schematized: the figures stand on a gold background and in general the landscape elements, when there are any, are reduced to a minimum, showing only what is essential: in the Raising of Lazarus the tomb is shown, in the Pharisee and the Publican, the temple with pediment and knotted veil before the door, in the Denial of Peter, a small building dominated by a huge door from which the maidservant has emerged, and so on. The scenes are crowded with figures and the large human forms lack the flowing elegance of the dome of the Orthodox Baptistery and remain heavy in spite of the foreshortening. They are evidently the work of a Roman rather than of a Byzantine hand.

Arians and Marian cult The absence of scenes concerning the birth and infancy of Christ is of particular importance. The Virgin does not appear at all and this is significant in suggesting that the Arians did not practise veneration of the Virgin as Mother of God and that this constituted an essential difference from Catholic practice. In fact the Arian doctrine, which affirmed the indivisible nature of God and denied in effect the divinity of the corporeal form of Christ, could not concede to Mary the title and prerogatives of 'Theotokos', that is, of the Mother of God. Before the Council of Ephesus the question had perhaps not been openly discussed, but after the condemnation of the Nestorian heresy (which held that the Word was not born of Mary but dwelt within the son of Mary, inseparably united) it is probable that on this point the Arians had followed, with some differences, the doctrine of the defeated rather than those of the Orthodox.

As Emile Mâle has pointed out, we have clear evidence on this point. At the Council of Toledo in 589 Ricimer and his Visigoths renounced Arianism and accepted the decrees of the Council of Chalcedon of 459 in a long and detailed resolution which he signed together with his consort. The Council of Chalcedon had substantially attenuated the decrees of that of Ephesus, which had centred on the validity of the title of Theotokos attributed to the Virgin. This document repudiated those who 'imprudently preach that the son of the Virgin was merely man' (Mansi IX, col. 982); and in the affirmation of faith drawn up by the bishops and leaders of the Goths those who did not accept the

Mausoleum of Theodoric the Great, Ravenna. *Cf. p. 58.*

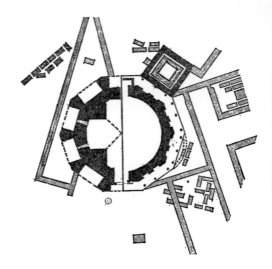

FIGS. 23, 24 – *Mausoleum of Theodoric, Ravenna: (left) exterior, reconstruction; (right) plan showing tombs excavated during last century*

decrees of the first Council of Ephesus and that of Chalcedon were condemned (Anathematisma xxi, Mansi ix, col. 987).

Ravenna,
Mausoleum of
Theodoric
FIGS. 23, 24

The best known of the buildings erected by Theodoric is however his own mausoleum which, according to the Anonymous Valesian, the king had made during his life, covering it with an 'ingens saxum'. It stands outside the city, apparently in the middle of a Goth cemetery. It is decagonal in plan with deep blind arches on the exterior and a cruciform chamber within. The material of the building is well-joined

PLATE P. 57

ashlar, the blind arches have lunettes with dentils, the barrel- and cross-vaults within are also of well-cut stone and the corners are decorated with scallop shells in relief. The upper storey is decagonal externally and circular internally and is surmounted by a cover hewn from a single block of Istrian limestone, obviously transported by sea and raised into position by means of twelve spurs projecting from the extrados. Within, on the intrados of the monolithic dome, can be seen traces of a large cross on a blue disc. Around the upper storey ran a gallery of small-barrel vaults carried, on the outside, on small columns raised along the perimeter of the lower decagon. The intermediate barrel-vaults were cylindrical; those at the corners opened out into a

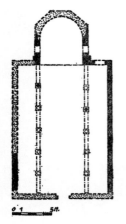

FIG. 25 – *S. Massimo Basilica, Collegno (Turin): phases I and II*

58

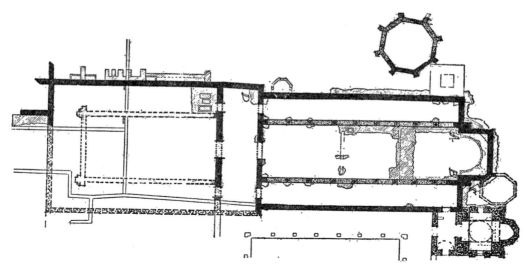

F IG. 26 – *SS. Felice e Fortunato, Vicenza: plan of phase II*

fan vault with a trapezoidal front. This is the form which, as De Angelis d'Ossat has shown, best corresponds to the shaped masonry that remains. The arrangement of the front of the building around the doorway is not clear: a rough corbel seems to have been intended to support the low-pitched roof of a pediment; a roof probably also covered the gallery with supports resting on the large projecting ring which is still in evidence. Access to the upper floor was perhaps by means of a stairway within a tower, of which traces have been revealed by excavation and which may correspond to the lighthouse mentioned by Agnellus.

The general arrangement is late Roman and Byzantine: the two Theodosian mausolea near St. Peter's, Rome, and that of Makry-Köy near Istanbul provide examples of funerary buildings with circular plan, and that at Makry-Köy has a cruciform chamber as well; so, too, has the mausoleum opposite the 'Temple of Romulus' on the Via Appia, Rome.

Clearly the mausoleum of Theodoric shows some individual features which may indicate peculiar Gothic characteristics. It is possible that the shape may have been suggested by domed tents: some nomadic oriental tribes used structures with light wooden hooped frames lashed together with strips of leather and covered with felt (a specimen is to be seen in the museum at Afyon). It is possible that these structures, which are clearly ancient in origin, were used by the Huns and the Goths and that the royal tent, as Ferri suggested, was of this kind but larger and perhaps surrounded by a gallery.

In any case, the monument certainly testifies to an original taste: not only are the ovoli and other decorative carvings stylized in a way that is very far removed from their Roman models, but their use, in decorative strips disposed at random in the blind windows of the first floor, has no classical precedent. The wide ornamental frieze which surrounds the cupola is of a type completely unknown to the Greeks and Romans but which is found again in a delicate work in gold filigree and garnets which was once in the Museo Nazionale at Ravenna, known as 'Theodoric's breast-plate'.

Ravenna,
Palace of Theodoric

The construction of a palace near S. Apollinare Nuovo has also been attributed to Theodoric, but excavations carried out between 1908 and 1914 showed that the building which we know as a peristyle courtyard surrounded by rooms of various sizes belongs to a period well before the fifth century; and that Theodoric's work was in fact a restoration in which the floor was remade and some new rooms added, among which was a three-apsed triclinium like that at Piazza Armerina. The triclinium was decorated with an allegoric mosaic floor featuring the four seasons and their respective fruits, and appropriate Latin inscriptions.

CEMETERY
CHURCHES
Collegno,
S. Massimo
FIG. 25

Two cemetery churches of north Italy can also be attributed to the third quarter of the fifth century. The three-aisled church of S. Massimo at Collegno, near Turin, was brought to light during restoration work to the Romanesque chapel. The ground-plan was revealed, with traces of columns (foundation slabs and two re-used Roman bases in place), five to a side, and the strongly projecting presbytery, probably polygonal externally and curved internally, with a door within a horse-shoe arch on either side. Tradition claims this as the burial site of St. Maximus, Bishop of Turin, but since there was a second bishop of the same name (452–465) and it seems likely that it was the custom of bishops in early times to be buried within a church built by themselves, both edifice and burial may be dated to 465. It is possible that the church was originally rectangular, with three aisles but without the projecting apse.

Vicenza,
SS. Felice e
Fortunato I and II
FIG. 26

The foundations of the second cemetery church, that of SS. Felice e Fortunato at Vicenza, have also been fully excavated. The earliest building was a simple hall of modest dimensions, of which only the mosaic pavement, of interlacing octagons and circles, remains; it dates from the first half of the fifth century. At a later date the building was reconstructed with three wide aisles and a large atrium, preceded by a transversal narthex. The building was hypostyle and the atrium was colonnaded on three sides. The apse was rectangular and, judging from the stout buttresses, covered by a barrel-vault. The floor is of square slabs with large discs at the intersections, in the style of the second half of the fifth century.

One of the few surviving examples of the artistic production of the Catholic communities in north Italy at the end of the fifth century is the five-part diptych in Milan Cathedral Treasury. It is the ivory cover of a codex. One of the leaves has a centre panel in *orfèvrerie cloisonné* (the Holy Lamb in silver with oriental garnets) within a garland of leaves, fruit and vine tendrils. Above are the symbols of the Evangelists Matthew and Luke, and below their busts, each within a wreath. The upper panel shows the Nativity, the lower panel the Massacre of the Innocents, and on the lateral panels in three registers are, on the right, the Annunciation, the Magi observing the star and the Baptism of Christ, and on the left, the Presentation of the Virgin in the Temple, Christ among the doctors and the Entry into Jerusalem. The other leaf has in the centre a jewel-decorated cross above the four springs of Paradise, and above and below the symbols and busts of the other two Evangelists. The scene of the top panel is the Adoration of the Magi with the Virgin enthroned, on the bottom panel is the Wedding in Cana. At one side are three miracles of Christ, on the other Christ on the celestial globe between two saints offering wreaths, Christ and the Apostles at the Last Supper and, at the bottom, the Widow's Mite. The iconography of these scenes is typically western (north Italy and Provence) and the attribution of this work to the last quarter of the fifth century is generally accepted.

Milan, ivory book-cover

Between 450 and 470 Gaul remained subject to the Empire with the exception of the region under the Visigoths and the Rhineland, which was now an area of Germanic settlement. While the peoples who had crossed the Rhine were infiltrating here and there, the great land-owners of Christian Gaul were still, in this autumn of civilization, linked in spirit to the classical world. Cassian, the founder of the monastery of St. Victor at Marseilles, wrote that even in moments of religious contrition there came to his mind 'lines from a poet' or memories of battles of the heroes.

GAUL
History 450–470

Christian civilization grew up within the framework of these survivals. In one of his letters (*Epistolae* v, xvii) Sidonius Apollinaris brings to life for us a celebration of the anniversary of the martyrdom of St. Julius, which did not differ greatly from such occasions in Italy or in the

Eastern Empire. So numerous were the participants in the procession that there was not room for them within the church and crypts 'although they were surrounded by capacious porticoes'. After the singing of psalms 'we withdrew so that we should be ready when the divine office began, at the hour of tierce,' says Sidonius. While they waited, some of his friends played dice and ball-games; the poet himself improvised a few lines of verse.

This society which sought to reconcile tradition with Christianity, the excessive power of a cultured few with the discontent of a huge majority, collapsed after 478 when the last Emperor of the West disappeared from the scene and the Franks, Burgundians, Alemans and Visigoths were left as masters of the situation. In little more than thirty years the Franks succeeded in absorbing the other kingdoms.

Clovis Clovis (482–511), a man of outstanding genius, energy and foresight, occupied all northern Gaul; and his military achievements were matched by an act of great moral and political courage, his conversion to Christianity in 498. Having thus gained the support of the Gallo-Romans and of Catholics in general, he proceeded (after checking the Alemans at the battle of Tulpiacum, near Cologne, in 496) to win the aid of the Burgundians, who also became Catholics, and to defeat the Arian Visigoths at Vouillé (507). Nearly all the Visigoths were driven into Spain. Clovis's heirs completed his work, depriving the last Burgundian king of his throne in 534 and dividing up the kingdom.

Church architecture Ecclesiastical architecture naturally suffered a check in this period of intermittent struggle. Much destruction was wrought in the cities in the period of barbarian occupation, and they became partly depopulated. Yet despite the political changes and economic troubles of these years, due in part to the disappearance of the former ruling class, the Burgundian and Frankish kings made an attempt to favour religious building in some of the main cities. Such building was, after all, a necessary element in the exercise of their power.

Written descriptions of churches In the most important cities the churches of the late fifth century must still have been very elaborately decorated. Sidonius Apollonaris describes the episcopal basilica of Bishop Patiens at Lyons in about 470 (*Epistolae*, v.i), decorated by verse inscriptions written by himself. A 'forest of columns' divided the nave and aisles, covered by a ceiling of gilded coffering; 'within, marble covered the floor and the walls, and above shone a mosaic of blue and gold tesserae which depicted various figures; the atrium had columns of marble from Aquitania.' Gregory of Tours (*Hist. Franc.* II,12) describes Bishop Namatius' church at Clermont (*c.* 450): it was cruciform with a semicircular apse, and

FIG. 27 – *Lugdunum Convenarum*
(*St.-Bertrand-de-Comminges*) : *plan*

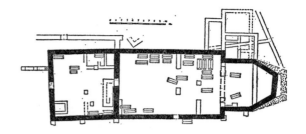

had seventy columns and eight doors. He also gives *(De virtut. Sancti Martini)* some details of the church of St. Martin at Tours, which was begun by Bishop Perpetuus (461–491) and completed twenty years later.

Unfortunately architectural evidence in present-day France is not as plentiful as literary evidence. The little oratory of St. Victor at Marseilles is said to be the work of the monk Cassian, founder of the monastery, who was active between 415 and 439. But the precious fragment of mosaic in the ancient atrium (vine scrolls issuing from an amphora on a gold ground) and the stucco work of an arcade appear from their style to be of later date.

*Marseilles,
St. Victor*

The church of Lugdunum Convenarum, now St. Bertrand-de-Comminges, on the Spanish border, was partially excavated by Dielaufoy and Lysop in 1913, but their account is not entirely clear. They brought to light a rectangular hall (31.6 by 12.4 metres) with a projecting pentagonal presbytery evidently covered by a roof or roof and ceiling, not vaulted, and with a double perimeter wall. Dielaufoy was unable to account for the different masonry of the walls, but the external polygon, which is irregular, appears to be the more recent, and the foundation of the inner, regular wall has an internal offset like that of the walls of the church. The excavators also found a wall, between the nave and the apse, which predates the church, and low down in this wall were four stone slabs. A fifth slab was found beneath the north side of the church.

*Lugdunum
Convenarum*
FIG. 27

Within the church were a number of sarcophagi with hipped covers (that is, with four sloping sides), one of which bore a Chi-Rho monogram. The church had two superimposed floors and the lower floor had been broken when the sarcophagi were placed in position. From this evidence the early church, as Grenier agrees, must have had a single nave, and not a nave and two aisles, ending in the inner apse. This church was built on the site of a pre-existing building, perhaps a villa with porticoes. The stone slabs were the foundations of the

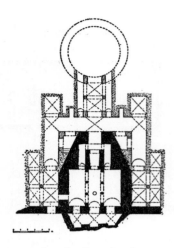

FIG. 28 – *St. Germain, Auxerre.*
Probably remains of 5th-century
presbytery in Carolingian crypt

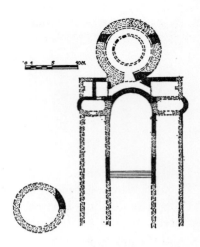

FIG. 29 – *St. Pierre, Geneva: plan*
showing results of excavations

columns of this older building, to which belong five coins datable to between 306 and 383, and a memorial inscription of 347.

The hall of the older church can be dated by the well-developed presbytery to the middle of the fifth century, the rebuilding with the wider apse, higher floor and burial of the sarcophagi, to the sixth. Clearly in the time of the first church interments within a place of worship were not permitted, and after the reconstruction customs had changed. A date *ante quem* would appear to be 585, the year in which the whole town was destroyed by Guntram, king of the Burgundians: the episcopal see must have been suppressed at this time, and it was not reconstituted until modern times (1788).

St. Maurice *d'Agaune* Another fifth-century building with a polygonal apse both internally and externally seems to have been the chapel of St. Maurice d'Agaune (Valais), which is built against a rock and constructed with small blocks of stone, with pilaster strips on the exterior. The fragments remaining are too few and uncertain to attempt a dating, and it is not impossible that it is some kind of ancillary chapel rather than the church proper (the sanctuary was already famous in the fifth century).

Auxerre, *St. Germain* *FIG. 29* Another church of this kind was perhaps that of St. Germain at Auxerre. In the Carolingian crypt can be discerned the outline of a pentagon which I think is the foundation of the presbytery of an earlier church. This would probably be the church built by Queen Clotilda (*ob.* 545) rather than the 'oratorium perexiguum' originally erected.

St. Pierre, Geneva, presents a very interesting problem. Excavation has revealed traces of an ancient small church with an apsed nave (St. Pierre I) and of a very large building with a nave and two aisles each terminating in apses, and with a rotunda with an annular ambulatory outside it which was evidently a mausoleum. Two pairs of sacristies, two of them oval and two rectangular, lay at the end of the aisles; a corridor ambulatory encircled the apse and joined the two rectangular sacristies and the rotunda. This complex structure has been attributed to Sigismund, king of the Burgundians, who may have built it after the burning of the city by his father Gundobad in 513–15: it is known that Pope Symmachus donated relics of St. Peter for the altar.

Geneva, St. Pierre II

FIG. 29

If we accept this date – and the agglomeration of rooms to the east is of a complexity that would seem to belong to a slightly later period – we have at Geneva one of the first examples of mausolea added to the outside of the apse. This arrangement recalls rooms built for burial purposes laterally to a nave and close to the presbytery, or the imperial mausolea erected beside the great sanctuaries of Milan (S. Lorenzo, S. Vittore) or Rome (the Theodosian tombs, St. Peter's); but the royal tomb here was on the main axis of the church, close to the relics, which were beneath the altar.

While the Western Empire was crumbling, just before the revolt of Odoacer, the Visigoths, who had been occupying part of France – the kingdom of Toulouse – became dissatisfied with their situation there and turned towards Spain. They first conquered the province of Tarragona, and then, around 470, spread throughout most of the peninsula. The state ruled by Henricus (467–85), of which the capital was Toulouse, was for a short time one of the most powerful in Europe. Soon this was changed by Frankish intervention. Clovis, as has been mentioned above, became Catholic and won the support of the overwhelming Christian majority in Gaul; in 507 he defeated and killed the Visigoth king Alaric II at Vouillé. The Visigoths then abandoned their territory in Gaul with the exception of Narbonne (Septimania), but now controlled the entire Iberian peninsula except Galicia (the kingdom of the Suevi) and the northern coast (Cantabria).

SPAIN

Visigoths

Franks

Spain was far from being a prosperous land. Already before the Visigoths appeared, its remoteness from Italy and even more from Byzantium had deprived it of reinforcements and aid. Franks and Alemans had raided Catalonia after crossing the Pyrenees as early as 257. Later, larger bodies of Alans, Suevi and Vandals, also from Gaul, had penetrated to the heart of the peninsula and settled there. Paulus

65

Orosius, writing early in the fifth century, lamented over the poverty of the little episcopal sees ('parvae et pauperes sedes') nestling within the ruins of what had been great cities.

Church architecture

Ampurias

Elche

Tarrasa

FIG. 30

Cabeza del Griego

FIG. 31

The churches revealed by excavation are indeed very simple, generally a single apsed nave, halls similar to the most modest examples in France and north Italy. Such is the one at Ampurias, which has a single nave terminating in an apse within the rectangular perimeter and preceded by a spacious narthex (or atrium). The tiny hall at Elche shows a similar arrangement. The bishopric here was founded between 514 and 520 and this may suggest a dating. The primitive church at Tarrasa, the Roman Egara, was probably built soon after 450, the year in which Egara was made a diocese by Nundinarius, bishop of Barcelona, who appointed Irenaeus its bishop. This church was rectangular with a small apse which was trapezoidal internally and projected externally: it is possible that at a later period a curved funerary apse was added to one side. The mosaic pavement is of interlacing octagons, ribbons, a scale pattern and a large circular field with ornamentation arranged radially – all late Roman motifs; and there are also arrangements of rectangles, lozenges and intersecting circles-popular motifs which became prominent in the sixth century. Attribution to the second half of the fifth century seems reasonable, especially since Irenaeus had a long life, and may not have died until the end of the century. In 464 he was nominated to the see of Barcelona but was not accepted, and so remained at Tarrasa (Egara). Puig y Cadafalch attributes to him a tomb in the church, with a mosaic inscription. Behind the apse was a simple octagonal baptistery containing a quadrilateral font with slightly concave sides, apparently surmounted by a four-columned ciborium.

In the most important towns and in areas which were spared the destructive effect of war it is natural to expect that larger, three-aisled churches were erected, but excavations have revealed very little trace of them. The church at Cabeza del Griego was discovered in the eighteenth century and excavations were not carried out systematically. It was a large hypostyle church with three aisles crossed in the presbytery area by a funerary crypt. Such crypts were not customary at that time in Europe but were frequent in the churches of North Africa. The one at Cabeza del Griego was narrow but extended laterally beyond the walls of the basilica; on the east it gave access, through a door within a horse-shoe arch, to another oval chamber containing two sarcophagi, possibly the subterranean chamber of a mausoleum of the type found at St. Pierre in Geneva. In the north

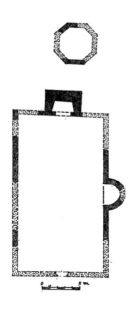

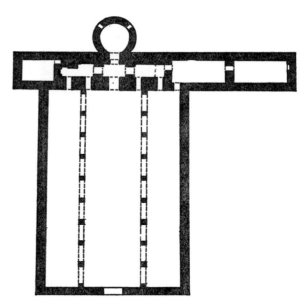

FIG. 30 – *Cathedral, Egara: plan of original church*

FIG. 31 – *Cabeza del Griego: plan of church excavated in 18th century*

arm of the principal corridor was the epitaph of Bishop Sophronius, who died in 550, the *terminus ante quem* of the building. Some of the plutei have designs which suggest a date around 550; one slab has a continuous ribbon interlace with interlacing octagons, another square diapering with rosettes, and two confronted peacocks with a laurel-wreath enclosing a Chi-Rho between them.

The Balearic Islands deserve a chapter to themselves. Laid waste by the Vandals for the first time in 423, they remained part of the Empire until 455, when the Vandals occupied them until Justinian's reconquest. Traces of three ancient churches have been found in the islands. The first S. Maria at Palma has been destroyed, but drawings of it remain which show the ground-plan and the large mosaic which decorated the central nave. It presented figural scenes in several zones, including the Garden of Eden, Adam and Eve, and episodes from the life of Joseph. The decorative hangings in the lateral aisles had a motif of cabalistic knots in four *peltae*, characteristic of the fifth century.

At Manacor the foundations of a church have been found with a

BALEARIC IS.

Palma, S. Maria

Manacor

67

mosaic similar in style to that of S. Maria at Palma. In the same district, at S. Peretó, there are traces of a three-aisled church preceded by a rectangular baptistery with a central font and an ambulatory. The apse area contains a square presbytery flanked by two other square rooms, chapels or sacristies; a kind of crypt, a subterranean space for relics, was situated underneath the presbytery. The arrangement of the churches at Manacor seems to derive from certain churches in Syria, Egypt and Algeria: the baptistery directly adjoining the façade is reminiscent also of that at Fréjus. An inscription found on the site, dated 493 and relating to a priest named Sabas, who was perhaps sent on a mission to intercede on behalf of the Catholics after the Vandal conquest, provides a *terminus ante quem* or at least a useful chronological pointer for dating the building. Similar groups of ecclesiastical buildings have been excavated recently in Corsica by Mme. Moracchini.

GERMANIC METALWORK IN ITALY AND GAUL

The artistic production of the Germanic peoples is best studied in their goldsmith's work, decorative metalwork and weapons. These objects have sometimes been found in small hoards, hidden and not recovered, but more often in tombs. It was customary with these peoples to bury men with their weapons *(Heergewate)* and women with their personal jewellery *(Gerade)*; after the eighth century this custom fell out of use and these objects were passed on instead to heirs or to the church.

At the beginning of the fifth century, bow and disc fibulae were commonly used in men's attire. Bow fibulae (and cruciform brooches) consisted of a strip of metal, partly flat and partly curved in order to hold the folds of material, with a pin and a transverse bar ending in knobs, pear- or tower-shaped. They were usually made of plain or gilt bronze and were widely used by soldiers; the well-to-do had them in gold or silver, but retained essentially the same form. In the Monza diptych, Stilicho and his son are wearing this type of brooch on the right shoulder, similar to so many that have been found in both East and West. One was found at Desana with the foot decorated with small spirals.

Disc brooches, on the other hand, were used for ceremonial dress and were decorated with gems or coloured glass pastes inlaid in cells. (One can be seen on the votive shield of Theodosius at Madrid.) The polychrome style which they exemplify was well established in Europe in the fourth century and is generally acknowledged to be Scythian or Sarmatic in origin, but, especially in the early stages, links are hard to trace, and Byzantine reliefs of the beginning of the fourth century (such as the porphyry groups of St. Mark, Venice) show imperial ornaments in gold and precious stones (arms, belts, greaves) which must be considered as reproductions of aristocratic examples in the polychrome style; another instance is the thrones reproduced in the Ravenna mosaics, also of gold and precious stones; other examples are shown in relief on porphyry statues.

Besides these masterpieces of polychrome work, other precious articles can be attributed to the fifth century, such as the pierced gold-work which is a refined version of the open-work bronzes *(durchbrochenen)* of the late Empire. A brooch found at Reggio Emilia (*c.* 490) consists of an open-work plate above three vertical bands surrounded by a raised frame. The two lateral bands are decorated with florets; the central band has arches with delicate foliage and a cross. A bracelet in a similar style was found in the Desana hoard (*c.* 450): the decorative motif is a sinuous inhabited vine pattern with amorini and a pecking bird on a ground of slender tendrils.

In the third quarter of the fifth century the polychrome style produced some very elegant articles of personal adornment. In this work, which combines gold with almandine garnets, the stones are not raised as in some Sarmatic work but inlaid in narrow cells so as to present a smooth surface of brilliant colour veined with gold (cloisonné). A magnificent sword of this type was recently discovered at Altlussheim (Baden), but the most distinguished example of this work was found at Tournai in 1685 in the tomb of Childeric, the father of Clovis, king of the Franks.

In this rich treasure, part of which is still in Paris, there were found a ring bearing the portrait of a long-haired man and the inscription 'Childerici Regis', weapons, a bow fibula, a mounted crystal ball and three hundred gold cicadas – symbols of eternity – which adorned the royal robe. The sword which remains has the hilt and the upper part of the sheath decorated with garnets set in cells divided by wavy cloisons. Among the objects now lost was a bull's-head mask with a kind of wheel ornament between the down-curving horns. *Childeric treasure*

Discoveries of polychrome metalwork in Italy show that the technique of gold and garnet cloisonné was not confined to the Rhineland but was widely diffused. In 1854 at Ravenna, for example, workmen found two fragments of bracelets and two symmetrical oval objects in gold and garnets, which were clearly ornaments for some article of personal use (once thought to be a breastplate and now believed to be a saddle). The metalwork was fine filigree in several symmetrically arranged strips with herringbone cells and small triangles each surmounted by a circle, like the decorative cornice of the cupola of Theodoric's mausoleum.

Finds at
Reggio Emilia Jewellery found at Reggio Emilia, which included ear-rings in the form of cicadas in cloisonné garnet inlay, pearl ornaments and a large fibula in pierced gold-work, was accompanied by coins which date the burial to *circa* 490. Almost contemporary with this is another cloisonné piece, the Holy Lamb of the ivory book-cover (475–500) in the Cathedral Treasury at Milan, which has already been discussed. Spirals take the form of small cloisonné triangles.

Some emphasis must be given to several articles, of an intrinsically modest nature, in cast and gilded bronze or silver, which have been thought to possess Germanic elements. These are bow-type fibulae having a semicircular head with projections (three, or more often five, whence they are sometimes called 'digital') and a lozenge-shaped or oval foot. In the Danubian or Nordic prototypes the decoration of these fibulae usually consists of straight lines or spirals, and at the end of the foot is a flat animal head shown frontally, a typical Germanic motif. A pair of large silver-gilt brooches of this kind was found among the Reggio Emilia treasure, but in these the decoration of the head of the brooch is Italian in taste – Constantinian interlace instead of spirals – and there are four small round garnets arranged around the foot.

Desana treasure The two large brooches of the Desana treasure, which are of gold cloisonné with red and green glass paste on a bronze base, also have Constantinian interlace (double continuous interlacing with a compass-drawn pattern) within a border of small circles. The semicircular head has wavy cloisonné cells within the same border, and on the edge there are four bird heads facing each other in pairs.

Plaque brooches Another group of ornamental articles in metal which are of importance in the study of the origins of early medieval taste are the rectangular plaque brooches, the so-called 'gotische Schnallen'. These generally have five inlaid garnets arranged in a diagonal cross on a field enclosed by a decorative band, with four other small round stones at the corners. Sometimes the border is more important (as at Ascoli Piceno, and in Romagna, also at Barete, near Aquila, which have interlacing) and sometimes the stones are set in the centre (as at Tressan and Hérault). Other plaques are in cloisonné or enamel (a cheaper imitation of cloisonné), i.e. in gold with stones or gold and paste (Leuc, Monceau).

Several of these plaques have a pair of confronted bird heads with inlaid stones (those from Norcia, Spoleto, Barete) or cloisonné enamel

(Lambrate). It is generally agreed that these eagle heads are Pontic in origin but the attribution of some Sarmatic fibulae to the second or third century needs verification. Eagle heads with a bright eye of garnet or almandine were popular in sword-hilts (the fourth-century Byzantine porphyry statues on St. Mark's, Venice) and in fifth-century spoon-handles (*ligulae* from Desana), and animal forms along edges (*Randtiere*) were widely used by Roman bronze-workers and imitated with significant differences in the Scandinavian countries.

A separate category is that of eagle brooches which show the whole bird: they are found in gold cloisonné, bronze and enamel (S. Ambrogio, Milan; Cesena, etc.).

Jewellery similar to these types is found in Spain, but the chronology is somewhat later than that of the French and Italian finds since the Visigoths occupied Spain only after the battle of Vouillé (507). As Zeiss has shown, before the year 500 only plain fibulae were used, and the first type of plaque brooch, that with five garnets arranged as a diagonal cross, is found only in tombs dated between 500 and 550, together with some oval brooches and plain belt-ends.

Metalwork in Spain

In general it can be said that an objective examination of the motifs used in these fifth-century articles of personal adornment show no elements which are exclusively Germanic: continuous ribbon interlace and basketwork were part of the most widely diffused Mediterranean repertory and filigree, polychrome work and eagle heads were common also among the Byzantines.

III. FURTHER SPREAD OF BYZANTINE CULTURE IN THE MEDITERRANEAN COUNTRIES UNDER JUSTINIAN (527–568)

HISTORY
Justinian's reconquest

Between 526 and 554 Justinian reconquered the Mediterranean countries for the Empire in the course of the Vandal and Gothic Wars. The African campaign was brief: in the years 531 to 534 the Vandal king Gelimer was overcome and the trophies of conquest, including the furnishings of the Palatium of Rome which had been taken as booty, were sent in triumph to Constantinople. A revolt of the Berber tribes (534–5) was the occasion for further severe repression, but eventually the country was reorganized, the Arian churches reconciled, and the cities rebuilt and defended with well-placed forts. Sardinia and the Balearic Islands were also retaken by the imperial forces, and these conquests revived commercial activity in the Mediterranean and provided secure supply bases for later operations.

Byzantine penetration into Spain

In 550 Byzantine forces entered Spain, but after some initial successes against the king, Agila, and the occupation of Cartagena, Cordoba, Malaga and Medina Sidonia, they were checked by the Visigoths under the energetic leadership of their new king Athanagild.

Italy: Amalasuntha

The campaign in Italy opened in 535. On the death of Theodoric in 526 power had passed into the hands of his daughter Amalasuntha, who by family tradition and by personal inclination, given her Roman upbringing, was attached to the Emperor of Constantinople. A cultured and energetic woman, she worked for harmony between Roman and Goth and perhaps also for the conversion of her people to Orthodox beliefs, realizing with prophetic insight the dangers of the situation. But the inclinations of the Gothic leaders were otherwise; Amalasuntha sought support from Constantinople and Byzantine activity increased, especially in Ravenna, accompanied by unconcealed supplies of money and perhaps also by troops. This phase was brought to an end after the premature death of Amalasuntha's son Athalaric (534), when the queen was imprisoned in a fortress in Lake Bolsena and there killed (535). Thus the Gothic War was provoked, which lasted for twenty years and reduced Italy to a state of prostration.

CHURCH ARCHITECTURE

As far as art and architecture are concerned, apart from the lamentable period of military activity during which, as Procopius records, the Gothic attack on the Castel S. Angelo was driven off by the Byzantine defenders using pieces of broken-up statues, two periods of artistic activity can be distinguished: the regency of Amalasuntha (526–35) and that which followed the final victory of the Byzantines over the Goths (554) – with the important qualification that Ravenna was occupied by the imperial forces as early as 540.

During the regency of the unfortunate daughter of Theodoric, Justinian's principal agent at Ravenna was, it seems, a certain Julianus Argentarius, a banker; and a powerful instrument with which to influence the population was naturally religion. Julianus in fact provided the means for the construction of some important churches connected with popular new religious tendencies which the Arians would not accept: the cult of the Virgin and that of the martyrs.

Ravenna, S. Maria Maggiore

The cult of the Theotokos spread rapidly in Italy: with the help of Julianus, Bishop Ecclesius built the church of S. Maria Maggiore on his own property ('in sua proprietatis iura', according to Agnellus) during Amalasuntha's regency. The new church of S. Maria in Cosmedin, in the Greek quarter of Rome ('ecclesia Graecorum'), was probably also built at this time.

Churches dedicated to the Virgin

After the defeat of the Goths and the Byzantine reconquest, there sprang up everywhere new churches dedicated to the Virgin, of which several still exist (S. Maria Antiqua on the Palatine, Rome, the rebuilt cathedral of Parenzo (Poreč), excavations in the crypt of the cathedral at Ancona, Castelseprio, Brioni). Also many cathedrals probably changed their title during this period of Byzantine occupation, and the hall in which episcopal functions were performed was dedicated to the Virgin. The Arian Baptistery in Ravenna was reconciled in the sixth century and re-styled S. Maria in Cosmedin, and chapels dedicated to the Theotokos were added even to funerary churches (S. Maria Mater Domini in SS. Felice e Fortunato, Vicenza).

Martyr cult

The cult of the martyrs was fostered alongside the Marian cult. The roll of those who had sacrificed their lives for Christianity included the names of Goths, but we do not know whether the Arian Ostrogoths accorded them any devotion, nor what form it may have taken, and still less do we know whether the Arians had any real veneration for other martyrs. It seems wise to doubt this: as a rule those Goths known to us do not bear the names of eastern martyrs such as Stephen or Damian or Eufemia, nor of western ones such as the Romans Lawrence or Agnes or the Milanese Victor or Satyrus, but either Germanic names – Uvimond, Theudila, Sindila – or names taken from the Old

FIG. 32 – *S. Vitale, Ravenna: plan*

73

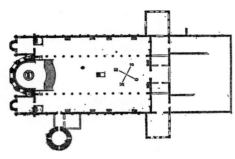

FIG. 33 – *S. Apollinare in Classe, Ravenna: plan*

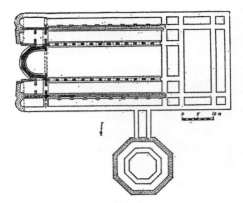

FIG. 34 – *Classe: basilica recently discovered by Cortesi*

Testament (Dannihel); as we have already remarked, it is known that by way of reprisals against the Catholics Theodoric ordered the relics of St. Stephen in the church named after him in Verona to be thrown to the winds ('Iussit ... oratorium Sancti Stephani idest altarium subverti' (Anon. Val. Ed. R.I.SS. II ed. p. 19)), which one assumes he would not have done had he professed any devotion to the proto-martyr. Only the Apostles were represented in Arian churches.

Other Ravenna churches
In the years of Amalasuntha's regency, Julianus Argentarius built in Ravenna, on a single site – probably the episcopal property on which S. Croce already stood – besides the church of S. Maria Maggiore, a church dedicated to the protomartyr St. Stephen himself and a third church to a local martyr, St. Vitalis.

Legend of St. Vitalis
FIG. 32
According to a legendary *Passio beatorum martyrum Gervasii et Protasii*, written some time after 526, St. Vitalis was a native of Ravenna, the husband of St. Valeria, who was martyred together with another Ravenna saint, Ursicinus. The great martyrium built in his honour was not only the expression of the piety of the people of Ravenna, but also a manifestation of local patriotic pride. A fourth church (S. Michele in Affricisco) was built not far from the other three by Julianus in association with a certain Bacauda and dedicated to St. Michael in gratitude for favours received. At the same time the church of SS. Cosma e Damiano was being raised in Rome.

Julianus Argentarius' churches at Ravenna are all constructed according to Byzantine building technique with thin square bricks and thick mortar joints. The same method is used in the church of S.

74

Arcangelo di Romagna, and in the upper part of the apse of S. Agata. The bricks were probably baked and laid by Byzantine masons or military personnel.

Another costly basilica was begun by Julianus at Classe, the military port of Ravenna, in honour of a local bishop, Saint Apollinaris. The basilica was begun during the episcopate of Bishop Ursicinus (532–6) and consecrated on 9 May 549, under Maximian. It is a three-aisled church with rich columns of grey marble, sent from the East, on large pedestals and with characteristic capitals of the 'wind-blown leaves' type. There are no women's galleries *(matronei)*, but the upper walls appear to have been reconstructed at a later date. The lateral aisles are decorated on the outside with the blind arcading which is traditional at Ravenna and Milan. The front of the present building was preceded by a two-storeyed narthex with projecting lateral chambers and by a quadriporticus, of which only one of the side rooms remains, largely a modern reconstruction. The narthex, and the polygonal apse enclosed between two apsed chambers are the most characteristic features; the spaces between the tribune and the side chambers are similar to those at S. Vitale and seem to suggest that the same architect was responsible for both buildings.

Classe, S. Apollinare FIG. 33

Another basilica which resembles S. Apollinare has recently been discovered at Classe only two kilometres away and excavated in part under the direction of Ing. Cortesi. It is too soon to form an opinion, but the building seems to have originally been three-aisled, and enlarged at a later date to a five-aisled church. The function of an octagonal space outlined by a double line of walls is as yet not clear.

Classe, newly discovered basilica FIG. 34

S. Vitale was begun after 526 and was built slowly (many pulvins bear the monogram of Bishop Victor, 538–45) and was consecrated by Maximian after 547. It is the masterpiece of Byzantine art in Italy. The plan of the building is octagonal; internally, an octagonal core is surrounded by eight semicircular niches pierced by arches. The presbytery niche is deeper than the others, which open out like festoons. The ambulatory is two-storeyed, that is, it has galleries for women as in the East; and it has a narthex *(ardica*, as the chronicler Agnellus calls it) preceded by a porticoed courtyard, which gives access to the building from the west. Other wide doorways open in the perimeter wall, one in each side. This multiplicity of lateral entrances, which is found also in S. Apollinare in Classe, is typically Byzantine, as is also the arrangement of two annexes (circular chambers with rectangular apses and a small space adjoining) on either side of the projecting presbytery.

Ravenna, S. Vitale FIG. 32

75

Presbytery of S. Vitale, Ravenna. *Cf. p. 75.*

FIG. 35 – *Cathedral, Parenzo: plan of phase III*

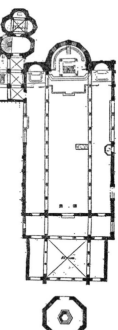

Sumptuous marble revetments, like those of St. Sophia in Constantinople (violet or green breccia from Africa) covered the walls, and some are still in place, with traces of intarsia borders. The presbytery has rich revetments of porphyry and serpentine, pierced transennae and mosaics. The sculptured work, including the columns with their deeply undercut capitals *(Tiefendunkel)*, like delicate lace-work, was transported in its finished state from the East; and some stucco work, rather clumsily executed scrolls of pointed leaves, resembling that of the cornices of the lateral doorway to St. Sophia, is also Byzantine in taste.

The ambulatory and gallery were originally covered by ceilings and roofs of timber, while eight large arches supported the dome. Western influence is seen only in the method of constructing the dome by means of hollow clay tubes, and in the blind arcading which decorates the exterior of the drum. The light construction of the building is found also in some eastern martyria of the sixth century, for instance at Korykos (Kiz Kalesi). Another western element, as we shall see later, is the taste for figural scenes apparent in some of the mosaics: evidently local customs had been respected in a matter which concerned religious tenets.

The two simple three-aisled churches of S. Michele in Affricisco at Ravenna and SS. Cosma e Damiano at Rome are more interesting for their mosaics than for their architecture. The former has some very fine pierced-work inverted-pyramid capitals.

The cathedral at Parenzo, built by Bishop Euphrasius between 543 and 554, according to a large inscription on the fascia of the apse, is remarkable for the marvellous marble revetments and its decoration in stucco and mosaic. It shows a new arrangement, of a nave and two aisles separated by columns and terminating not in one but in three apses, of which the central one is polygonal and projecting, the lateral ones recessed into the masonry of the wall. The columns with pierced pyramidal capitals and the cancelli of the presbytery were worked in eastern quarries and transported to Parenzo in their finished state. The stucco decoration on the soffits of the nave arches are among the few surviving examples of this art: they show lozenge or circular coffering with rosettes, an ornamentation showing the persistence of classical taste.

The *opus sectile* revetment of the apse is impressive: large panels are

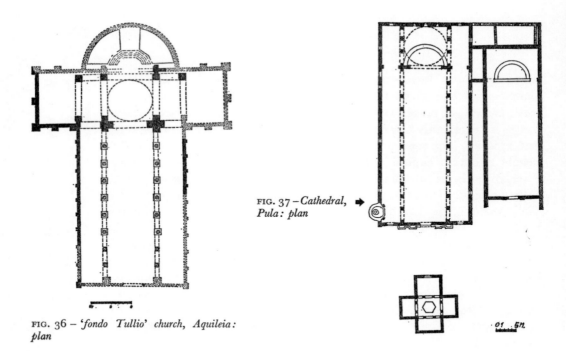

FIG. 37 – *Cathedral,*
Pula: plan ➡

FIG. 36 – *'fondo Tullio' church, Aquileia:*
plan

aligned beneath a band of smaller squares bounded above by stucco leaves. The panels are enlivened with mother-of-pearl insertions, discs and *guttae*. The motifs are late Roman (circles and lozenges) or simply primitive and popular rectangular patterns. Even the exterior was richly coloured: on the anterior gable was a mosaic (now partially restored) of the Transfiguration and on the posterior gable, the Adoration of the Magi.

Pula,
S. Maria Formosa
Another important church in Istria, similar to S. Apollinare in Classe, was S. Maria Formosa at Pula (Pola), also built by Bishop Maximian of Ravenna (546–56), who was a native of Pula: it has now almost completely disappeared. It was a three-aisled building with a nave and two aisles divided by columns; the apse was flanked by two pairs of chapels, one circular the other cruciform; of the whole edifice only one of these cross-shaped chapels remains, with traces of stucco decoration. The little church of S. Maria delle Grazie at Grado was also constructed with three aisles, of rather squat proportions, with two chapels beside the apse enclosed within a straight wall on the west, according to Byzantine custom.

Grado,
S. Maria delle Grazie

Deep presbyteries
In comparison with those of the early fifth century the presbytery of late fifth- and sixth-century buildings is generally extended, as in the

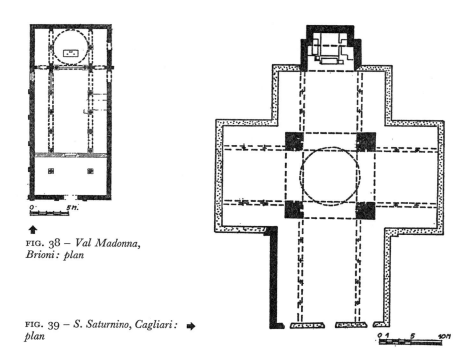

FIG. 38 – *Val Madonna,*
Brioni: plan

FIG. 39 – *S. Saturnino, Cagliari:* ➡
plan

Arian Baptistery, S. Vitale and S. Apollinare in Classe at Ravenna. This modification was the result of liturgical changes: a part of the eucharistic synopsis was celebrated out of sight of the congregation. A beam at the entrance to the presbytery, supported by columns, the iconostasis, had curtains hanging from it which were closed and then drawn back, according to an account of a service by John the Silentiary in his Description of S. Sophia.

The arrangement of the narthex also was further complicated in the sixth century: but unfortunately this part of ancient Christian edifices has been destroyed or modified in the West and the surviving *ardica* in the Ravenna churches (S. Apollinare in Classe and S. Vitale) are insufficient to elucidate what this was.

The narthex

The originality of the sixth century, however, is shown particularly by the spread of a new type of church, the domed basilica, which combined the ground-plan of the basilica with that of the martyrium. The earliest examples belong to the last quarter of the fifth century. These churches were generally cruciform and the dome was placed above the crossing, as in Romanesque churches. The supporting pillars are usually of relatively small section, a fact which has given rise to doubts as to the existence of a dome, but there is no question that there

Domed basilicas

were cupolas consisting of a timber frame covered with lead plates on the outside and cane and stucco on the inside: the perishable nature of these materials accounts for the disappearance of the structure.

Aquileia,
'fondo Tullio'
FIG. 36
One of the most important of these churches was that known as the 'fondo Tullio' church at Aquileia, excavated in 1903. The front part of the building was three-aisled, the central nave being twice the width of the side aisles, with two funerary chapels like transept arms communicating by two arches and a central column. In the presbytery area there were four compound piers, which indicate the existence of a light cupola. The apse was semicircular, and the mosaic floor, which is 58 centimetres lower than that of the nave, suggests that there was a polygonal ambulatory, possibly beneath a high synthronos behind the altar.

The exterior of the building was adorned with pilasters which functioned as buttresses and were particularly massive in the arms of the cross. The mosaic in the ambulatory showed rinceaux and lambs, and is the most reliable evidence for dating: the fleshy leaves of the acanthus clusters, from which spring vine stems with rudimentary leaves and grapes, squat lambs, ducks and partridges, all point clearly, according to Zovatto, to the early sixth century.

Pula II
FIG. 37
At Pula, the cathedral presbytery has an arrangement of supports which seems to indicate a high drum bearing a light cupola. The rhythm of the marble columns of the nave is interrupted by two cross-piers joined by the triumphal arch, and these together with the end wall of the building show a clearly defined square plan. This is a shape well suited to being roofed with a dome, which is not true of the rectangular crossings in S. Maria Maggiore or S. Pietro in Vincoli in Rome. The attribution of the building to the sixth century is suggested also by the plutei of the presbytery, which show ducks in relief.

Brioni, S. Maria
FIG. 38
On the island of Brioni, just off Pula, are the ruins of another similar church (Val Madonna). It has three aisles with a square presbytery area which was probably covered with a small dome. The triumphal arch is supported by two columns, and on either side are two arches with a central column. To judge from the reproductions of Garber, the shape of the capitals suggests a late dating (sixth or seventh century) and a local style somewhat removed from the delicacy of the Byzantine sculptors.

Castelseprio,
S. Giovanni
The various transformations of S. Giovanni, Castelseprio, make it a building of considerable interest. In a first phase it was a single-nave rectangular church (Mirabella-Roberti), to which an octagonal

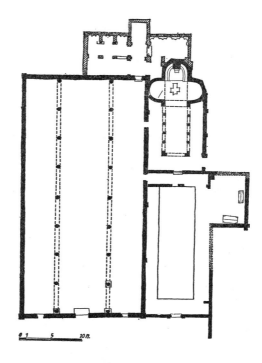

FIG. 40 – *Concordia Sagittaria: plan of phases II and III*

0 1   5   10 m.

baptistery was added, and a late fifth-century dating for this is suggested by the overhang of the exterior of the apse. This building contained a hexagonal basin for immersion preceded by a round basin (perhaps for the feet, after baptism), an arrangement similar to that which existed at Albenga and which has come to light recently also at Chieri (Turin). In a second phase the main projecting apse was added, apparently later than the baptistery, to judge by the appearance of the junction. This has two rows of arched windows. The nave was then divided by supporting columns fairly close together, of which the foundations have been found; but preceding the presbytery was a wider area with pillars which may have carried a light dome (7 by 5.5 metres).

An important martyrium of unusual shape is to be found at Cagliari, with a central core of four piers supporting a stone cupola which is still in a good state of preservation, and the foundations of perimeter walls. The four central arches lead to four short three-aisled halls, forming a cross, which were replaced by similar structures of the Romanesque period based on the old foundations. The east arm had a small projecting rectangular presbytery beneath which was a crypt of

*Cagliari,
S. Saturnino*
FIG. 39

81

three barrel-vaulted chambers, an unusual arrangement determined by the requirements of the African liturgy. Four small corner columns remain *in situ*, and impost blocks classical in style in the piers of the crossing. On the floor lie several pulvins from the old columns of the nave, which have stylized acanthus leaves with very sinuous lobes.

The building has always been attributed to the fifth century, although the presence of small columns inserted in the angles of the piers (a medieval rather than a late Roman practice) and the sinuous leaves of the pulvins would appear to indicate the sixth century, and the possibility cannot be discounted that this may be a reconstruction of *circa* 650–60 when, as Langoni has pointed out, the body of St. Augustine was translated from Hippo on account of the Arab invasion. King Liutprand ransomed it for a large sum and transferred it to Pavia.

Concordia Sagittaria FIG. 40 The cemetery behind the trichora at Concordia Sagittaria must have developed by several stages during the sixth century. First the chapel itself was transformed into a church by the addition of three hypostyle aisles in the front part, and at a second stage a portico was added, probably containing sarcophagi. It thus formed an open funerary area in communication with the most sacred part of the martyrium, as at St. Pierre, Geneva or later at Jouarre. Then the portico was enclosed by adding walls, and the chamber thus formed contains three curious trilobate niches to the east. In the central niche is a sixth-century sarcophagus with scallop niches and large crosses bearing the name of a certain Faustiniana. Finally another similar funerary chamber was built to the north with a slightly projecting rectangular chapel in the centre. The complex of buildings thus came to form the prototype of a strange arrangement of conjoined elements which we shall find again in S. Stefano, Bologna.

Buildings with central plan In the sixth century funerary chapels with a central plan are relatively rare: one of these is preserved laterally to the apse of SS. Felice e Fortunato at Vicenza, joined to it by a small octagonal space. Its title is S. Maria Mater Domini, the Theotokos dear to the Byzantines. The building is cruciform with a projecting apse which is polygonal externally, and it is preceded by a small vestibule in the form of a transverse corridor; vertical pilaster strips decorate the corners outside. The central vault is octagonal, roughly shaped as a hemisphere; all the others are barrel-vaults. The walls and apse are faced with slabs of Proconnesian marble surmounted by a small cornice; here and there are precious fragments of mosaics. On the north-east pendentive is the symbol of St. Mark and above it part of a medallion showing a female saint; in the north-west corner are traces of grape clusters, and

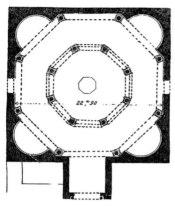

FIG. 41 – *Baptistery, Marseilles: plan*

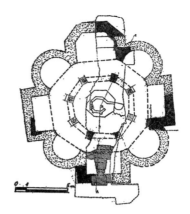

FIG. 42 – *Baptistery, Nevers: plan*

on the intrados of the arches are the remains of some frescoes with cornucopias and *clipei*. The attribution to the sixth century is indisputable, confirmed by the title, the structure and the decoration. In the sixth century baptisteries became rare, owing to the fact that baptism of adults by immersion, which involved a large piscina and various rooms for instruction, undressing and so on, had become infrequent, and infant baptism, by immersion in a small basin or by sprinkling, was a simpler matter. Some buildings, however, were quite complex and seem to have combined in a single chamber the traditional niched space and an ambulatory. The Arian Baptistery at Ravenna represents a transition from the fifth- to the sixth-century type, since it has four arches in the walls between the central core and the ambulatory. BAPTISTERIES

The baptistery at Marseilles (Provence remained culturally within the Mediterranean sphere for a long time), which was excavated in 1850, had a plan which was externally square and internally octagonal, with four niches in the angles and a projecting presbytery. Eight freestanding columns and eight others in the corners decorated the interior. The piscina was spacious and octagonal with an *opus sectile* floor; traces were also found of an *opus alexandrinum* pavement with a dodecagonal pattern. *Marseilles*
FIG. 41

A similar baptistery, altered in the Romanesque period, is still in existence at Riez (Basses-Alpes); the traditional square ambulatory appears to have surrounded it. *Riez*

The baptistery at Classe mentioned by Agnellus probably used the same type of structure; the chronicler attributes it to Peter II, describing *Classe* it as 'mira magnitudinis, duplicibus muris et altis moenibus structis aritmedice artis'. It is likely, however, that the work was due rather to Peter III, since a structure as lavish as this seems out of place in the age of Theodoric.

Nevers

FIG. 42
The baptistery at Nevers, excavated in 1947–9, had a central octagonal chamber of 5.40 metres in diameter, with a cupola supported on columns and surrounded by an ambulatory with eight niches, alternately curved and rectangular. The principal apse was polygonal and larger than the others (Louis).

SCULPTURE
Ravenna, transennae
The sculpture of the mid-sixth century at Ravenna includes in the first place the famous open-work transennae of S. Vitale, with simple or lobate rhomboidal mesh filled with a tracery of Byzantine pointed acanthus and small crosses. One has a series of touching rings folding back to form a triple leaf in the centre. There are fine transennae also at S. Apollinare Nuovo: one with crosses, vine scrolls and Greek fret which recalls some panels in the presbytery of St. Sophia, Constantinople. The pattern of another – thick vine scrolls with grape clusters rising from an amphora, a small cross and two peacocks – is found again on the cover of the Lamb sarcophagus in S. Apollinare in Classe.

Ravenna, sarcophagi
There are few sixth-century sarcophagi in Ravenna, and they show the same symbolic elements: peacocks, lambs, crosses and palms; that of Bishop Ecclesius (532–4) has in low relief, like the altar of S. Vitale, a border of characteristic quatrefoil rosettes. The workmanship of the front of a sarcophagus now in the Cleveland Museum of Art is more refined: it has columns and niches (two curved, one scallop and one pointed) and the ends are carved with large plain crosses, showing the new taste of the sixth century, a portent of the abstract decoration of the Iconoclasts.

Ravenna, episcopal throne
The episcopal throne of Ravenna, the greatest work of ivory carving which has come down to us from antiquity, is semi-cylindrical in shape. The framework is richly decorated with vine scrolls, peacocks, deer and small birds, and encloses a number of figured panels. On the front, within elaborate niches with scallop lunettes, are the four Evangelists and in the centre St. John the Baptist with the Lamb. Above, in the centre of a finely decorated band, is the monogram of Maximian, identical with one in S. Vitale.

The figured panels depict three separate cycles, and are probably the work of the same number of artists. On the anterior face of the back are panels, originally eight, showing scenes relating to the life of the Theotokos; on the sides are scenes from the life of Joseph, five on each side; and on the back there were originally twenty-four panels with

FIG. 43 – *Evangelistary of St. Lupicin: ivory cover*

scenes from the life and miracles of Christ. The work, which was once thought to be Alexandrian in origin, is now thought to have come from Constantinople, but it is accepted that some parts may have been executed in Egyptian workshops in the Byzantine capital. The vine scrolls show Asiatic taste, and the Evangelists and many figures in the Theotokos cycle suggest the elegant grace of Asia Minor rather than the vivacity of Alexandria. On the other hand, the stories of Joseph have many 'Egyptian' features; and the style of the small reliefs representing the life of Christ is still a matter of discussion.

Another piece of Byzantine ivory carving of the sixth century is the cover of the Gospel-book from St. Lupicin (Jura), now in the Bibliothèque Nationale, Paris. The two leaves are made up of five panels each, as was usual, and like those in Milan Cathedral one leaf depicts miracles of Christ and the other episodes in the life of the Theotokos. In each the upper panel shows two angels bearing a garland with a cross, like two winged Victories of the Classical period (e.g. the Barberini ivory panel, late fourth century, in the Louvre). The second leaf shows in the centre the Virgin and Child with two attendant

Ivory carving: book-covers
FIG. 43

85

angels, and at the sides the Annunciation, the Visitation, the Proof by water and the Flight into Egypt, depicted according to the Byzantine iconography which we shall discuss later. The lower panel, evidently taken from the 'Christ' leaf of another book-cover, shows the Entry into Jerusalem. Other Byzantine book-covers in five sections show a similar arrangement: in the Museo Nazionale, Ravenna, there is a 'Christ' leaf of rather rough workmanship, and at Etchmiadzin, Armenia, there are two covers almost exactly the same as the St. Lupicin one. The Virgin leaf has laterally the Annunciation, the Proof by water, the Flight into Egypt, the Nativity and, below, the Adoration of the Magi, with shepherds and an angel.

ICONS   Painting in the sixth century, compared with that of the earlier Christian period, shows a revolutionary change. From the beginning of the century images of a new type appear in mosaics and wall-paintings, which are related to the observer and not only to the other people in the picture, as was the general rule in narrative painting; and towards 550 icons became widespread. These were panels or paintings with isolated portraits of sacred personages, presented frontally. These objects of devotion constituted a new form of art which became widely popular and had great influence, and was soon imitated in both painting and mosaic.

Origin of icons   The origin of the icon probably derives from the imperial portraits which were carried in triumph in official celebrations and which implied the presence of the Emperor. On these occasions homage was paid to the *lauraton* – the official portrait with imperial insignia – with genuflection and candles. (Du Cange, *Glossarium Graecitatis, s.v.*). In a miniature of the Rossano gospels the two portraits of the imperial couple stand on easels behind Pilate seated on the judgement seat. During the fourth and fifth century portraits of sacred figures such as these had not been permitted. Christ, the Virgin and the saints had been depicted realistically only in narrative paintings or in such symbolic scenes as those of the Good Shepherd in the mausoleum of Galla Placidia at Ravenna, but the separate portrayal of their human form had been scrupulously avoided. Christ had been represented by the *etimasia* (from ἑτοιμάζο), the throne surmounted by a cross prepared for Him on the Day of Judgement; or by the Lamb (sacrifice) or the jewelled cross (triumph of martyrdom) and so on.

Frontal pose   The frontal pose of the icons was not incidental but essential, and was the result of the interest, typical of the late Roman world, in the spirituality of the face and the importance attached to the expression of the eyes. In religious portraits of the sixth century the gaze is not directed upwards to heaven as in some late Roman carvings, but is turned directly towards the observer, with an emotional intensity achieved by dilation of the eyes and elimination of expressive elements in the face in such a way as to effect an absolute tension, an intensity of spiritual communication of great power. This result was possible because artists who could still draw on the classical heritage of pictorial technique now turned to interpretation of the new religious and aesthetic principles. But the synthesis they achieved could not maintain itself for long: the effectiveness and emotional intensity of the icons and portraits of the sixth century were not achieved in their counterparts, however elegant, of the seventh and eighth centuries.

No icon incontrovertibly attributable to the sixth century has come down to us in the West, but a group of ancient Roman Madonnas painted on wood or cloth gives us an idea of them. They are images which have been exposed to devotion since very remote times and have recently been restored and carefully studied. They have proved to be of very early date, some time between the sixth and eighth centuries. The oldest is perhaps that of S. Sisto, which according to Bertelli is an imitation of the Madonna of the Blachernae quarter of Constantinople. The extraordinarily profound and sweet expression of the eyes, which seem at the same time veiled by sorrow, the purity of the lines of the nose and the small mouth, give a wonderful beauty to the head. The summary modelling of the face and of the neck was perhaps a device to give prominence to the more expressive features of the face, the large eyes and the mouth, which achieve an intensity of effect which could well belong to the sixth century.

Roman Madonnas

Madonna di S. Sisto

Other early icons in Rome, evidently executed by Byzantine hands or under Byzantine influence, are the large Madonna in S. Maria in Trastevere, of a type similar to the Madonnas of the St. Lupicin and Etchmiadzin ivories (sixth century), and those in the Pantheon and S. Francesca Romana; these works are related to prototypes of the Justinian period but seem to be of later date.

Other ancient icons in Rome

The first Italian mosaic composition to show the effect of the new principles of expression is that in the apse of SS. Cosma e Damiano in Rome, executed during the regency of Amalasuntha and commissioned by Pope Felix IV (526–30), and belonging therefore to the period of renewed Byzantine activity.

MOSAICS
Rome,
SS. Cosma e Damiano

The composition is dominated by a few large figures and thus differs in spirit and in form from the traditional composition. In the centre of the conch is Christ in a tunic with a purple stripe and a golden cloak against a background of dark blue sky, enlivened in the centre

87

by long thin clouds, streaks lit up by the red of dawn; at His feet runs the Jordan. This figure dominates the scene, holding a scroll on the left hand and raising the other in an emphatic gesture of imperial declamation. The large eyes are turned on the spectator, but the position of the body, slightly turned and with natural balance, seems to indicate a relationship also with the other figures; thus Christ is at the same time a figure participating in a collective act and an icon portrait.

The other figures behave as though they are part of a court presentation ceremony: St. Peter and St. Paul, at a respectful distance, introduce St. Cosmas and St. Damian who offer wreaths with veiled hands. At the ends of the curve of the apse was, on one side, the Pope bearing a model of the church (the present figure is a fresco painting re-done in 1572–85 and again in 1655–8) and, on the other, the martyr St. Theodorus of Amasea in Pontus, in the act of making an offering. (St. Theodorus perhaps had a particular appeal for the Goths: his name was later chosen for a reconciled Arian church in Ravenna.)

The composition appears to be the work of a Byzantine hand because of the refinement of its colouring: the golden mantle of Christ, the sky, the clouds, the silver of the Jordan and the green robes of the two physician saints combine in wonderful harmony, and the well-contrived space around the central figure gives it prominence and nobility.

Ravenna, S. Michele in Affricisco Another work showing the figures of St. Cosmas and St. Damian is the mosaic from S. Michele in Affricisco in Ravenna, a building consecrated in 545. It was removed from the church and after many vicissitudes and various restorations taken to Kaiser Friedrich Museum (now Staatliche Museen) in Berlin, where it is at the present day. This is a very interesting work because it shows a third cult spread by the Byzantines: that of angels. The founders Julianus and Bacauda wished to dedicate the church to St. Michael for favours received, according to the ancient inscription recorded by Agnellus. The apse in the Berlin museum accordingly shows new iconographical elements. In the conch is a beardless Christ with a crossed nimbus holding a long jewelled cross (Christus victor) and in his veiled left hand a book with a text from the Gospel according to St. John (XVI, 19 and X, 30) which perhaps has an anti-Arian significance: '*Qui vidit me vidit et patrem. ego et pater unum sumus.*' At the sides stand two archangels with their names, Michael and Gabriel, and along the edge are ten doves in profile.

The mosaic of the arch, besides two lateral panels with the two phy-

'Tempietto', Cividale: interior. *Cf. p. 192.*

sician saints, shows some smaller figures in the upper zone: a bearded Christ sits on a jewelled throne between the two archangels with tall ceremonial staffs, and upon these figures converge seven angels in two groups, shown frontally: the angels of the Apocalypse (VIII, 2), sounding trumpets as they approach among the clouds, sinuous streaks of red, green and blue.

Ravenna, S. Vitale The most elaborate of the mosaic complexes of Ravenna is that of S. Vitale, from the Justinian period. On the side walls of the presbytery, in conformity with tradition, are depicted two episodes from the Old Testament, but the composition of the scenes as a whole and the incomparably varied colouring of the rocky background, the strange, menacing tree which dominates the Abraham scene, belong to a world now far removed from the classical and strangely close to the taste of our own times.

A series of fifteen clipei, medallions showing busts of the Redeemer, the twelve Apostles, and St. Gervase and St. Protase, adorn the large arch at the entrance to the presbytery. The subjects are shown frontally except St. Peter and St. Paul, who are slightly turned away from the observer. These portrait medallions are really icons but derive from the *imagines clipeatae*, portraits of heroes painted on shields for funeral or honorative purposes in the Classical period. These circular icons of S. Vitale are enclosed in a decorative surround of dolphins and little shells within a richly ornamental border.

In the cross-vault which precedes the apse of the presbytery there is a magnificent design of acanthus scrolls, and the groins are covered by tapering festoons which ascend to the border of the garland in the centre of the vault, which encloses a representation of heaven with the Lamb of God; four small angels standing on coloured globes along the main axes of the vault support with raised arms this symbol of Paradise. In the apse is a beardless Christ, enthroned upon a large blue globe, against a background of gold. He is holding out a crown to St. Vitalis, an elegant figure in his official chlamys and richly embroidered tunic; on the other side is Bishop Ecclesius, the founder of the church, who holds a model of it. These two figures are presented by two attendant angels with long staffs, who indicate them with a hand on their shoulder. From the rocks beneath Christ emerge the four mystic rivers, which flow away into a meadow crossed by low rocky terracing broken by wide vertical fissures; flowering shrubs enliven the green ground. Beside the windows of the apse, on a lower level than the heavenly scene just described, are the two famous processions: one of Justinian, with nimbus and purple mantle, accompanied by two dignitaries and his guard, and preceded by Bishop Maximian and his clergy; the other of Theodora, bearing a rich offering in a chalice. The Empress, with nimbus and crown beneath a scallop canopy, is dressed in purple and brings gifts to the church; she is preceded by her officials and followed by ladies of the court. The fame of these two masterpieces is still inadequate to their beauty: the two monarchs, Justinian's three courtiers, Maximian, the two young and beautiful ladies of Theodora's retinue, are portraits worthy of immortality, and for the liveliness and boldness of its colouring the composition as a whole is one of the most sublime harmonies of colour ever achieved.

The frontal pose, the intent gaze of the imperial pair and of several members of the retinue suggest a by no means unintentional connection with icons. This kinship between the earthly court and the heavenly one is accentuated by the embroidery on the Empress's mantle, which shows the Epiphany.

The mosaic of S. Apollinare in Classe, finished during the episcopate *Classe, S. Apollinare* of Maximian and dedicated with the church on 9 May 549, is of extreme interest because it epitomizes the style of two eras: that of symbolism and the succeeding one of icons. In the conch of the apse the first bishop of Ravenna stands frontally with his arms raised and open, in the *orans* position, and gazes with a profound, sad expression at the faithful who turn to him; his large eyes seem to convey a supra-human emotion which makes a deep impression on the beholder. The abstract landscape surrounding him underlines without disturbing this concentration and spiritual solitude. It is a large, almost deserted meadow animated only by a few small trees, some rocks and large flowers springing up here and there. But in the airy sky above there is a large starred disc with a jewelled cross bearing in the centre a small icon of Christ, representing heaven, while busts of Elijah and Moses among the clouds and three sheep – Peter, James and John – at the edge of the mystic field symbolize the Transfiguration.

Twelve sheep turned towards St. Apollinaris symbolize his faithful flock, suggesting an analogy with Christ and the Apostles. The arch which encloses the apse bears in the centre another disc with an icon of Christ with a pointed beard, similar to but larger than that in the centre of the jewelled cross; and at the sides, among clouds, are shown the symbols of the four Evangelists. Along the edge of the arch ascend two lines of angels and the twelve Apostles, rising from the symbolic Jerusalem and Bethlehem. A border of pointed leaf scrolls, typical of the sixth century, surrounds the composition; on the piers are two

archangels carrying banners with the threefold acclamation ΑΓΙΟϚ –
Holy, holy, holy.

This work, which succeeds in presenting a sacred figure within a world of thought and abstract symbolism, is a masterpiece of faith and of theological subtlety.

Parenzo III Another wonderful mosaic, which rivals those of Ravenna, is in the cathedral at Parenzo, the work of Bishop Euphrasius (*c.* 550). It is a glorification of the Virgin, evidently in connection with the title of the church. Mary is in the centre of the semi-dome of the apse, seated on a richly jewelled armless chair with cushion and footstool. Two attendant angels guard her, and on the right approach St. Maurus offering a wreath, the donor of the basilica carrying a model of it, and an archdeacon with his son; on her left are three unnamed saints, and below, beside the windows, where at Ravenna there are the processions of Justinian and Theodora, are two large scenes depicting in a human and moving way the Annunciation and the Visitation.

In the barrel-vault of the presbytery before the apse there is a series of large round *clipei:* the top one shows the Holy Lamb in a circle of stars and those down the sides contain the busts of twelve martyr saints with their names, a garland of holy women to pay homage to the divine Motherhood of Mary. On the triumphal arch is Christ on a blue globe among the twelve Apostles.

The small south apse also contains priceless traces of mosaic: a young Christ in the act of crowning two saints – St. Severus and perhaps St. Ursus, two bishops of Ravenna – with a pattern of stylized pointed acanthus scrolls, typical of the sixth century, surrounding them.

Ravenna,
S. Apollinare Nuovo The last of the great Ravenna mosaics executed before the Lombard invasion of Italy are the two processions in S. Apollinare Nuovo. These were made by order of Bishop Agnellus (553–66) who after the dissolution of the Arian church wished to erase all memory of the heretical Theodoric from the building which had been his palace basilica, and to give prominence to the Virgin and martyrs. The church was dedicated to St. Martin, patron of the Catholic Franks, and accordingly the figure of the saint precedes the line of martyrs, and is dressed in purple whereas the others are in white. The procession files slowly towards a Christ in majesty between four angels: twenty-six male saints, sixteen of whom belong to the Ambrosian canon according to the names which are inscribed above, bear offerings of crowns on a background of gold, and between each saint is a palm-tree with dates hanging from it. They walk lightly over a meadow of large flowers, a mystical landscape like that of the apse of S. Apollinare in Classe.

On the other side of the nave is the procession of female martyrs (twenty-two, of whom eleven belong to the Ambrosian canon) who, preceded by the Magi, approach the Virgin and Child enthroned. They are richly dressed in many-coloured silks with embroidery and jewellery, magnificent robes signifying triumph through sacrifice. Here again each martyr offers a crown with veiled hands.

The significance of this glorification of martyrs and of the Theotokos is obvious: these two cults were not admitted by the Arian Goths, and the substitution of these for the former scenes of Theodoric's day was a form of consecration of the reconquest.

The only figures shown in profile are the Magi, who are dressed in oriental fashion and face the group about the Virgin, to whom they offer their gifts. Christ and the Virgin, with their attendant angels, are in frontal pose, and both groups of martyrs, although their bodies sway slightly forward, all look with lively intensity towards the spectator in the manner of icons. The emotional effect of these two compositions, in which the almost magnetic force of the single figures is given additional power by repetition, has never been surpassed in medieval Christian art.

The formal unity of the processions of martyrs and the two divine groups towards which they move is sufficient to counteract the widespread opinion that the groups showing Christ and the Virgin with the angels belong to the earlier state of the S. Apollinare Nuovo mosaics; of secondary importance are the observations of detail that might be made to this effect, such as the far smaller figures of the Theodoric mosaic, the identical treatment of the mystic meadow with large flowers throughout, and the analogy of the Virgin group with that of the cathedral at Parenzo.

A similar Virgin between two angels is found as a fresco in the Catacombs of Commodilla which were renovated by John I (523–26). She wears a nimbus and is seated with the Child on her lap between the martyrs Felix and Adauctus. The latter has a hand resting on the shoulder of the widow Turtura whose face, enlivened by the unearthly expression of the large eyes, is famous for the realism with which a master hand has painted it. The sacred figures are true icons.

FRESCOES
Rome, Commodilla Catacombs

Another fresco icon of the Virgin is in S. Maria Antiqua, also in Rome. It is the oldest painting in the famous building which formed part of the Palatium and was accordingly frequented mainly if not exclusively by Byzantine military and official personnel of the Palatine and their families. The church had been converted from two large rooms of the imperial period beside the approach passage which rose directly from

Rome, S. Maria Antiqua

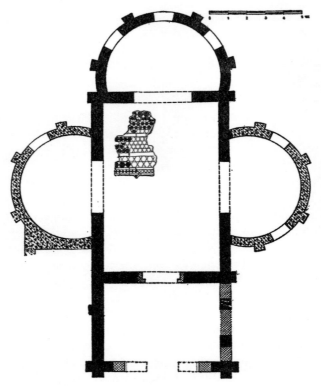

FIG. 44 – *S. Maria, Castelseprio: plan*

the Forum to the Palatium, as though under its protection. The fresco in question was painted on the end wall of the second room, to the right of a kind of niche, beneath other layers. It depicts Mary as Queen between two angels who bow in the act of offering, and is unanimously attributed to the middle of the sixth century, the period of Byzantine occupation of the Palatine under Belisarius and Narses, or the years immediately following. The iconography of the Madonna with a crown, and the technique of almost flat colours of the fresco seem to indicate a local artist rather than a Byzantine one. In the same church, the stronghold of the Greeks, other frescoes were painted later in a style far freer and more confident which form part of a particular artistic trend which deserves a brief but careful study.

Throughout the sixth century and continuing into the time of Heraclius (610–41) a classicizing school was fostered by a refined aristocratic milieu, which revived even mythological subjects with Roman and

Hellenistic plasticity of form, and this trend developed parallel with the other manner, that of the icon, whose abstract tendencies and linear colouring, albeit with a certain formal magnificence, appealed to the unsophisticated popular taste.

The starting-point of this distinction of styles was given by the silver dishes in classical style now in the Hermitage Museum made known by Mazulevitch together with the set of imperial control stamps from Justinian to Heraclius which provided proof of dating. Other investigations and discoveries have added further evidence: apart from these silver dishes there are the mosaics of the Great Palace at Constantinople which, although they are relatively late (Baster's attribution to the beginning of the fifth century is far more convincing than the recent attribution to the sixth), show the persistence of Hellenistic taste beyond the limits usually assigned it.

In the wake of Justinian's armies, painters working in this refined style were active in sixth-century Italy. The surviving masterpiece is in S. Maria at Castelseprio, a small Lombard town which was the stronghold and base of a Byzantine garrison.

Castelseprio, S. Maria

FIG. 44

The architecture of the little church shows features which are a departure from the local norm: a rectangular nave with a horse-shoe apse separated from the nave by a narrower arch. At either side there were two other niches, also horse-shoe shaped, of which the foundations have been discovered, and a small narthex with masonry arches precedes the building. The building technique is of a simple kind; the walls are roughly made of stones, and there is a flat wooden ceiling throughout, even over the apses, following Lombard and Gallic practice. Decoration was simple but not neglected: the pavement was in geometric *opus sectile* of white and coloured marble slabs, and some of the rather small windows have an archivolt which continues beyond the arch.

The pride of this small building is the series of frescoes illustrating the Theotokos cycle, which not only have the exquisite formal beauty already mentioned but include episodes typical of Byzantine iconography, deriving in part from the apocryphal gospels. The faithful of Asia Minor delighted in certain 'human interest' interpretations of the mystery of the Nativity and liked to see them depicted. One of these is the Proof by bitter water of the purity of the divine conception, by Joseph and a priest, another the miracle of the midwife who doubted the virginity of Mary and was punished and then cured, the bathing of the divine Infant according to ancient tradition, and so on. The Byzantines spread these appealing subjects among the local population in Italy. At Castelseprio this Byzantine choice of incidents is illustrated in the paintings in panels on the curved wall of the apse. In the upper zone are 1) the Annunciation; 2) the Visitation; 3) the Proof by bitter water; 4) the appearance of a reassuring angel to St. Joseph, who is shown asleep on a mattress, in the eastern fashion, out of doors with a background of distant architecture which seems inspired by Hellenistic paintings; 5) the Flight into Egypt, with the Virgin on an ass preceded by an angel and followed by St. Joseph. In the lower zone is a portrayal of the Nativity, with the Virgin lying wearily on a mattress, the Infant between the ox and the ass, the midwife with a withered hand, and above a star bearing a cross; in the foreground are two women preparing to wash the Infant, St. Joseph and the shepherds to whom the angel is announcing the birth. Then comes the Epiphany, with the three Magi offering gifts to the Virgin who is seated in an elevated position with the Infant, protected by a hovering angel. The Presentation in the Temple is the last decipherable scene and shows the Virgin holding out her son to Simeon beneath a scallop conch. The names which accompany some of the figures are in Latin but some of them are in Greek: Emea (the midwife), Zumeon for Simeon etc.

PLATE P. 97 Above in a clipeus is a bust of Christ holding a closed scroll; on the posterior of the triumphal arch are a crown and a cross upon a throne and symmetrically on either side an angel bearing a globe with a cross. Low down in the apse runs a festoon and beneath this are low arches in perspective and a curtain hanging from a beam with birds perched upon it. At the centre of the plinth the Etimasia is depicted again, a throne with a book on a purple cushion.

The work is certainly that of a Byzantine hand but opinions on its date vary between the sixth and the tenth centuries: a date between 526 and 580 is the most probable. During the last century a seventh-century tomb was excavated within the building; the freedom of execution, the Hellenistic taste for figures posed against space with a background of barely indicated architecture and trees, indicate a period not far removed from the classical. On the other hand it is not easy to believe that the Lombards, implacable enemies of the Byzantines, would make use of an artist of the nation they detested in a place like Castelseprio, far from the remaining centres of Greek influence. Some details are however indicative of the Constantinople school, such as the architectural elements consisting of arches slanting askew (in the Flight into Egypt, for instance), which have antecedents in the mosaics of the Great Palace (*c.* 400) and will appear again in a cruder style in the Münster frescoes (*c.* 800).

Fresco of Christ. S. Maria, Castelseprio. *Cf. p. 96.*

The most substantial evidence for the attribution of the Castelseprio paintings to the sixth century is given by the characteristic iconography of the Theotokos cycle, which is portrayed with similar conciseness only in works of that period. The six panels of the throne of Maximian FIG. 45 show the Annunciation, Joseph's dream, (the Visitation is now lost), the journey to Nazareth, the Nativity and the Epiphany with the Magi, and all these scenes, although very economically expressed, are full of warmth and humanity as are those at Castelseprio. Mary, the divine Mother, shows the feelings of a woman rather than of a divine being. She shows amazement at the Annunciation, leans on Joseph in the Flight into Egypt, appears exhausted in the Nativity, gentle in the Adoration of the Magi, holding the Infant with one hand and bending her head over Him.

FIGS. 45a-d – *Ivory panels on throne of Maximian, Ravenna*

*Other
sixth-century works* But the Ravenna throne is not the only work of the sixth century that offers comparisons with the Castelseprio paintings. We have already mentioned the Byzantine five-part leaves of St. Lupicin and Etchmiadzin, with Mary in majesty and the typical episodes of eastern iconography inspired by the apocryphal gospels. There is another work which can be added to this canon, the silver censer with gold and niello work found at Korydella in Lycia as part of a marvellous hoard of religious silverware of the sixth century, which was displayed in the museum at Antalya.

Korydella censer The censer is cylindrical (about 20 centimetres diameter) and has along the edge a dedication from a bishop, the 'insignificant' Eutychianus of the church of the Theotokos. It is dated by the control stamps of Justinian, identified by the Director of the museum. There are six scenes depicted in gold: 1) the Annunciation, with the angel and the Virgin, with a basket of wool, beneath an arch; 2) the Proof by water; 3) the Visitation; 4) the Journey to Nazareth (these are identical with the Castelseprio scenes); 5) the Nativity, with the Virgin lying on a mattress, St. Joseph and a large building on the left, and

98

two women washing the Infant in a large pod-shaped cantharus on the right; 6) the Annunciation to the shepherds: the Infant lies in a cradle between the ox and the ass, with a star above, while a shepherd points to this sign and a second follows carrying a gift on his shoulders. Other Byzantine frescoes with a classical flavour are to be found in the diaconal church of S. Maria Antiqua in Rome. We have already mentioned the painting of the Virgin enthroned in the early funerary chapel. The church properly speaking, that excavated by Boni at the beginning of the century, was made in 570 by substantial alterations to two large rooms already existing on the site. The first, a former piscina, became the atrium while the second, which had been some kind of peristyle court, was transformed into a hall for worship by replacing four pilasters with columns, freeing one side from the supports and opening an apse at the end, which partly cut into the ancient fresco of the Virgin. The date of this adaptation is shown by three coins of Justin II (565–78) which were found beneath one of the lateral columns, and it is reasonable to assume that by this stage the church had already been decorated with frescoes. Two panels in the most

Rome,
S. Maria Antiqua
FIG. 46

99

conspicuous place on the piers of the triumphal arch probably belong to the time of the alteration under Justin II or a few years later. These are the famous frescoes attributed to the time of Martin I (649–53). The first is the Annunciation, with the angel erect and enveloped in robes, which are partly clinging and partly flowing out behind the figure as though blown by a strong wind, with tapering wings and a large nimbus which give the slight figure an air of great nobility. Little of the Virgin is now visible except for the throne and footstool.

The corresponding panel on the other side of the arch is in a better state of preservation, and shows St. Solomonia with her sons the Maccabi, and Eleazar. The mother, a noble elongated figure, wears a draped tunic and is wrapped in a dark cloak with a *palla* covering her head, leaving only her face exposed. On her left is a figure wearing a light-coloured pallium which conceals the left hand, while the right hand points to Solomonia; in front is a boy wearing a red chasuble over a white tunic, also pointing to his mother, with a second boy beside him. On the left is Eleazar with a pink tunic and light brown pallium; the two other figures are in a fragmentary state. The inscriptions are all in Greek, and the painting is executed in a free and graceful style; it shows its dependence on the Hellenistic tradition also in the spaciousness of its composition. The figures have an air of nobility and are freely grouped, yet all contribute to the concentration on the mother, who alone wears a nimbus – an obvious reference to the Theotokos. The figures are painted with great plasticity in tones of red and brown and stand against a blue ground with wide streaks superimposed on it.

The mosaics of the little church of Casaranello on the Salentina peninsula, once cruciform like the tomb of Galla Placidia, have a particular interest in connection with Christian symbolism rather than with the complex figural composition of the sixth century. The vault of the presbytery has exclusively geometric motifs, like those of an oriental carpet. The border consists of five bands: jewellery, a three-ribbon interlace, corbels in perspective, running dog, and jewellery again. The main area is divided into three zones: a central one of multi-coloured stripes, and lateral ones of interlacing forming large and small circles, the wide ribbons of the interlacing being either tapering or continuous. There are branches with fruit, fish and small animals – rabbits, ducks and so on – in the spaces of the composition.

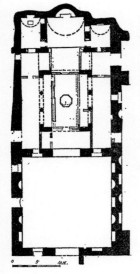

FIG. 46 – *S. Maria Antiqua, Rome: plan*

The dome recalls that of Albenga. In the centre is a small cross of yellow stones in a blue disc with three circles of stars (the highest heaven): around this is a wide band of rather deeper blue with two circles of stars (the heavens of space) and at the base of the cupola a rainbow-coloured ring. From the pendentives rise foliage scrolls stylized in a particular way, found also in the stuccoes of S. Vitale, Ravenna and the top entrance to the narthex of St. Sophia, Constantinople: rinceaux with pointed leaves and a little seed pod like a poppy-head at the end. The arches on imposts are decorated with leaves and jewellery. The abstract composition symbolizing heaven and some elements of the decorative repertory ('running dog', bands of leaves and jewellery) seem to belong to the fifth century, but the presence of continuous ribbon interlace and plaits in a vault mosaic, and above all the typical pointed leaf rinceaux indicate the middle of the sixth century.

Italian illumination of liturgical manuscripts is represented very modestly by what survives from the sixth century: the Vatican Gospel-book (Lat. 3806) has the canons of concordance of the gospels framed in a quadruple arch with columns and gilded capitals. The top of the arch has a rich decoration of foliage and two graceful blue birds (in another example these are peacocks) standing out against the page at impost level.

Illuminated manuscripts
PLATE P. 102

In the sixth century the Franks, led by the Merovingians, consolidated their rule in Gaul by occupying in 523 the kingdom of Burgundy. Provence alone remained precariously under the control of the Goths of Theodoric. During the Gothic Wars the Franks attempted to instal themselves in the Po valley but were driven away by Narses; but once the Ostrogoths had left, they kept a hold on Provence and thus after 553 found themselves securely established on the shores of the Mediterranean, no longer merely as vassals of the Empire but as conquerors. The situation in the Frankish kingdom did not become stabilized during the sixth century, however, due to the fierce dynastic wars and to the heterogeneous nature of the population. The remaining Romans did not fuse with the Germanic settlements, even when the alliance made by Clovis with the Christian episcopate had removed the religious obstacle that separated the two peoples. Thus to a large extent the cities were deserted because the Franks usually lived outside them, and the bishops, who were generally of aristocratic Gallo-Roman families, came to be the dominant factor in both church and society, defenders of the persons and rights of the citizens and helpers of the poor. These bishops sought to keep in existence, or to revive, the urban

GAUL
Merovingians

Abandonment of cities

nuclei, reconstituting sees that had been abandoned after destruction and sacking. Those of the southern provinces remained on normal terms with the Papacy, but those of the centre and north were obliged to obey the Frankish kings, who considered themselves the protectors of the French Church.

The Merovingian kings built large basilicas, all of which are now destroyed but of which a little is known. Ste. Geneviève, Paris, built by Clovis over the tomb of the saint, was approached through an atrium of marble and its walls were covered in mosaic with stories of the Patriarchs, Prophets, martyrs and confessors. Ste. Croix and St. Vincent (the present St. Germain des Près) in Paris was built by King Childebert and finished in about 558: it had marble-clad walls, mosaic pavements and a bronze roof. *New churches in Paris*

Rather more is known of the church of Notre Dame de la Daurade in Toulouse, which received its name from the mosaics which decorated the interior. It was a strange decagonal domed building with a hole in the apex and three rows of arcading on marble columns in the walls. The building, which had been altered in the Romanesque period, was demolished in 1761, apparently after some incompetent attempts at restoration. The mosaics, as described by a friar, Don Lamothe, were in niches: those in the topmost zone showed the Adoration of the shepherds and the Magi, with the visit of the Magi to Herod and the Massacre of the Innocents; in the middle zone were Christ and the Virgin with four archangels (Uriel, Michael, Gabriel and Raphael) and Twelve Apostles or Evangelists; in the third row were scenes from the Old Testament, prophets, Joseph and Benjamin, the Children in the Fiery Furnace. *Toulouse, La Daurade*

A few remaining pillars and bases give a clue to the style of the sculptural decoration: the capitals are decorated with foliage treated according to classical taste, and the shafts are covered with vine-leaf arabesques. The building, as Mâle points out, cannot have been constructed in the fifth century because the dedication and the Marian iconography were not admissible during the domination of the Arian Visigoths; at the earliest it may be from *circa* 560. The strange structure with the superimposed arcading; the iconography, entirely western in subject-matter but with isolated figures; and the presence of the archangels, including Raguel, suggest a date in the seventh or even

Fragment of an evangelistary. Canon table of Eusebius of Caesarea. *Biblioteca Apostolica, Vatican City (Vat. Lat. 3806). Cf. p. 101.*

the beginning of the eighth century. The suggestion that Notre Dame de la Daurade is to be identified with the basilica of Ste. Marie in which Chilperic's daughter Rigonthe sought sanctuary (Gregory of Tours, *Hist. Francorum* III, 10) is hypothetical.

Geneva, St. Germain An interesting church was excavated beneath St. Germain, Geneva, in 1906. It was a square building about 10 metres in length, with a small projecting apse. Beside the presbytery was a little room, a kind of *prothesis*, and there was a small narthex. The plan gives the impression that it was a domed chapel like that of S. Vittore, in S. Ambrogio in Milan, which was intended as a funerary chapel for the saint. At

APPX. PL. 21 Geneva fragments were in fact found of a monument about 1.25 metres high with confronted deer and lambs facing a jewelled cross on a ground of slender trees, each with three small leaves. Another find

APPX. PL. 19 was a wide decorative band with large stylized leaves (in typically non-classical style) pointed alternately up and down and separated by narrow ribbons curving S-wise. The leaves are striated in the intaglio 'chip-carving' technique with two slanting surfaces *(Kerbschnitt)*. Other fragments, with vine scrolls and grapes issuing from a cantharus, show sixth-century Byzantine influence, but the terminal curling of the tendrils shows not only a very individual type of stylization but also a relatively late date (middle or end of the sixth century).

METALWORK These finds are important in that they show the transformation of Byzantine motifs at the hands of Frankish and Burgundian artists and the new characteristics of their work.

In southern Germany the type identification of tomb finds, especially of fibulae, is made possible by coins which can be dated. Fibulae in silver-gilt decorated with small garnets and a bird-head foot (Weimar no. 84), spiral-decorated bronze fibulae and S-shaped fibulae (Weimar no. 86) belong to the period 520–50; a fibula with S-shaped body and a flat-headed foot (Mannheim no. 57) and one with an S-shaped body and a digital bow fibula (Tomb 12, Mengen) to the period 550–60. The S-shaped brooches deserve special mention: serpentine in shape, they have two heads with open beaks arranged diametrically opposite each other, sometimes with a round garnet eye (Werner).

The finest specimens of this form of art were found in the royal tombs at Cologne and in that of Queen Arnegunde, who died between 565 and 570, at St. Denis. An important item in the latter tomb is the great silver belt-buckle decorated with gold plates and gold filigree and small garnets. The design is very different from usual cloisonné work and exemplifies the creative originality of the Franks and their excellent craftsmanship. There are traces of the zoomorphic style in the

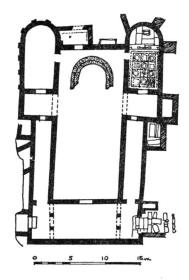

FIG. 47 – *Church, Teurnia: (left) exterior; (right) plan*

pattern of the narrow silver ribbon, expressive of tension and latent strength; at the ends on either side are symmetrical bird-heads in profile with long half-open beaks and at the central join there are frontal bull heads. The smaller buckles have bird-heads in profile, disposed symmetrically on long sinuous necks, with long beaks grasping a ribbon with curling ends. These heads are notably more dynamic than the Gothic eagle-heads, whose ferocity is only potential, in that they are birds of prey, and not really expressed.

During the phase of expansion in the Mediterranean the Byzantines occupied the Balearic Islands and some coastal regions of Catalonia and Spain, but they were contained by the Visigothic defenders who gave ground only very gradually. As time passed it became harder for the Byzantines to keep a foothold on the mainland because of increasing pressure from the Visigoths, who succeeded in re-occupying much of the territory they had lost. The last centres of Byzantine occupation were overrun by Sisebut (612–20) and Swinthila (621–31). Leovigild himself added Catalonia (574) and Galicia (585) to the Visigothic kingdom, so that almost the entire peninsula was subject to his rule.

SPAIN
Byzantine occupation

Apart from the effect of military occupation, direct contact with the Byzantines had a great influence on the Visigoths. The churches in the area occupied by the Greeks (Algeciras, S. Pedro de Alcántara etc.)

Influence on Visigoths

appear to have more in common with North African churches than with Byzantine ones. But Leovigild, the liberator, adopted Byzantine ceremonial and struck coins imitating those of the Empire.

Sculpture Decorative sculpture of the late sixth century includes some imported from Byzantium (a capital in the large church of a Merced, Barcelona, from the Justinian period, and another capital in the diocesan museum at Palma de Mallorca, from the time of Justin II) as well as imitations of Byzantine work (the sarcophagus of Ithacius in the Panteón de los Reyes, Oviedo Cathedral, and the relief at Salmasas (Lugo) which has squares containing animals like the two ambos at Ravenna).

Metalwork Visigothic work in bronze of the sixth century still includes plaque brooches of the usual rectangular type and, in the second half of the century, plaques with roughly fashioned birds projecting from the edges. Bronze objects and crosses, with and without open-work, date from 550 onwards, as do the Byzantine type lyre-shaped fibulae (Zeiss).

NORICUM
Architecture
FIG. 47 The most important sixth-century church excavated in Noricum, at Teurnia, had a single nave terminating in a straight wall, and the usual clergy-bench at the eastern end. In the front part of the building there were long narrow corridors flanking the nave but communicating only with the narthex, a wide transverse space running along the front of the building, two pairs of columns continuing the line of the nave walls. Laterally to the presbytery there were two chapels ending in apses whose curve sprang directly from the walls. Fragments of altars and of plutei carved with crosses, doves and triple rosettes of acanthus leaves were found here.

IV. THE MEDITERRANEAN WORLD ENDANGERED BY THE ARABS AND GERMANIC TRIBES. FIRST MANIFESTATIONS OF INDEPENDENT CULTURE IN NORTHERN EUROPE (568–700)

The important political events of the seventh century and the resultant changes in taste make this a period of decisive significance in the evolution of medieval art.

After the death of Justinian (565) and the ending of the fear inspired by that energetic ruler, Italy, which had already been weakened by the Gothic War, was invaded by the Lombards. On 2 April 568 these barbaric warriors, under King Alboin, crossed from Pannonia into Friuli and the Veneto. They captured Aquileia, then moved on to occupy Lombardy and other parts of the peninsula. Milan submitted to them on 13 September 569.

The reigns of Alboin (assassinated in 572) and Cleph (572–74) were followed by the so-called decade 'of the dukes', during which the Lombards became subject to independent commanders, and penetrated into central and southern Italy. Some of the small states created during this period of expansion survived after the monarchy had been restored in 584. The Lombards infiltrated everywhere, in groups headed by enterprising leaders, yet they failed to round off their gains by depriving Byzantium of the main maritime cities and the places on which their defensive fleet was based.

When Lombard expansion came to an end some regions, particularly coastal ones, remained under imperial rule. In these areas a Byzantine way of life, centred on various cities or large ports, survived. For a long time the emperors of Constantinople continued to regard the Lombards as merely temporary occupiers of the land: the will of the unfortunate Emperor Maurice treats Italy as the inheritance of his second son. These illusions did not vanish until after the onslaught of Islam.

Whereas the Ostrogoths had administered Italy through 'Romans', the Lombards proceeded to exploit it systematically by levying local tribute without any administration or economic organization. Hence the chaotic situation of Gaul in the fifth and sixth centuries was repeated in Italy in the seventh. The invasions led to general disorder: institutions were not reorganized, and towns were partially or even wholly abandoned by their former residents, while the conquerors

HISTORY

Italy invaded by Lombards

settled in fortresses, fortified camps or small towns in good defensive sites.

CHURCH
ARCHITECTURE

This was not a propitious climate for art and architecture to flourish, yet both Greeks and Lombards constructed new buildings, particularly churches, making use of such materials as they could find at hand, that is, columns and marble which had already been used.

Spoils

In western churches from 550 onwards the expense of marble columns had often been avoided by the adoption of very simple architectural schemes, plain halls: in large or important buildings (hypostyle basilicas or martyria) the shafts and capitals, if they were made expressly for the building, came generally from the East, and occasionally, as at Verona, from local quarries and workshops.

The use of columns which were spoils from older buildings had originally been the practice in towns which were well provided with classical monuments; in Rome, for example, the church of S. Sabina (*c.* 440) had a series of beautiful Corinthian columns, all matching, but salvaged from an earlier building, and at S. Stefano Rotondo (*c.* 475) there are shafts grouped in series and a regular architrave. In general, however, the re-use of classical components was approved only in important basilicas in Ravenna and Rome.

An edict of Majorian of 458 (Nov. III, 11 July) threatened dire penalties for any damage inflicted upon ancient edifices in Rome ('aedificia quaeve in templis aliisque monumentis a veteribus condita') in the course of repairs to buildings. Exceptional cases had to be sanctioned by the highest authorities with the obligation to transfer the artistic parts ('ornamentum') to other buildings.

Destruction of classical buildings

In the second half of the sixth century all this changed completely; the use of marble spoils became the norm and the few surviving buildings were destroyed without compunction. The last temples which had been preserved as noble memorials of the past were pulled down and decorative buildings, such as nymphaea and triumphal arches, and public buildings, such as basilicas and theatres, were stripped. Even houses in the devastated cities were robbed of their columns, and the removal of these coveted marble supports usually involved the collapse of the whole building.

The spoils from classical buildings, which obviously became increasingly rare, had a great influence on the architecture of the late sixth, the seventh and eighth centuries. Churches built of salvaged materials had from the first supports that were not uniform, and as material became scarcer the lack of uniformity increased. With the passage of time it became usual to incorporate large or small marble columns into piers by way of embellishment, until the noble rhythm of marble columns had disappeared from basilicas, its place taken by a restless display of contrasts.

Simultaneously with the re-employment of individual components of buildings, whole classical temples were transformed for Christian worship. Pagan observances had been prohibited under the Theodosian emperors (the destruction of rural sanctuaries had been ordered as early as 399, although 'sine tumultu et turba'), but in spite of the affirmation of Theodosius II (Cod. Theod. XVI 10, 22) 'we believe that there are no longer any pagans', and the threat of grave penalties, paganism continued.

Justinian finally decreed a relentless campaign against the ancient religion: the nobles who practised it were sought out and punished; the philosophers who defended it were persecuted and the School of Law in Athens closed (529); the remaining temples were destroyed or turned into churches. Evidently in this period the temple buildings, with podium, peristyle and pediment, were not at all unpalatable to the Christians, since the religious authorities themselves sought permission to transform temples into churches. The Pantheon was donated by Phocas between 608 and 610 at the request of Boniface IV, who dedicated it to the Virgin and to all martyrs. At this time the cult of angels was becoming popular.

These immaterial beings had been the object of religious speculation *Spread of cult* from the earliest times. For the faithful of the fifth century, the good *of angels* angels dwelt in the sphere of fire which was the seat of the Divinity, and radiant with this warmth, they were depicted as red in colour; the wicked angels on the other hand were blue, like the air of which they were formed, and they are shown thus in the scenes of the Last Judgement in S. Apollinare Nuovo, Ravenna.

In the sixth century the cult was spread in the West by the Byzantines. *Ravenna, S. Michele* At Ravenna angels were depicted guarding Christ and the Virgin, and a church was built dedicated to St. Michael (S. Michele in Affricisco) with a rich angel iconography.

The treatise of the Pseudo-Dionysius concerning the celestial hierarchy (late fifth century), which defined the nature of the nine heavenly choirs, attracted the attention of Gregory the Great in Constantinople (579–86), who summarized and popularized its conclusions. From then on the celestial beings became the object of a cult that was widely diffused in the West, growing to such an extent that angels were accepted as interceders for grace in the same way as martyrs.

In the seventh and eighth centuries churches and oratories dedicated *Spread of angel cult in West*

109

to angels arose in all the cities of the West. These centres of the cult were often situated in high places since these were thought more pleasing to the archangels, inhabitants of heaven, who preferred mountains for their appearances. (Among them were Mt. Gargano, from 492(?), and Mont St. Michel, from 709(?).) When no elevated site was possible, oratories in honour of archangels were set up in towers or the galleries of churches. Pope Boniface IV (608–15) built the church of S. Michele inter nubes on the top of the mausoleum of Hadrian (Castel S. Angelo).

The cult of St. Michael, imported by the Byzantines, was particularly successful among the Lombards, and in the opinion of recent writers this devotion constituted a national characteristic. Exaggerated ideas and superstitions arose in connection with angels, which were firmly dealt with by the Council of Rome in 745. In this consistory Pope Zacharias had a resolution passed to the effect that only three names of Archangels were admitted to human knowledge, Michael, Gabriel and Raphael; but other angels, particularly Raguel, continued to be mentioned sporadically even after this.

Transformation of iconography Besides accepting the material of new cults, religious iconography was undergoing a fundamental transformation. Before the seventh century Crucifixion scenes are very rare (the door of S. Sabina, an ivory in the British Museum) and they are certainly not cult images. Only at the end of the sixth century do we find representations of the Crucifixion, on some Monza lead ampullae from the time of Gregory the Great. The two crucified thieves are shown realistically, wearing loin-cloths; Christ is indicated by a nimbed head above a symbolic cross, with the sun and moon on either side. This is an intermediate form between the purely symbolic jewelled cross and a true Crucifixion scene, and it is found also in the mosaic in S. Stefano Rotondo, Rome, where a clipeus bearing the head of Christ is depicted above two crossed pieces of wood. The representation of the Crucifixion with the whole body of the Saviour on the cross is seen on other Monza ampullae (two of which show also the Virgin and St. John), but Christ is shown wearing a long tunic.

The long garment of Christ on the cross was obviously a mark of respect. At the end of the sixth century Gregory of Tours mentions a representation of Christ on the cross which aroused the indignation of the faithful because he was shown naked, which was in consequence then covered with a garment: and all the oldest portrayals of the Crucifixion (Rabula Gospels; crystal cross of Monza Cathedral; the Volto Santo, Lucca; a Roman fresco in S. Maria Antiqua) show Christ in the long garment.

The Monza ampullae, which appear to have been executed in Constantinople and not in Syria, are also of great importance for the frequency with which the Anastasis, the Holy Sepulchre at Jerusalem, is represented on them; but this will be discussed later. FIG. 48

GERMANIC ART

In almost the whole of Europe from the end of the sixth and throughout the seventh centuries, Germanic art flourished in the decoration of small articles of personal adornment worn by the Anglo-Saxon, Lombard, Frankish, Burgundian and Aleman peoples. Some of these tribes, such as the Franks and Burgundians, had already been settled for a considerable time in their areas of western Europe but had not used the developed forms of the Germanic style before this time, when it reached them, as it did the newly immigrated tribes, from eastern Europe and Scandinavia, brought either by single individuals or by masses on the move. It acquired variant characteristics although the different branches all remained clearly related to a common cultural background and representational tradition.

Germanic art is essentially introspective, in which the artist seeks to express what he finds within himself and not what he sees around him; and this is reflected in the zoomorphic ornament and in the dynamic interlace.

Zoomorphic ornament

Zoomorphic ornament (and the word 'ornament' is a debatable one because the depiction of animal forms may have had at that time a prophylactic function even if not explicitly admitted as such) originated, as we have said, in the small figures of quadrupeds or bird heads which decorated the bronze objects (brooches, etc.) worn with uniforms and some late Roman and Gothic garments. In true Germanic art these animal forms lose the naturalistic character of their Roman provincial prototypes and are deformed and broken up to accentuate their strongest features, ferine or beaked heads, sinews, or talons.

In the first phase of Salin Style I animal or human forms (or in some cases, parts of them) were represented in a caricatured or surrealistic form, but with their constituent elements arranged according to nature. In the second phase of the same style the animal forms were broken up into separate limbs and used without co-ordination – a procedure analogous to that of the Cubists and Futurists, which emphasizes the tendencies which they have in common – systematic abandonment of naturalism, conscious expression of force and movement, accentuation of some features and wilful omission of others, all of which constitute a break with tradition and attempt to convey 'the spontaneous form which springs from the drama of the object in its surroundings' (Boccioni).

An ornamental motif suggested by the work of basket-makers had already been widely used in the late Roman period: plaited work and interweaving is found in the mosaic pavements and transennae of Pope Hormisdas (514–23) in S. Clemente, Rome. In this 'Constantinian' interlace, the basic tracery, whether straight or curved, is simple and static and forms part of the repertory of geometric ornament common in Roman popular art.

In Germanic interlacing, which spread from the sixth century onwards, this regularity is completely lacking. In some areas where culture was primitive, motifs are found with irregular, asymmetrical windings and knots which depend entirely on the whim of the artist; in these uncontrolled movements a 'dynamism of disorder' finds expression. Other interlace patterns, including knotwork which is typical of Insular art, are more considered and planned, executed on a tracing of lines drawn with ruler and compass, yet still dynamic in movement, knotted and plaited.

The fundamental rule for obtaining this regular 'dynamic' interlace, as Romilly Allen has shown, is by 'cutting' certain strands and rejoining them. This practice of breaking and joining gives a 'feeling of strength in action' which brings a curious quality of excitement to the composition. The system of 'breaks', however, is not used in all cases and many regular patterns, also 'dynamic' in style, derive from simpler combinations of curves and straight lines, especially diagonals, or are purely geometric compositions (Bain). A basic geometric grille was used also by the Umayyads, as the stucco plaques at Khirbet-el Mafjar show. Examination of the pattern structure, however, cannot entirely explain the extraordinary poetic power of this totally abstract, unrepresentational art.

The supple play of this dynamic interlace is made more obvious by

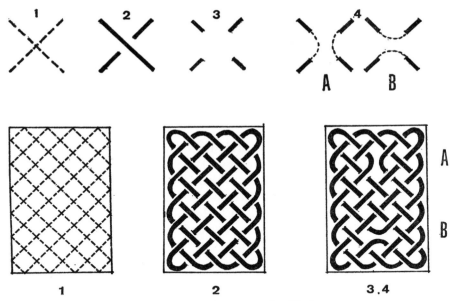

FIG. 49 – *Patterns of 'dynamic interlace' (after J. Romilly Allen)*

the many colours of the ribbons or, especially in the work of the Merovingians, by the different patterning of the ribbons (smooth strands combined with granulated or studded ribbon, for example), so that variety of effect is achieved and the movement of the single strand is more evident.

The transformation of stylized animal motifs to conform with the practice of dynamic interlacing produced the Zoomorphic Style II, which was widespread in Europe from the late sixth century. In this style the animal bodies are intertwined irregularly, almost as if in a struggle to the death; or they are elongated and combined with ribbons, as in Merovingian work. More often some animal elements, such as feet or tail, are reduced to long threads which interweave with the elongated body as though they were narrow ribbons, and end in a small clawed foot or a tuft. Zoomorphic interlace, too, can be classified as irregular or symmetrical.

Salin Style II

After the Lombards had settled in Italy, the stronghold of Ravenna, the bridgehead for the putative reconquest of the Po valley, remained the fulcrum of the defence of the peninsula and the seat of the Byzantine governor, the Exarch.

ARCHITEC-
TURE IN
BYZANTINE
AREAS

Within the city no building remains which can be dated to the time of the Lombards. It is known that Peter III (578) began the church of S. Severo in Classe, which was completed by John II (578–95), who also built a chapel near S. Apollinare in Classe; but that is all. S. Severo is, however, at present in the course of excavation: the plan, of grandiose dimensions, has been revealed and consists of a nave and two aisles with a single apse and a mosaic floor with typical early medieval motifs.

Within the territory of the exarchate, a church of the second half of the sixth century or the beginning of the seventh exists almost in its entirety: S. Michele d'Acervoli, which has given its name to the town in which it stands, S. Arcangelo di Romagna. The building, as its title shows, can be associated with the spread of Byzantine religious influence; it is fairly large (about 11 metres wide), rectangular in plan, with an apse to the east. The masonry is of thin bricks in horizontal courses with thick mortar joints, as in the Ravennate churches built employing Byzantine technique (S. Vitale, apse of S. Agata). On the outside are vertical pilaster strips, four on the longer sides and one each side on the front. In each of the side walls are two large arches, one with a span of 2 metres, the other of 1.4 metres. There are two doors in the east wall, one on either side of the apse. It is possible that these arches were intended to lead to lateral funerary chambers, and indeed these may have even been built and later destroyed. The windows are not very large; there are two in each side surrounded by a projecting concentric arch. Clay tubes and mosaic tesserae from the conch of the apse have been found. The building appears to be close in date to S. Vitale, to judge by the masonry technique and the clay tube vaulting. The rather small windows are very unusual for the sixth century and the arched lintels are found in buildings of a later date (S. Salvatore, Brescia; S. Maria delle Cacce, Pavia).

A second Byzantine centre arose at Grado. As the Lombards approached, Paulinus, the Patriarch of Aquileia (557–69), took his treasures and sought shelter in the neighbouring lagoons where he could be defended by the imperial fleet, and transferred his episcopate there. From 606, after the death of Archbishop Severus, there were two archbishops who styled themselves of Aquileia, a Byzantine one at Grado and another, a Lombard, at Cividale. Duke Lupus succeeded in sacking Grado in 662, but he could not hold it.

Bishop Elias, who was a devoted subject of the Byzantine Emperor and naturally supported him in the 'Three Chapters' controversy between the churches of East and West, built a cathedral in the new

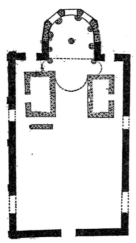

FIG. 50 – *S. Michele d'Acervoli,*
S. Arcangelo di Romagna: plan

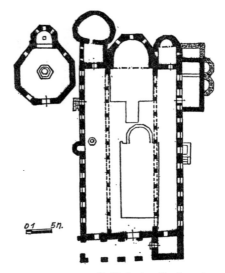

FIG. 51 – *S. Eufemia, Grado: plan*

see dedicating it to S. Eufemia, the martyr of Calcedonia, and con- *Cathedral of*
secrating it on 3 November 579. This building, which stands on the *S. Eufemia*
site of an earlier church, is three-aisled with columns and capitals of FIG. 51
spoils. The external walls have regular projecting pilaster strips and
large arched windows. The apse, polygonal externally and semicircular
internally, is flanked by an apsed chapel on the south and a trichora
on the north. The original floor is almost completely preserved: it is a
mosaic bearing inscriptions from those who have made offerings, and
decorative motifs. In the nave there is an undulating pattern, and
panels with lozenges and circles containing emblems on a circular
field. The trichora has an elaborate composition of discs within a large
circle and a dedicatory inscription to Elias. The presbytery still has
marble plutei showing a Chi-Rho from which flow two twisting ribbons
bearing crosses at the ends. The octagonal baptistery has a projecting
apse: it stands beside the basilica to the north and is a little older.

A third Byzantine nucleus formed around Rome, and the city was *Rome and its*
never occupied by the Lombards. The Byzantine defenders were *hinterland*
supplied by sea, through Ostia, and formed a ring of fortified towns
(Bomarzo, Orte, Amelia, Terni and Perugia), with the result that the
Lombards remained in the Apennines and set up a duchy with Spoleto
as its capital. Thus Rome was able to continue relatively undisturbed
as a Byzantine colony, and during the seventh century new churches
and chapels were built within the city.

At the end of the sixth century Pelagius II built what is now the east part of the present building beside the great fourth-century church dedicated to St. Lawrence. It is a small hypostyle building with *matronei* (women's galleries), raised over the tomb of the saint and hence a basilica 'ad corpus'. Pelagius II was a loyal subject of the Emperors of Constantinople, as his part in the 'Three Chapters' controversy shows, and received favours from them; the typical Greek feature of the women's galleries is symptomatic of Byzantine predominance.

APPX. PL. 8

The church is three-aisled with five large Corinthian columns on each side, of spoils. The monolithic architraves came from different pagan edifices and were cut to a uniform length: some parts have the epistyle more or less intact, others have only the frieze and cornice. The galleries have smaller columns, also of spoils, in different shapes and sizes, supporting arches with roughly carved dosserets, wide and squat, interposed. The narthex opens into the nave, with two columns between, on both storeys; the parapets of the gallery were slabs of porphyry. The windows are wide but not large; the triumphal arch still has its mosaic; beyond it there was a semicircular apse and then, outside, a kind of *sub divo* sanctuary. The apse underwent transformations at various later dates up to the time of Honorius III (1216–27), who doubled the size of the edifice by joining another basilica to it.

As at S. Lorenzo, a lesser basilica 'ad corpus' was erected at S. Agnese, to the south of the atrium of the great basilica of Constantine, on the site of an earlier church. Pope Honorius I (625–38), who also enjoyed the favour of the Emperor Heraclius in recompense for his activity in religious matters, commissioned the new building in honour of the saint, who was popular with the Romans. Again Byzantine in type with galleries, the church has a nave 9.43 metres wide, nearly three times wider than the two aisles. Nave and aisles probably all ended in apses, since besides the central apse there is another one to the south gallery. On the walls of the principal apse are symmetrically disposed plaques of paonazzetto marble and in the conch the splendid mosaic which will be discussed later. The columns, seven on each side, are of spoils; at the west end is a narthex, now open towards the interior, with three wide arches and also provided with a gallery.

APPX. PL. 7

Of seventh-century Italian mosaic and fresco painting very little remains; only two panels in S. Apollinare in Classe are undoubtedly from the late sixth or early seventh century. But to this period probably belongs a group of mosaics usually attributed to the time of Theodoric, the mosaics of the Archiepiscopal chapel.

This little church is cruciform with a cross-vault, preceded by a small transverse passage covered with a barrel-vault, and it is on the first floor of the Bishop's palace. This is probably the chapel of S. Andrea which the chronicler Agnellus attributes to Peter II, supporting his assertion by citing a long mosaic inscription of which traces have been discovered in the course of restoration work carried out by Gerola. In my opinion, however, the mosaics are closer in style to those of S. Vitale than to those of Theodoric's time, and it is possible that Agnellus has confused the actions of the two Peters, or that the erection of the chapel coincided with that of the episcopal palace at Tricoli (τρία κῶλα – three arms or parts of the building), which was begun by Peter II, according to the same passage in Agnellus, and was completed by Maximian (546–53).

Ravenna, Archiepiscopal chapel

The mosaics of the narthex consist of a gold ground with a pattern of rosettes formed of four stylized triple acanthus buds, and a variety of birds, some of which have bodies covered with small chequers, a typical late sixth-century motif. On the soffits of the arches around the perimeter of the main chamber are clipei containing busts of saints similar to those in S. Vitale, but of inferior workmanship. The frontal presentation of these portraits makes them 'icon clipei', and their emotional content suggests an affinity with portraits of the Justinian age, at the earliest. The iconography of the cross-vault, with four angels supporting a Chi-Rho monogram symbolizing heaven, is found in a rudimentary form on the presbytery vault of S. Vitale and later in that of the chapel of S. Zeno in S. Prassede, Rome (Paschal I, 817–24).

These mosaics seem to belong to the time of Maximian or even of Peter III rather than to that of Theodoric and Peter II, when figures tended to be strongly foreshortened and heavy.

The more important of two panels in the apse of S. Apollinare in Classe shows the Emperor Constantine IV Pogonatus and his brothers Heraclius and Tiberius, followed by a dignitary holding out a roll of privileges – 'PRIVILEGIA' – to Bishop Reparatus (671–7) with three attendants, two of whom are deacons. The figures are in frontal pose within a perspective edifice; this has a polychrome conch with a scallop shell flanked by two doves within it, and a pattern of zigzag and dentils with a scalloped edging in a variety of colours—a good example of the development away from naturalism in art which had taken place during the hundred years since the time of Justinian. The figures, composed of line and colour only, lacking physical life but possessing great spiritual intensity, stand out against the curtains of the

Classe, S. Apollinare

background in a design that is essentially hieratic, all reality sublimated into formal abstraction.

The matching panel, with identical architectural elements, brings together the three mystic sacrifices of Abel, Abraham and Melchizedek which are also to be found, but differently composed, in the S. Vitale lunette.

Four lesser panels between the windows show single portraits of bishops of Ravenna and have some similarities with the two compositions that have just been described, notably the architectural frame, but their dating is uncertain. So indeed is that of the Reparatus panels, which remain subject to conjecture because of the restoration and reworking they have undergone.

Rome, S. Lorenzo The mosaic of the triumphal arch in S. Lorenzo, Rome has in the centre Christ seated on a blue globe and bearing a long-stemmed cross, in the act of blessing, and at the sides St. Peter with his cross and St. Paul with his book. Laterally is St. Lawrence carrying an open volume showing an inscription relating to his final act as a deacon, distributing to the poor the valuables in his charge, and beside him, smaller in size, is Pope Pelagius with a model of the church. On the other side of the arch are St. Stephen, also wearing a deacon's dalmatic, and St. Hippolytus (one of the soldiers ordered to guard the saint, and who had been baptized by him) bearing crowns of martyrdom; and at the ends, on either side beneath the windows, the mystical cities, Jerusalem and Bethlehem, decorated with gold and precious stones (*Apocalypse* XXI).

Although partly restored (in the lateral areas), the mosaic is imposing because of the expressiveness of the figures, depicted without relief. Christ, in a purple pallium, has almost the severe, unearthly expression of the Pantocrator. All the figures gaze intently at the observer, drawing him into the scene.

Rome, S. Teodoro(?) At the foot of the Palatine is a small round edifice, S. Teodoro (?), which was perhaps originally covered with a dome. It has three apses, one of which, the presbytery, is deeper than the others and retains its mosaic covering. The building already existed in the time of Gregory the Great (590–604). The iconography of the apse seems to indicate the second half of the sixth century: in the centre is Christ on a globe, as in S. Vitale, bearing the staff-cross, with St. Peter and St. Paul on either side presenting two martyrs who carry crowns, as in the church of SS. Cosma e Damiano, on a background of gold.

Rome, S. Agnese In the apse of S. Agnese, against a gold ground, stands the saint, richly
PLATE P. 119 dressed as a Byzantine empress. She carries a book in her hands and

Apse mosaic. S. Agnese, Rome. *Cf. p. 118.*

at her feet are the instruments of her suffering – the flames which left her unharmed and the sword which ended her life, as it did St. Paul's. At the apex there are curving bands of blue and a disc, the empyrean, with the red clouds of dawn and the hand of God crowning the martyr. On either side, at a respectful distance, are two Popes, of which one, Honorius I (625–38), on her right, holds out a model of the church. A verse commentary on the composition conveys the effect of the noble colouring on the faithful of the time: 'The picture rises, gilded with sharp-cut metal, and daylight itself is enclosed therein, with the light sent out by the rainbow amid the stars and the purple peacock glow, blazing with colour . . .'

This mosaic can be compared in its effective simplicity with that of S. Apollinare in Classe; the result of the colouring is to reduce form to an almost abstract composition. The two Popes seem merely ceremonial figures, and the virgin saint herself stands out on the vast gold surface with a deep, serene gaze which captivates the beholder.

Rome, Lateran:
S. Venanzio chapel

The most important seventh-century mosaic is, however, that of S. Venanzio in the Lateran. The chapel is very simple, almost square in plan with an apse (perhaps once covered by a light cupola); it was commissioned by the Dalmatian Pope John IV (640–2) to receive the relics of ten martyrs which had been rescued from Salona, at that time threatened by the Avars. The decoration was completed under his successor Theodore.

The iconography contains new elements: at the centre of the conch is a large bust of Christ Pantocrator, not enclosed within a disc but emerging from the clouds between two large angels, also busts. Beneath is the Virgin *orans*, between St. Peter and St. Paul, St. John and St. Theodore, the patron saints of the donors, St. Venantius and St. Domnius, the two most important of the Salona martyrs, and finally, still within the semi-dome of the apse, the two donors, Popes John and Theodore.

Along the walls come next the remaining eight saints, four on each side, the lay saints bearing the crown of martyrdom, the ecclesiastics with scrolls or books. In the upper register at the sides are jewelled representations of the mystic cities Jerusalem and Bethlehem, and in the two centre zones the symbols of the Evangelists, in pairs.

The backgrounds are all gold; the borders include, besides the jewellery, which is used with sensitive moderation, the large archivolt border with crosses, lozenges and florets; and the tympana are decorated with a fine thread-like rinceau pattern. The frontal presentation of the figures is similar to that of other contemporary mosaics but it is finer

FIG. 52 – *S. Stefano Rotondo, Rome: apse mosaic in chapel of SS. Primo e Feliciano*

work, and the decoration includes freely stylized flower and ornamental motifs which are very different from traditional types.

The decoration of the chapel of SS. Primo e Feliciano was carried out in the time of Pope Theodore (642–9), who had the bodies of the two martyrs transferred from Via Nomentana to the martyrium on the Coelian hill. It is the first example known of a translation of this kind. The iconography of the apse mosaic follows at a distance that of S. Agnese, but the two martyrs are not the fulcrum of the composition: a large jewelled cross, which seems to foreshadow that of the Iconoclasts, takes the central place in the conch, which is covered in gold. At the top of this symbol of triumph is a disc containing a bust of Christ with a crossed nimb, as he appears on some of the Monza ampullae; above is a representation of the two celestial regions, the starry sphere and the empyrean, with the hand of God and a crown. St. Primus and St. Felician stand with their feet on a green meadow strewn with red flowers; they are dressed as officials of the Palatium (purple tunic, white chlamys with a purple tablion), and each holds a book.

Rome, S. Stefano Rotondo: chapel of SS. Primo e Feliciano

FIG. 52

Rome has many early medieval frescoes in the church of S. Maria Antiqua, and some of these are of the seventh century. The figures of the Fathers of the Church painted on the end wall (known as the 'Palimpsest wall') are attributed to the time of Pope Martin I (649–55), but the quotations shown on the open scrolls held by these figures, referring to the theological questions debated at the Council of 649, cannot be taken as sufficient proof for a dating. Following that council, Martin I was arrested, deported and put to death, and it is unlikely that the Exarch Calliopa would have permitted texts hostile to the Monothelites in the very church of the Greek stronghold. I think it more probable that these frescoes were done after the death of the Emperor Constans II (668).

SCULPTURE
Two ambos at Ravenna — There are two large marble ambos at Ravenna which belong to the second half of the sixth century. They were originally massive pieces of furniture, with two stairs, a curving centre-piece and a domed canopy carried on columns. One of these is in the cathedral and is dated by a long inscription of the time of Bishop Agnellus (557–70). The two curved central parts of it remain, decorated in square panels: the borders have a repeated ribbon motif, and the central area contains horizontal bands of symbolic animals – lambs, peacocks, deer, doves, ducks and fish. The relief is very low; the animals and the border seem to have been cut out in card and applied to a flat ground.

FIG. 53 — The other ambo, formerly in SS. Giovanni e Paolo and now in the Archiepiscopal Museum, is smaller and of more slender proportions, but the decoration of animals within squares is very similar, and the inscription attributes it to Bishop Marinianus (597–606).

APPX. PLATES 14, 15 — With these should be grouped two similar fragments (one of which comes from S. Apollinare Nuovo) showing single figures in panels in the upper part: one figure is shown in the act of receiving, with hands veiled.

ART AND ARCHITEC-TURE IN LOMBARD ITALY — In the areas of Italy under Lombard occupation art followed two directions. Architectural monuments seem to be linked to classical or local tradition, which is logical since the Lombards had neither the habits nor the traditions of a firmly settled people, and so made use of local architects and skills, in the same way that the Arabs, after they had conquered Syria, used Byzantine architects for their castles and mosques. The most sumptuous goldsmith's work, with wrought gold, precious stones and enamel often came from Constantinople or was imitated locally from Byzantine models, because the capital of the Eastern Empire was unrivalled in the production of luxury articles, but there are also examples of local taste. Metal objects used for their

FIG. 53 – *Ambo, formerly in SS. Giovanni e Paolo, now in Archiepiscopal Museum, Ravenna*

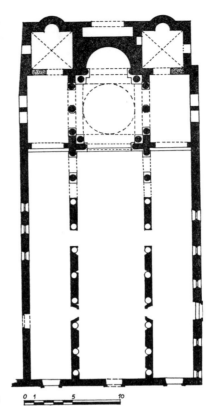

FIG. 54 – *S. Salvatore, Spoleto: plan*

adornment by the people often show a very different characteristic style, of Germano-Scandinavian origin, and these, in spite of their intrinsic simplicity, are of great interest both culturally and artistically. Foremost among the more elaborate buildings erected by the Lombard rulers should be included, I believe, two buildings whose chronology is the subject of sharp controversy among scholars: S. Salvatore, Spoleto, and the little temple of Clitumnus.

S. Salvatore, Spoleto, was a basilica with three aisles covered by timber roofs and by a light dome over the crossing (of clay tubes or a stucco intrados on a timber frame covered with lead). The nave walls, with arched clerestory windows, are supported on Doric columns and entablatures, of spoils; between the window level and the columns is a band of panels divided by axial pilaster strips, with the columns in a disposition similar to that of S. Maria Maggiore, Rome. At the crossing there are compound piers with large Corinthian columns on

Monumental architecture
APPX. PL. 2

Spoleto, S. Salvatore
FIG. 54

dados decorated with foliage, four arches tall enough to contain pairs of windows at the same level as those of the clerestory. On either side below are Doric colonnades like those in the nave.

Externally, the height of the building is indicated by the drum, a kind of tower like that at Alahan in Cilicia (475 or later), which clearly was originally surmounted by a light cupola.

The building thus belongs to the eastern group of domed basilicas like Salona Cathedral, S. Maria, Brioni and so on. In S. Salvatore, moreover, the curved apse is flanked by two square chapels with cross-vaults and absidioles which derive from Byzantine models and can be compared with those of S. Apollinare in Classe.

Internally, the decorative elements are almost all spoils from classical buildings (one exception is the foliage dado beneath the arches of the cupola; there are others) but many components of the façade, although not dissimilar from those of the imperial Roman period, are con-temporary with the church. The masonry of the façade seems to have been of small blocks of ashlar, as in pagan temples, and it is arranged in two levels: the lower sector, which contained a narthex, is remarkable for the three doorways with elaborate but delicate consoles, a frieze with rinceaux, and a corbel-table cornice. The upper section has four tall Corinthian pilasters which perhaps supported an architrave and pediment; between the pilasters are three windows, two gabled and one arched with an aureole of sixteen strange skittle-shaped candle-sticks and a cross; the jambs are short pilasters rising from dados. At first sight this ornamentation, which closely resembles that of third-century buildings in Asia Minor, appears classical; but the crosses in the frieze of the doorway and over the central window, and several completely unexpected details such as the cornice which includes the rinceaux of the doorways on a 'sofa-shaped' ground and at either end strange palmette acroteria, and the curious features projecting from the extrados of the central arch (candlesticks on the curve, large curving palmettes at the impost and a cross above) show that the work is obviously not of the Classical or late Roman periods.

Temple of Clitumnus

PLATES PP. 125, 126

Equally rich in contrasts is the famous 'temple of Clitumnus': the façade has four columns imbricated behind two others (there is no evidence that the outer columns were added later) and two wings at the sides (two small porticoes with stairs which served as entrances, since the front gave no access from outside) have no parallel in Roman temple plans, although there are some affinities. The decorative reliefs of the pediments, moreover, are puzzling because of the 'free' elements grafted on to the classical manner of the composition as a whole, from

'Temple of Clitumnus', Perugia. *Cf. p. 124.*

'Temple of Clitumnus', Perugia: interior. *Cf. p. 124.*

the spirals at the foot of the cross, taking the place of the traditional tuft of leaves, to the bunch of grapes hanging from each of its arms. Inside the building, the disposition of the aedicule of the apse is a definite break with late Roman taste: four tall and narrow pilasters and a sharply angled tympanum frame the niche; the projecting carved entablature which continues within the niche, lacking frieze and architrave, and the rinceaux of the archivolt and the tympanum, with helically-arranged leaves, are clearly early medieval in taste. The rather cruder manner of the carving in this small building seems to suggest that it is later in date than S. Salvatore. The invocations on the pediments to the God of the Angels, the Prophets and the Apostles, to the Resurrection and so on, are to be found also in Insular and early Carolingian litanies (Marrou). With this in mind it is impossible to base a reliable judgement of the chronology of the style on the Roman elements, and it must be remembered that classical elements persisted strongly in the fifth, sixth and seventh centuries in Rome, which was not far away and with which Spoleto clearly was in close communication.

S. Salvatore, Spoleto, is distinguished among other early Christian *Spoleto, S. Salvatore* churches for the way in which space is treated. The spacious single-aisled churches of S. Croce, Ravenna and S. Stefano, Verona, or the hypostyle basilicas of Aquileia II or S. Apollinare in Classe represent an attempt to enclose a vast space within walls and roof. The silent dignity of these large halls was accentuated by the rhythm of noble columns and of numerous wide windows. The same sensitivity is manifest in the unified treatment of the external mass. The martyria, dominated by a cupola representing the heavens, show the same taste. In S. Salvatore, however, the handling of space internally is different: the narrow nave is flanked by two rows of columns supporting high walls, and the rhythm of the columns is interrupted by the massive pillars of the cupola, which assert different values of volume of masonry and of contrast between light and shade. The exterior, with the towering cupola and the chapels of the presbytery, lacks the traditional unity of mass.

The strange combination of elements of volume in the little church of Clitumnus, with its two projecting wings, shows that it cannot have been a temple; nor can it have been erected as a Christian building before the sixth century, since only then did buildings in the form of a temple, with rare exceptions, cease to arouse hostile feelings among Christians and only then were they taken over for purposes of Christian worship.

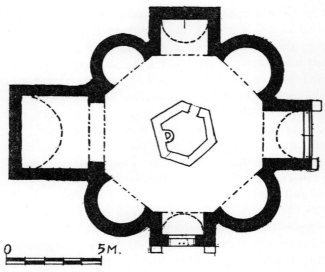

FIG. 55 – *Baptistery, Lomello: plan*

History provides an important *terminus ante quem* for these buildings: a document of 815 mentions the 'monastery of S. Salvatore' among the daughter houses of the abbey of Farfa, and it seems probable that two 'luxury' buildings such as those we have just described, which were constructed with valuable material of spoils made available for their construction, would have been built by the Lombard dukes, and only by them, and that some 'Roman' elements would have been included on purpose as an anti-Byzantine gesture and as a manifestation of monarchical prerogative. To provide the uniform columns of S. Salvatore, for instance, porticoes or buildings of ancient Spoletium must have been demolished, which only a ruler could do.

The dukes of Spoleto, who twice conquered Classe and who succeeded in developing a policy of their own towards the Papacy, flourished from 571 (Faroald I) to 729 (victory of King Liutprand); and the dependence of the monastery of S. Salvatore on Farfa, which is mentioned in the letter of 815 cited above, makes it possible that this was a Lombard foundation, assigned to the famous Sabine monastery when Faroald II (703–20) restored and enriched it. The most probable theory is that the two buildings were commissioned by the dukes during the seventh century from Roman workmen.

FIG. 56 – *Baptistery, Nocera: plan*

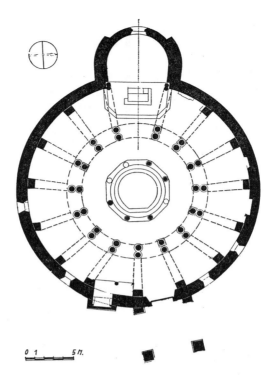

0 1 _____ 5 *m.*

The construction of baptisteries was certainly rare in Lombard Italy in the seventh century, but a few examples can be given. There is one at Lomello at the side of the church of S. Maria Maggiore, not very unlike baptisteries of the fifth century. It was a niched octagon like that at Novara, but without corner columns and with a deep presbytery apse. The wide windows in the drum are enclosed on the outside within two pointed arches.

At the height of the lower edge of the windows runs a rough cornice of projecting bricks and of dentils cut out of brick or formed of small bricks laid vertically.

The hexagonal font is very interesting, with frescoes of painted bricks and Byzantine motifs of painted marble lozenges. On one side is a painted cylindrical basin bearing a cross within an arch and the word *piscina:* evidently holy water for sprinkling was kept here. Baptism by immersion was no longer practised in this baptistery (which has no outflow), and this fact, together with the unusual depth of the presbytery and the pointed arches on the exterior suggest a date at the end of the sixth century or the beginning of the seventh. This site was in fact of some importance during that period: according to Paul the Deacon it was at 'Laumellum oppidum' that the betrothal of Duke

Buildings with central plan: Lomello, Baptistery

FIG. 55

Agilulf and Theudelinda took place, the site of the romantic scene in which the queen gave her consent.

The baptistery at Nocera Superiore, in Campania, is very large. It is circular in plan, with an inner supporting ring of fifteen pairs of columns, of spoils, and a projecting curved apse, where the space between the arches is wider. The cupola is of masonry and begins low, just above the level of the arches; originally the extrados must have been apparent outside, protected by a roof upon pillars. The ribbed barrel-vault of the ambulatory is also very solid, and in front of the apse there is a groin vault. In the centre is a large piscina with steps to descend, and eight columns; it has plutei decorated with coloured pastes inlaid in cells in very simple designs of lozenges, crosses, discs and zigzag.

The masonry work is carefully executed; the central chamber and the cupola are in small blocks of stone with rows of brick; in the archivolts ashlar alternates with bricks laid in pairs. The dating of the rotonda to the seventh century is suggested by the style of the plutei, the simple geometric intarsia of coloured pastes, and the pulvins, which are simple blocks remote from classical taste, and the small paired columns decorating the sides of the entrance to the apse.

Theudelinda, who was daughter of the king of Bavaria and wife first of Authari (in 589?) then of Agilulf, and finally regent until 625, was the chief ally of Gregory the Great in the conversion of the Lombards to Catholicism, and she received from him some historic gifts of religious jewellery, relics and even a copy of his *Dialogues*. Her palace near Monza has been destroyed, but Paul the Deacon gives some information about it, mentioning the 'pictures of the ancient Lombards' (probably paintings) it contained, and their clothing, similar to that of the Anglo-Saxon contemporaries of the chronicler (787–99).

Theudelinda built the cathedral at Monza, but it was rebuilt in the fourteenth century and the only remains of the Lombard edifice are two marble slabs very simply carved in low relief—rare surviving examples of Lombard decorative sculpture. One has two crosses with an α and ω, and a 'wheel' Chi-Rho monogram; the second has a cross between two lambs.

In the Cathedral Treasury of Monza is a valuable collection of ancient jewellery, part of which belonged to the Lombard queen and of which other items may have been gifts from other Lombard monarchs. The

most important of these works is a rich Gospel book-cover: each of the leaves (34 by 26 centimetres) is of plain gold plate with a border of champlevé red enamel and a large jewelled cross with pearls,

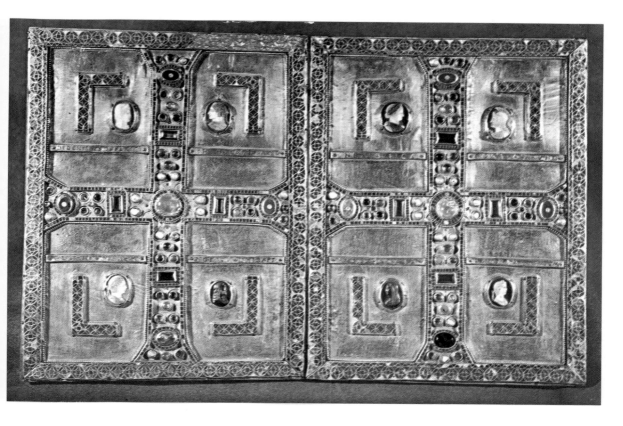

Cover of Theudelinda Gospel. *Cathedral Treasury, Monza. Cf. p. 130.*

sapphires and emeralds, also surrounded by a narrow enamel border. In each of the four divisions are antique cameos and strips of red enamel squares in relief, in the shape of an L. Two narrow bands of gold nailed across the divisions bear an inscription to Theudelinda. The enamel is set in zigzag cells and interlaced circles: this motif, elaborated from circles, is common in the Roman and late Roman periods, but an identical band of champlevé enamel is found in the crown of Recceswinth (653–72), and the narrow band of granulation which borders the four divisions and the central jewel seems to suggest a Constantinople workshop.

Similar in style and technique is the cross of Agilulf, which also has borders of granulation and large and small gems, both round and rectangular, but the workmanship is less careful and the design less

Cross and crown of Agilulf FIG. 57

131

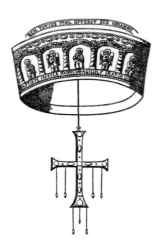

FIGS. 57a-b – *Cross of Agilulf and lead ampulla. Cathedral Treasury, Monza*

refined: the surface is crowded with stones and pearls touching one another, and there is no enamel. This cross hung from a crown, now lost, which bore the inscription 'rex totius Italiae': a drawing by Frisi shows it decorated in relief with a series of small arches containing single figures – Christ in the centre between two angels, and saints around the band. The columns of the arches were twisted and each supported two laurel branches leaning to form the arch. In an upper register round the band were alternating oval stones and pearls. This work, however, is now referred to the twelfth century by Schramm. Tradition attributes to Theudelinda a gold crown decorated with discs of mother-of-pearl (outer rows), small pearls and round gems (two inner rows), stones, large pearls and lozenge-shaped jewels (centre row). Its simplicity suggests that it is local work.

Silver-gilt hen
PLATE P. 133

The silver-gilt hen with seven chicks grouped around her, pecking corn scattered over a plain disc, is shown with Theudelinda and her gifts in the thirteenth-century relief in the lunette in the cathedral. Its execution, with the firmly marked lines and punched dots of the feathers and the inlaid garnet eyes, recalls late Roman techniques. In the tomb of the Lombard goldsmith at Paysdorf (Austria) the skeleton of a hen in a ritual position was found. The effective plasticity of the structure of the hen, with the mass of the body apparent beneath the light covering of feathers, and the head with the fixed yet lively eye, still retains something of Roman naturalistic tradition. This seems to exclude attribution to the Romanesque period, yet it has little to do with Byzantine art. Thus the object was probably the work of a local or a Lombard craftsman.

Silver-gilt hen and chicks. *Cathedral Treasury, Monza. Cf. p. 132.*

The 'iron crown', the most famous object in the Monza Treasury, is no longer considered to belong to the Lombard period. The multi-coloured enamels which form a background for the oval stones and the gold repoussé flowers suggest an affinity with the altar of Volvinus at S. Ambrogio, Milan, a work of the ninth century.

PLATE P. 134

Iron crown. *Cathedral Treasury, Monza. Cf. p. 133.*

Cf. p. 133.

Silver ampullae
FIG. 57

Also of interest to scholars in the Monza Treasury are the ampullae, which are particularly valuable for the study of iconography in the early Middle Ages. They were originally made to contain oil from the lamps which burned around the tombs of famous martyrs and were objects of veneration considered to have protective powers against disease.

A papyrus belonging to the basilica explains their origin: a priest, John, brought more than seventy of the ampullae to Rome in the time of Gregory the Great, with the names of the saints concerned. Sixteen of these remain, some still bearing the label with the name of the martyr thus venerated. The flasks, probably sent to the queen by the Pope, were made in Constantinople and present scenes of unusual iconographical interest (the Crucifixion, Ascension, Resurrection and the Holy Sepulchre) and have appropriate inscriptions in Greek.

Other ampullae, not of silver but of base metal, were found at Bobbio in the crypt of the church of St. Columbanus, and are thought to have been given by the pious queen to the Irish saint at the time the famous monastery was founded.

Germanic art prior to the Lombard period is represented in Italy by grave goods – small personal articles which were buried with the body up to 650. All these objects are thus datable to between 580 and the middle of the seventh century (Werner). The cemeteries where these finds have been made are generally considered to be Lombard, but it is not impossible that they were used also by the local population and even the garrisons of Byzantine fortresses. *Lombard grave goods*

Bow fibulae continue to reproduce sixth-century types with some modifications: they generally have a small bow and a broad head, semicircular or rectangular in shape, with the perimeter decorated with knobs. The foot usually has an animal head shown frontally. The ornament is of lines and zigzag (Museum of Cividale) or of irregular dynamic interlace or zoomorphic motifs, sometimes reminiscent of Salin Style I (Cividale) or sometimes clearly of Style II. *Fibulae*

The small crosses of gold-foil which were sewn to the breast of garments, a characteristic Lombard adornment, have punched decoration, simple geometric designs or Constantinian interlace, sometimes dynamic interlace (Brescia) or zoomorphic motifs (another example at Brescia). The so-called cross of Gisulf has small heads and inset coloured stones. The influence of the Mediterranean tradition is shown in general in the use of Constantinian interlace, but the taste and skill of the gold-smiths of the Eastern Empire is more directly evident in some individual objects. Typical is the use of chip-carving to outline fish, animal heads, vine scrolls and leaves on a plain ground. This technique was used on gold-foil (sword sheaths, Chiusi) or more often on cast bronze plaques, loops and brooches. The saddle ornaments (?) of tombs v and 119 at Castel Trosino have the same motifs punched. The pierced gold-foil intended to stand out on the background of leather or cloth is of great elegance. The sword scabbards of the Castel Trosino tomb have a design of acanthus palmette; the gold brooches of Chiusi have a double vine rinceau. *Crosses* *Technique*

Other evidence of Byzantine craftsmanship can be seen in the gold filigree work. The cross from the so-called tomb of Gisulf has only a narrow border of granulation around the stones in the Germanic fashion, but in the round brooches of tombs B, C, S2, 115 etc. of Castel

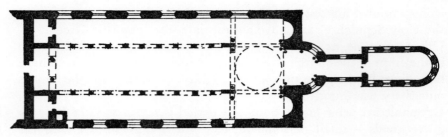

FIG. 58 – *Former church of St. Martin (now destroyed), Autun*

Trosino filigree work covers the whole surface and even the knobs with a fine lace-like design.

GAUL
Merovingian rule

The barbaric struggles of the Merovingian kings in the late sixth century came to an end with the massacre of Thierry's sons, and finally Chlothar II (613–29) was able to reign in peace.

Gallo-Roman and Frankish elements had now fused in a landed aristocracy, a ruling class which provided the 'mayor of the palace', an official who controlled the administration of the court and, later, that of the state as a whole. Gradually these 'majordomos' substituted their authority for that of Chlothar's successors. The last Merovingians were deprived of power by Charles Martel, who in 715 took over the reins of government and set out to reunify and reorganize the state. During the crisis of the Merovingian monarchy some regions of ancient Gaul had attempted to reassert their independence; one of these was Aquitaine, which from 670 was organized under the leadership of Duke Lupus. This movement accounts for the formation of

Cultural centres

local centres of culture and independent artistic schools in the seventh century, whose originality deserves emphasis.

Moreover the influence of the energetic monasticism of the British Isles became very strong in France in the course of the seventh century. Starting with the foundation of Luxeuil, Irish and Anglo-Saxon missionaries were extremely active in Gaul, and the cultural interaction between the two countries naturally included artistic influences.

ARCHITEC-
TURE

Little remains of seventh-century ecclesiastical architecture, but what there is possesses considerable interest.

Autun, St. Martin
FIG. 58

The baptistery of St. Martin at Autun, which was built by Queen Brunhild in *c.* 590 and destroyed in the seventeenth century, is known only through a plan made in 1658. It was three-aisled and terminated in three apses, of which the centre one was semicircular internally and externally and communicated by means of a passage with a funerary chapel which stood to the east and had an apsed nave. The two lateral absidioles were recessed into a wall which was straight on the outside.

In the presbytery area there must have been a tower with a small cupola: this is shown by the thick piers in this area with columns which evidently supported transverse arches.

Another four columns stood before the apses, an arrangement anticipating that in S. Maria d'Aurona (*c.* 735) and at Malles (*c.* 800). The windows were large, but it is not known whether these were the original ones; similarly the façade, which had a tower at either end of a narthex forming a primitive 'westwork', is not necessarily part of the original building. Early descriptions of the building say that it was rich in 'admirables mosaïques' and tall marble columns; an elaborately decorated wooden ceiling concealed the roof timbers.

According to ancient tradition and to documents that have survived *Jouarre, crypt* in a seventeenth-century compilation, the foundation of the monastery at Jouarre was suggested by St. Columbanus and carried out by an important personage, Adon. The first abbess appears to have been the niece of the latter, Theodechild, who died about 680, and the church was commissioned by her brother Angilbert, bishop of Paris, who towards the end of his life came to live near her. Angilbert was one of the leading prelates of the seventh century. He had studied the scriptures for ten years in an Irish monastery and occupied the see of Dorchester before coming to that of Paris.

The early building was probably rectangular, with a funerary sacellum *FIG. 59* behind the altar, continuing the nave, in which were buried Adon, *APPX. PL. 20* Theodechild, Angilbert, Angilberta the second abbess, and her aunts St. Balda and St. Moda. The funerary nature of the whole building, and not merely the chapel of the family of the founder, is beyond question. In the excavations of 1870 sarcophagi were found in the nave area at several levels, the lower ones of stone, the upper of stucco. The second, narrower, aisle adjoining the south of the building seems to have been built in a second phase towards the end of the seventh century by Angilberta's brother Ebrigisilus, bishop of Jouarre, who was buried in a funerary chapel to the east. At the present day only the crypts (the funerary chapels) remain; in the Romanesque period these were joined together and covered with a cross-vault.

The fabric is particularly interesting in the wall of the older crypt, St. Paul, near the nave, where it shows three kinds of masonry, the bottom one of rectangles and squares, the middle one of lozenges, and the top one of hexagons and small sharp lozenges—a motif associated with paving. Touching this wall, but not joined to it, are small pilasters, close together and joined by a continuous architrave; it is probable that they once supported a barrel-vault, constructed at a later stage not long after the original foundation.

Some of the capitals, which were used again in the Romanesque rebuilding, are very elegant; some, such as no. 3, with finely indented acanthus leaves, are in late fifth-century Byzantine style, while others belong rather to the beginning of the seventh century, such as nos. 4 and 6, which are deeply carved in Corinthian style with a single row of corner leaves and thick caulicoles, reminiscent of those at Ravenna. No. 1 has four corner leaves with pointed lobes and an abacus design of narrow tongues and beads. Capital no. 5 is unique of its kind, with four corner leaves decorated at their bases with pairs of curling leaves from which rise slender, partly detached corbels to support the abacus.

Poitiers, tomb of Mellobaudès The small tomb known as the 'hypogeum of the dunes', Poitiers, was a small rectangular subterranean chamber roofed with a barrel-vault; a pair of small columns, one each side, supported a transverse arch beneath which there was a step. The chamber was thus divided into two parts, in the second of which was a small altar on whose left stood the sarcophagus of the builder, Mellobaudès, in a small painted sarcophagus niche. Access was by a passage and a few descending steps.

The building would be of little value were it not for the original reliefs and the wording of the inscriptions, which are evocative of the strange, primitive faith of the Dark Ages in the north. Within the monument there are small ornamental reliefs arranged in an unusual way: three of the steps have carvings of respectively a sinuous stem bearing heart-shaped leaves, two fish, and three twining snakes forming a plait. The strip of paving that divides the chamber has discs with rays, one of the door jambs a band of circles containing flowers with petals of different shapes – ray-shaped, ball-shaped and even small animal heads, and the other jamb has a winding ribbon with trefoils.

Sometimes the inscriptions bear evidence of distress and superstition: '+α and ω+, the beginning and the end, because every day everything goes from bad to worse, for already the end approaches...' 'In the name of God, I, Mellobaudès, debtor and servant of Jesus Christ have prepared this cave for myself; I have made it in the name of the Lord Jesus Christ, whom I love...' And he ends with a curse upon whomever should dare to destroy the work.

The figured reliefs have considerable interest: one chest for relics bears the symbols of the Evangelists Matthew and John, and the Archangels Raphael and Raguel; on another are two cherubim and two bound figures on a pedestal, their hands behind their backs, and a strange cross with wide arms; another has St. Simeon. The many names of saints in the inscriptions are astonishing: there are names sanctified in Roman martyrology, such as the sixty-two martyred at the tombs of St. Chrysantus and St. Daria, together with St. Simeon Stylites, the national saint of Syria, Gallic saints and well-known local saints (Martinus, Agnanus) or unknown ones (Varigatus, Lauritus) and angels.

In short, the monument contains artistic, hagiographic and iconographic elements derived from and inspired by both Rome and the East together with local elements, all transformed by a spirit that is essentially of the north and of the Dark Ages. The composition, the polychrome pastes inlaid in the marble, and some of the zoomorphic ornaments are new elements which afford valuable evidence of the monumental art of Europe in its earliest phase.

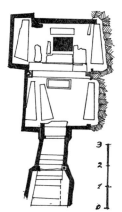

FIG. 60 – *Tomb of Mellobaudès, Poitiers*

139

Support for a dating in the second half of the seventh century is given by typical decorative motifs, like the plait of three serpents, which is found again in other reliefs, on Merovingian fibulae (St. Saturninus etc.) and on Lombard gold crosses, all seventh-century work. The palaeography of the inscriptions also indicates the seventh century.

SCULPTURE

Decorative sculpture and reliefs in seventh-century Gaul are of great interest. At Poitiers, Jouarre, St. Dizier and Metz, ornament similar to that of the niello work of Merovingian belt buckles is found carved in stone. Thus no clear distinction can be made in northern France between artist and craftsman, between the 'Roman' heirs to the classical tradition and the 'Germanic' exponents of popular taste – the style which emerges is original and 'Frankish'.

Jouarre, sarcophagus of St. Angilbert

The most important group is at Jouarre. Here one of the sarcophagi, that of St. Angilbert (*ob.* 672), bears a large scene with figures. In the centre is Christ in majesty holding open the scroll of the Law, and at either side is a group of standing figures, naked except for a loin-cloth, with an angel at each end. The scene probably represents the Resurrection of the Body at the Last Judgement. At the head is a relief showing the vision of Ezekiel: Christ, beardless and nimbed, in the celestial region between the symbols of the Evangelists, with long-stemmed round flowers at either side. The cover was decorated with large three-leaved rinceaux.

Sarcophagus of St. Theodechild
APPX. PL. 20

The sarcophagus of St. Theodechild has only decorative motifs: along the sides are two rows of scallop shells, one row inverted, which are separated vertically by short stems bearing triple leaves above and below, and horizontally by three bands with inscriptions. The cover is very worn, which is particularly regrettable since the motif was an interesting one, a splendid pattern of rinceaux with vine-leaves and bunches of grapes.

Sarcophagus of St. Angilberta
APPX. PL. 17

The sarcophagus of St. Angilberta has a design of lozenges containing florets of three Byzantine acanthus leaves along the sides and a cornice of key pattern all round it. The cover is decorated with small cavities delineating an intersecting circle pattern with a lozenge-shaped point in the centre—a motif widely used in the late Roman period and in Visigothic Spain. The cavities perhaps contained glass pastes. The tomb of St. Balda has two figures in the round, an angel with a thurible on a corner and a female saint, both shown frontally like the figures in the temple at Cividale.

St. Dizier

Of especial interest as examples of Merovingian carving are a mausoleum and a sarcophagus at St. Dizier, in Alsace, which were made for a bishop named Desiderius and another prelate, Regenfrid, who were

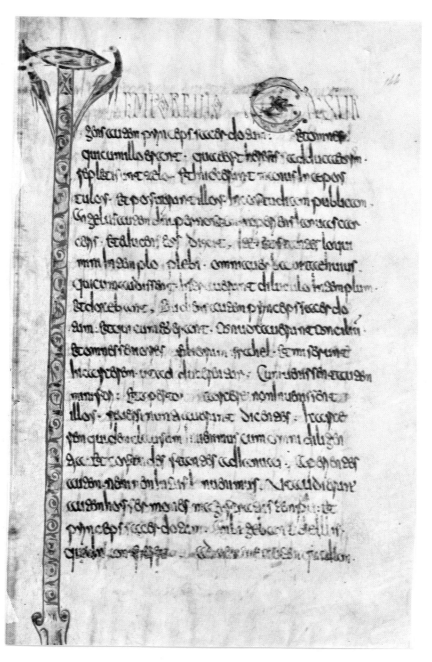

Lectionary 'T' from Luxeuil: illuminated page. *Bibliothèque Nationale, Paris (Lat. 9427, fol. 144). 28.2 × 17.8 cm. Cf. pp. 145, 146.*

killed in the reign of Childeric II (663–75) according to a *Passio S. Desiderii* published by the Bollandists (*Acta Sanctorum*, September 5th, 788/92). Excavations carried out in 1880 revealed the foundations of an octagonal building erected as a first tomb by a faithful servant, Willebert, who had witnessed the murder. The two prelates must have been interred in a simple stone chest, which is still *in situ* in the centre of the building. Some years later a monument was built over the tomb, which Jean Hubert identified as a kind of sarcophagus of honour, still to be seen, with a cover with two richly decorated sloping sides. On one of these, plain ribbons form a zigzag interlace above a row of small arches and enclose palm leaves, the whole being contained

APPX. PL. 16

within a sinuous Merovingian-type ribbon decorated with dots; on the other sloping side, ribbons form two rows of interlocking heart-shaped rings with palmettes in the interstices; and on the ridge is a simple continuous interlace.

At a third stage, according to the *Passio Sancti Desiderii*, a *loculus* was erected with a silver tablet recording the name of the donor, Duke Rabiacus. The silver part – perhaps an altar – has of course disappeared, but the main part of the monument Hubert has identified

APPX. PL. 18

in a stone chest, richly decorated with carving on the front and having two hollow cavities within. Evidently preparations had been made for translation several years after the first burial and the cavities served to contain the bones of Desiderius and Regenfrid.

The front of the *loculus* has two ornamental bands, the lower with lotus flowers, and a central band with symmetrical pairs of leaves, treated very plastically, with striations in the centre lobes; the upper part is damaged. In the lotus flowers and the curling leaves some remote connection with Byzantine acanthus can be sought, but substantially the *loculus* is original in conception and datable to the beginning of the eighth century. (The *Passio* must have been written in the second half of that century.)

Carvings at Metz

Other important fragments of carvings were found among re-used material in the church of St. Pierre at Metz. Some slabs are clearly related to Byzantine models from the Mediterranean area. One has a saint in a pointed arch, another rinceaux of heart-shaped and acanthus leaves, a third panels with arches and small crosses and a fourth a row of three vases and curving leaves. Other reliefs have Merovingian motifs, woven patterns or plaitwork terminating in small heads, like coiled or intertwining serpents. The interlace of one piece is a dynamic

Sarcophagi in Aquitaine

type of knotwork rather than a Constantinian plait.

Of a very different and clearly Mediterranean type are the many

FIG. 61 – *Sarcophagus of St. Raimundus, Moissac*

FIG. 62 – *Sarcophagus from Moissac, now in Bordeaux Museum*

FIG. 63 – *Sarcophagus from St. Severin, Toulouse, now in Toulouse Museum*

sarcophagi found in the south-west of France, between the Rhône and the Pyrenees, carved in a local marble. The number of these is constantly increasing as research continues; so far eighty-six examples are known, of which thirty-six are in Aquitaine, and eighty-nine fragments, of which thirty-eight sarcophagi are in Septimania (Narbonensis I). Formerly attributed to the fifth or sixth century, they were dated correctly by Hubert in 1938 to between 650 and 750. He showed that throughout the sixth century attempts had been made in Aquitaine to imitate ancient Provençal figured sarcophagi, with varying degrees of skill, in Pyrenean marble. Examples of these are a sarcophagus made probably for St. Clarus, bishop of Euze, who died *c.* 510, and another for Duke Regnovaldus (*ob.* 593). He then used four sarcophagi with the Aquitainian type of ornamentation to support a correct dating: two from the abbey of Moissac (founded *c.* 640), that of Drausius, bishop of Soissons (*ob. c.* 680), now in the Louvre, and that of Bishop Lentadus (*ob. c.* 718).

FIGS. 61–63

An examination of the decorative elements confirms the chronological attribution to the seventh and eighth centuries of this large group of carvings, which seems to fit in with the relative economic recovery of western Gaul after 650, subsequent to the achievement of independence of Aquitaine (685). Figural representation is rare and in any case is restricted to the oldest examples, taking the form of single figures on the front of the trough (Valbrant) or of small scenes, such as Daniel and the lions, on the cover. Christ and the Apostles appear on the cover of a sarcophagus at St. Guilhelm du Désert, which is perhaps later than the trough beneath.

The composition generally consists of panels with different subjects repeated symmetrically. The vocabulary of motifs in general derives from the sixth-century Byzantine repertory, but interpretations are usually rather free renderings of the models: trees of curving acanthus palmettes arranged regularly, or vine scrolls with small bunches of grapes. Sometimes the vine leaves have twisted lobes, the stems rise one from another in a kind of 'cornucopia' motif (trumpet pattern), and the convolutions end in small round flowers indented in the centre—all typical of the late seventh and the eighth centuries. The division into panels each mirroring its neighbour derives perhaps from pavement mosaics, and the use of heterogeneous composition, made up of different decorative panels, is a clear sign that these precious relics of early medieval sculpture are late works.

Some of the long sides of the sarcophagi, however, bear a single motif: rinceaux rising from the centre and developing symmetrically towards the ends. This design remained in vogue for a long time and is frequently found again in closure-slabs of the eighth and especially of the ninth centuries in Italy.

The inventive originality of the Merovingian Franks is naturally also shown in their manuscripts. In northern France of the seventh century a new script was evolved, which was inspired by cursive but transformed it into an elegant and lively hand. This minuscule calligraphy appears in a codex of 669 at Luxeuil (Haute-Saône), a monastery founded by St. Columbanus in 590, and again in a perfected form in the *Missale gothicum* and the Lectionary.

MANUSCRIPT
ILLUMINATION

The books chosen for illumination were usually liturgical or theological works, missals, sacramentaries, patristic writings and so on, the requirements of a well-established and relatively cultured clergy. From their ornamentation of manuscripts it is evident that the Frankish miniaturists of the seventh century were oblivious not only of classical art but also of Christian symbolic art. They produced neither 'episodes' nor symbolic compositions, and sought neither to represent nor to suggest, but principally to decorate; and in this they were following a similar path to that of their counterparts in Britain.

The illuminated decoration emphasized the first letter or the first line of the chapters. Only rarely was a whole page taken up by a large cross within an arch. Sometimes the initial page contained besides the cross the title of the book or the prayer.

A fine manuscript of the seventh century is the Sacramentary of Gelasius, which came from a Frankish church and was given by Christina of Sweden to the Vatican Library (Reg. 316). It is written in uncial but two folios (2v and 45v) have passages in Merovingian cursive. There is no figural representation in the miniatures, only ornament and symbols: one page contains a large cross within an arch, bearing an alpha and omega and differing little, in effect, from the Byzantine Chi-Rho which is also often shown within an arch. Other traditional motifs from Constantinople appear in the ornamentation: on the arch can be recognized quatrefoil acanthus rosettes, and on the arms of the cross are other rosettes. Other elements, however, are remote in spirit and form from Mediterranean models, such as the zoomorphic decoration, with quadrupeds, birds and fishes, and the gaudy colouring in which browns accompany complementary greens and reds.

*Sacramentary
of Gelasius*

The initial page of the second book is similar in type and has rows of large multi-coloured letters and zoomorphic motifs. The bottom line contains the word NOVERIT formed of birds and fish, a widespread

Merovingian practice. There are no very large letters: the I of INCIPIT is only three lines high; but on the left side of the page is a large Chi-Rho richly decorated with animals, with the Lamb in the centre. These miniatures do not, however, show any trace of the distortion of animal forms of which Germano-Scandinavian art was particularly fond. Deer and other animals and birds, and even typically Germanic subjects such as the four birds with curved bodies and long beaks at the foot of the arch, are all shown complete. The iconographic symbols, the Byzantine decorative elements and the palaeography all indicate a seventh-century dating for the Sacramentary.

Luxeuil Lectionary The Luxeuil Lectionary also has illuminated initials. The zoomorphic subjects do not have the exuberant vitality of the Gelasius Sacramentary: the fish are confined within outlines drawn with the compass, and other decoration has floral elements. There are peacocks, a favourite Byzantine motif, perched at the top of long stems, the height of the page; there are stilt-birds, and delicately drawn flowers. The colours are green and red, with yellow used mainly for the background.

METALWORK The key to an understanding of the spirit of seventh-century Mero-
Personal ornaments vingian Gaul is, however, to be found in the small metal articles used for personal adornment. The motifs of this type of decoration reveal the cultural level of the different regions and the degree of fusion attained after two centuries by the local population and the various tribes of Germanic origin.

We have already remarked how by the sixth century certain objects such as the large silver brooch with gold-foil and filigree of Queen Arnegunde were not of the usual polychrome inset type but had markedly original elements, with traces of zoomorphic decoration in the animal heads. This independence increases in seventh-century work, which can no longer be identified as clearly Mediterranean or Germano-Scandinavian in type, but rather as 'Frankish'.

The most interesting articles are nielloed iron belt buckles, often plated with silver and having inserted bronze ornament. These have been found particularly in the formerly Burgundian districts of Switzerland and neighbouring areas. Brooches and plaques in cast bronze are also numerous. The decorative interlace work is of a special kind: frequently there is no regular symmetrical weaving of the Constantinian type, nor even of the typically Germanic and Irish knotwork. The

Sacramentary of Gelasius: illuminated page. *Biblioteca Apostolica, Vatican City (Reg. Lat. 316, fol. 131). 26 × 16.7 cm. Cf. p. 145.*

132

INCP
LIBER
SIGN
DUS
ORAGO
ETPRAE
DENATALICIISSCORUM,DENUN
CIACIONATALICII.IUNIUSMARTYRUS.
NOUERIT

strands are often 'free-flowing', that is, they are not closely interwoven or knotted, but loose, with wide loops, and the effectiveness results from the variety of wide or narrow, smooth or grooved or dotted strands. The grooved ribbons are found also in Oriental art, for example in the diptych of Philoxenos (525). An instance is a cross at Fétigny on a trapezoid ground.

Zoomorphic ornament is often used in conjunction with interlace, a development of a tendency widespread in Germanic prototypes, already noted in the Arnegunde brooch, to use an animal head at the ends of the strands so as to transform them into serpents, thus creating a kind of reptile interlace or plait. *Zoomorphic ornament*

In the Swiss examples the ribbons are often interrupted, and they are always alternately wide and narrow. The narrow ones are often animated with a stylized zoomorphic element: small beaked circles, like heads. This type of decoration, with few exceptions, thus preserves traces both of Constantinian and of Germanic traditions, but re-elaborates and combines them in compositions of high technical quality and originality.

Besides the 'damascening' technique, Frankish popular art includes work in cast bronze. This generally takes the form of plaques showing compositions with *orants* and griffins in a neo-naturalistic style. The griffins are generally paired, facing towards a central human figure indicated more or less schematically or even abstractly, a grouping in which can be recognized the subject of Daniel and the lions. *Bronzes*

In Würtemberg and Bavaria the Germanic element is naturally felt more strongly, with lively zoomorphic interlacing and knotwork, frequently with large beaked heads.

In Aquitaine the 'Mediterranean' decorative elements predominate. Constantinian plaited work is more frequent; serpentine ribbons have no animal heads; and sometimes rather plump birds with their heads facing backwards are introduced in interstices, perhaps suggested by the animal reliefs of Byzantine ambos of the sixth century.

The anti-Byzantine, anti-Roman attitude of the Visigoths during the struggle with Justinian's forces slackened after the liberation. Reccared I, the son of Leovigild, made an ostentatious public renunciation of Arianism, but the support of the local nobility and of the prelates, who were invited for the first time to participate in the government at *SPAIN / History*

Sacramentary of Gelasius: page with ornamental lettering. *Biblioteca Apostolica, Vatican City (Reg. Lat. 316, fol. 132 v.). 26 × 16.7 cm. Cf. p. 145.*

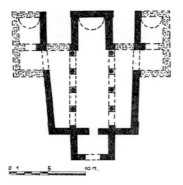

FIG. 64 – *San Juan de Baños: plan*

the Council of Toledo (589) – the 'Reconciliation' Council – was offset by the resistance of a section of the Visigothic nobility. Another step towards unity was the promulgation by Recceswinth (649–72) of a judicial code common to both Romans and Visigoths. These reforms, however, accentuated rather than eliminated the glaring social inequalities which existed in the country. A few great landowners (Visigothic and Roman nobles and high prelates) held a tight grip on economic power, and the impoverished mass of the native population failed to identify itself with the new state, so that the restoration of political and religious unity was followed by the moral weakening

Arab invasion of the Spaniards. From the outset of their invasion the Arabs found the peninsula devoid of strength, shattered by internal revolts; these had led King Witiza (701–9) to raze the walls of many of the cities.

In 711, therefore, the fanatic Islamic armies found no difficulty in overcoming the scanty forces sent against them, and succeeded in taking Toledo, the capital, with very little interest shown by the greater part of the population. This attitude did not change even when in the following year the incursions turned into permanent occupation. Only the north of Spain avoided this fate and later became the base for the reconquest. Discoveries of hoards of jewellery, buried and never recovered by clergy fleeing before the ferocity of the Islamic invaders, bear witness to the phase of struggle and violence inseparable from invasion.

Visigothic The only authentic example of Visigothic monumental architecture
architecture which survives is the little church of S. Juan de Baños at Cerreto
FIG. 64 (Palencia), which was built by King Recceswinth and dedicated on 3 January 661, according to the inscription over the arch of the apse. In plan it is a three-aisled church with a projecting rectangular presbytery at the end of the nave (4.67 metres in length). The side

aisles also end in chapels but it seems that originally they ended in a straight wall. On the other hand, in 1898 excavations revealed the foundations of two small lateral wings leading to two projecting rectangular presbyteries. A small narthex preceded the nave, and restorers have indicated porticoes at either side, on what evidence it is not known.

Decoration is typical of local popular taste: horse-shoe arches are used repeatedly, in the presbytery vault, in the colonnades of the nave, in the windows, in the principal doorway. This was a frequent feature in Europe from the sixth to the eighth century, but it is particularly widespread in Spain where, as is well known, overhanging arches were common by the late Roman period. The capitals are Corinthian in type, some closer to Roman types, others deriving from western early Christian models with broad caulicoles: the technique of these anticipates the effect of 'Kerbschnitt' which is common in the eighth century; little or nothing is owed to Byzantine precedent.

The carving of the impost blocks and the two archivolts of the main doorway is late Roman in taste, with florets of intersecting circles and a central boss; that of the side chapel has a continuous interlace of ribbon with a line of dots in the centre. Other impost bands carved with lozenges and crosses or with a scale pattern herald the effects of the eighth century. A fragment of a pluteus in the Archaeological Museum at Madrid, with a bunch of grapes and crude acanthus foliage, seems also to anticipate the taste of this century.

Important evidence of the aristocratic luxury arts of the last years of the Visigothic kingdom are the two treasure hoards of Guarrazar and Torredonjimeno. The Guarrazar treasure was found in a small cruciform chapel in the neighbourhood of Toledo in 1859. Some pieces went to the Musée de Cluny, others to the Armoury and to the Archaeological Museum at Madrid. Unfortunately many were sold and melted down. These included lamps (one of which bore the date of 587), thuribles, gold and silver vases, belts, chains, collars, gold doves and processional crosses, apparently coming from a church of S. Maria 'in Sorbaces'.

Guarrazar treasure

The oldest piece that could be dated was the crown of Swinthila, who reigned from 621 to 631. It consisted of a band of pierced gold decorated with pearls and coloured stones and was suspended by small chains formed of palmettes enclosed in a heart-shaped ring. From these hung the letters of an inscription, and drops of crystal, pearls, and a large hooked-armed cross adorned with pearls. To this group, which is now lost, belonged also a plain cross with an inscription to

Crown of Swinthila

Crown from Guarrazar (Toledo). *Musée de Cluny, Paris.*
Cf. p. 151.

Crown of Recceswinth from Guarrazar (Toledo). *Musée de Cluny, Paris. Cf. p. 154.*

Lucedius and small pendant stones, a crown in pierced gold-foil dedicated to St. Stephen by Abbot Theodosius, and a crown of large golden circles with stones at the intersections and other pendant stones.

PLATE P. 152 A crown of this type is to be seen in the collection of the Musée de Cluny (n. 4982), with a knob above in the usual Byzantine fashion, and a large pendant cross below. Another crown, probably of local craftsmanship, was the offering of Sonnica to the church of S. Maria 'in Sorbaces', according to the inscription on the back of the cross; it has stones on the crown (three rows) and in the front of the cross.

Crown of Recceswinth The crown of Recceswinth (king from 635 to 672) is the richest of the collection. It consists of a hoop in embossed and pierced gold which is hinged and can be opened into two parts, suspended from chains with palmette links depending from a knob above decorated with enamel and precious stones. The letters of the dedication, RECCES-VINTHUS REX OFFERET, are suspended from it, and through the centre hangs a simple cross set with large gems. These same motifs are used on a large processional cross.

PLATE P. 153 The style of the great crowns of Swinthila and Recceswinth, the processional cross and the link cross of the Musée de Cluny is certainly Byzantine. The upper knob and the chains (the palmettes of the Recceswinth crown are typical) are obviously Byzantine in origin, the borders of the crown are in champlevé with red enamel and intersecting circles like the Monza book-cover, and the letters are also in red vitreous enamel. It is evident that at the beginning of the seventh century the Visigothic court employed Byzantine artists or ordered this jewellery directly from the capital of the Eastern Empire.

The other crowns, the offerings of private citizens, are different in character, simple gold-foil embossed with elementary motifs – arcading or zigzag – and decorated with pearls, and their dependence on Constantinople seems indirect.

Torredonjimenos treasure The other treasure hoard had an unfortunate history. It was discovered by a peasant at Torredonjimenos (Jaén) and thought to be of tin, and almost completely destroyed. Apart from pieces of chain with links of heart-shaped leaves, only a few gold-foil crosses remain. One of these bears a dedication to St. Justa and St. Regina from a certain Trutila, and has four shells at the extremities and a central stone; a second is covered with rough vine scrolls. Other have stones of various sizes inset on the arms, with plain borders. The composition and decoration of these articles are again almost exclusively Byzantine in taste.

The continuing influence of Byzantine culture throughout the seventh century is confirmed also by objects of personal adornment in metal. The primitive rectangular belt plaques with inset stones had disappeared from 550; the sheet metal fibulae with oval foot and the later plaques with crude projecting bird heads lasted until the end of the seventh century, and eagle brooches and decorated bow brooches continued until about 650. *Metalwork*

The characteristic types of the last phase date from the beginning of the seventh century to the Islamic invasion and show Byzantine or Mediterranean motifs uncontaminated by those typical of Germanic art. In the last decades before 711 even the Visigothic language seems to have fallen out of use, surviving only in proper names of persons and places. Fibulae often present two Byzantine acanthus leaves arranged symmetrically in profile on a circular base so as to give a lyre-shaped appearance to the piece; this is an original and typical form in Visigothic Spain.

The belt plaques however represent Frankish and Aquitainian influence, and bear stylized animals and versions of the Daniel-and-the-lions group. Some pieces (Castiltierra and Cordoba) have damascening, obviously influenced by the popularity of this technique in Gaul, but the subjects are always 'naturalistic', i.e. not deformed, animals, horses and deer. *Gallic influence*

In the Balearic Islands, which the Visigoths never took from the Byzantines, metal objects are exclusively of Byzantine types.

Ireland had never been subjugated by the Romans but had gradually absorbed some elements of Mediterranean culture. Christianity reached Ireland from Gaul and southern England, and was spread particularly by St. Patrick (432–66). By the end of the fifth century many monasteries had been founded, and frequent exchanges of missionaries took place between the two islands of Britain. IRELAND

The christianization of Ireland was achieved through the proliferation of monastic foundations with widely varying rules – as many as 3000 houses – each attached to the life of the clans into which the population was divided, the monks fulfilling pastoral and other functions relevant to the communities as well as leading the contemplative life. At Armagh 365 monks were devoted to perpetual praise of God, like the Byzantine *acoemeti*. These religious centres were of extraordinary vitality, to which contributed the unshakable faith of the neophyte, *Monasteries*

FIG. 65 – *Lyre-shaped fibula. Archeological Museum, Madrid*

the physical robustness of a race accustomed to a hard life, and the longing for culture of a people which allowed exceptional social privileges to the intellectual. Fruitful contacts were established by the Irish monks with England and the continent. It was no mere spirit of adventure that impelled the missionary Irish to their travels; love of their native land and ties of family and friendship were strong, and to abandon green Ireland for the 'solitude of strange peoples' involved sorrow and suffering. They faced a life of wandering, often never to return, because they considered themselves *commilitones* of the *militia christiana* and professed absolute obedience.

St. Columba
The first wave took place towards the middle of the sixth century under the inspiration of St. Columba, who after founding Derry in the north and Durrow in the centre of Ireland established the monastery of Iona, off the coast of Scotland, in 563 and began evangelizing from these houses. Iona remained the headquarters of the order. Towards
St. Columbanus
580, St. Columbanus, a monk of the abbey of Bangor, 'began to long for pilgrimage', as his biographer Jonas writes. He left for Gaul with twelve companions and there founded first Luxeuil and then Jouarre, Faremoutiers and Rebais; later, passing over the Rhine, he left one of his companions at St. Gall to establish the famous monastery, and crossed the Alps to found his last house at Bobbio, where he died in 615. The intrusion of these zealous missionaries into continental Christendom was not accomplished without difficulties. Although they had always recognized the authority of the Pope, the Irish differed from the rest of Christianity in some liturgical matters and in the dating of feasts. They were reproached in 663 – 'a few men, even if they are saints, lost in a remote island, cannot prevail against the universal Church of Christ in the whole world' – and the Synod of Whitby (663–4) forced them and their English followers to conform to the rules and practices common to the whole Roman Church.

Architecture and sculpture
No buildings datable to the seventh century are known; what will be said later of eighth-century architecture is obviously relevant here. Sculpture is represented by two very early examples of monumental crosses which are typical of the plastic art of the islands in the early Middle Ages; these, however, consist of carving on ashlar or on fragments of rock erected like stelae.

Illuminated manuscripts: Cathach
The art of illumination is the most satisfactory evidence of the artistic activity of this time. The *Cathach* (which is believed to have been written by St. Columba, and was carried into battle by the O'Donnell as a talisman) appears to be of earlier date than the seventh century. It is a fragment of a Psalter, of which the first large page is unfortunately

missing. The surviving decoration consists of initials at the beginning of each Psalm. These are in black, emphasized by dots, enclosing ornamentation in yellow in which Celtic elements are recognizable – spirals and 'trumpets', crosses and small animal heads.

Another codex, probably from the second half of the seventh century, has greater artistic significance: this is the Book of Durrow, from the monastery of that name. There is little doubt that this famous manuscript (now in the library of Trinity College, Dublin) is the oldest of the great Insular 'monumental series'. As Kendrick pointed out 30 years ago, on the great monogram page 'XPI autem generatio sic erat' the monogram itself is not overdeveloped, and there is room for seventeen lines of genealogy. In the Lindisfarne Gospels (c. 700) there is room for only four lines of text, and in that of Kells (c. 800) the monogram takes up almost the entire page with only three words following and closely joined to it. Analogous comparisons can be made between all the illuminations with regard both to size and to complexity of design.

Book of Durrow
PLATE P. 158

The arrangement of the illuminated pages follows a certain 'Insular system' which seems to impose a rigidity similar to that demanded by iconoclasm in the East. Like Merovingian miniature art, the Irish offers no figured scenes or episodic illustration. The Gospels are decorated by whole-page designs with crosses and symbols of the Evangelists. The beginning of the text is ornamented with a large initial on a ground of red dots. The art of the Durrow Book is essentially abstract: the pages with large crosses having single or double arms are barely distinguishable from those which are pure decoration, and even the symbols of the Evangelists are highly schematized.

The decorative elements are typical of the Scandinavian-Insular repertory in their very simple forms; some pages have patterns of spirals of ancient local Celtic origin, borders of repeated multicoloured animal forms, intertwining looped bodies with thread-like tails and claws (Salin II). On other pages the designs are composed of close knotwork in two alternating colours, or of spiral and trumpet patterns. These compositions are very carefully controlled and ordered, never capricious or irregular. Even the figures which stand on a spacious ground are dominated by the overwhelming vitality of the ornamentation: the body of St. Matthew appears as a plaque of millefiori enamel; the body of the ox *(vitulus)* is covered with dots and spirals project from the extremities; the lion has a harlequin pattern of lozenges and part of the body is covered with small dots. The work exemplifies all the characteristic motifs of the Insular style, and the

colouring and arrangement of each illuminated page effectively emphasize the different parts of the whole composition.

Unfortunately very little remains of seventh-century Irish jewellery, *Jewellery* and that little is doubtful. There is however no doubt that the decorative motifs used in enamel work included the spirals of ancient Celtic local art and the simple dynamic interlace which appear in the Book of Durrow.

Christianity came to England in the late Roman period. A very small ENGLAND church consisting of a rectangular hall with two lateral chambers and a narthex, similar to S. Abbondio, Como, was excavated at Silchester in 1892. The floor was of uniform red mosaic with a checkerboard design in the presbytery. A second church has apparently come to light at Caerwent.

The withdrawal of the Romanized minorities from the island and the *Teutonic invasions* arrival of the Teutonic invaders from the fifth century onwards changed the direction of the ethnic and cultural evolution of the island. Of many leaders of the settlers, such as Cerdic, the traditional founder of the kingdom of Wessex, and Ida, the ancestor of the Northumbrian kings, only the names are known. The struggle of the Christian Celts against the pagan invaders, the memory of which survives in the Arthurian legend, was an unsuccessful one, though Scotland remained independent of Anglo-Saxon authority for centuries. By the beginning of the seventh century bands of Germanic settlers were grouped in regional kingdoms. Among these the small kingdom of Kent is famous on account of the mission of St. Augustine, who was *St. Augustine* sent with forty monks by St. Gregory the Great and who began the conversion of the whole island. In the seventh and eighth centuries the outstanding kingdom was that of Northumbria, founded by Aethelfrith, which rapidly achieved a position of supremacy.

The wholesale conversion of the Anglo-Saxons occurred in the second half of the seventh century. The rich treasure discovered in 1939 at Sutton Hoo, in a ship cenotaph within a tumulus, belonged to a pagan king towards the middle of that century.

Ecclesiastical buildings are of modest dimensions but normal con- *Architecture* struction—that is, with walls and roof, and not made of stones by some primitive method; this is evidence of an urban standard of life, or at least of civic organization. Kent, the seat of the mission sent by

Book of Durrow (St. Matthew?). *Trinity College Library, Dublin (fol. 32 v.). Cf. p. 157.*

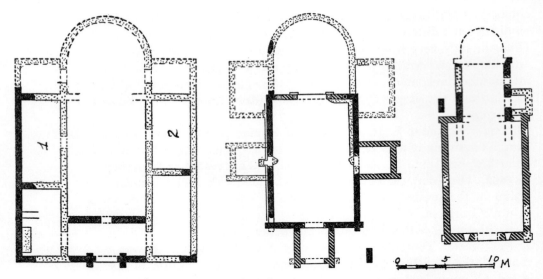

FIGS. 66, 67, 68 *(from left to right) – St. Peter and St. Paul, St. Pancras, St. Martin, Canterbury: plans*

St. Gregory the Great, contains some venerable examples. Of the seven churches which can be dated from Bede, six (at Canterbury, Lyminge, Reculver and Rochester) are in Kent and only one (Bradwell-on-Sea) in Essex.

Canterbury, abbey church

FIG. 66

According to Bede, the abbey church of St. Peter and St. Paul at Canterbury was founded by St. Augustine (*ob.* 604) and consecrated by his successor St. Lawrence; it is known only from the foundations, which were excavated in 1905–7. It consisted of a fairly spacious nave preceded by a narthex with buttresses at the sides of the doorway. On either side were two long rectangular chapels, that to the north-east being dedicated to St. Gregory; in this St. Augustine, St. Lawrence and four succeeding bishops were buried.

Canterbury, St. Pancras

FIG. 67

Parts of St. Pancras are still visible above the ground; it was originally rectangular in plan, with an apse and four columns across the nave forming a kind of screen, to separate the presbytery area. At the corners were supporting pilaster strips. In a second phase a front porch and two side chapels were added. The existing wall, at the west of the 'porticus', is in Roman brick with thick mortar joints in Byzantine style.

Canterbury, St. Martin

FIG. 68

St. Martin, also mentioned by Bede, was a plain hall with pilaster buttresses; red mortar containing pounded brick was used in the masonry. There were three large windows in the façade; the projecting

160

FIG. 69 – *Church, Reculver: plan*

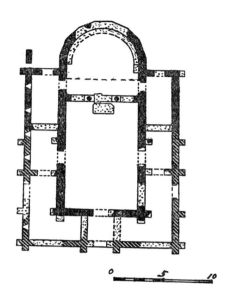

chancel was narrower than the nave and was considered to be the oldest part of the building.

In 669 Egbert, king of Kent, entrusted the building of a 'minster' at Raculf to a priest, Basse; ten years later a donation by King Lothair of Kent is recorded to the abbot of Raculf. Monastic life seems to have come to an end there in the tenth century, but the church remained in use until 1805, when it was almost entirely demolished. From drawings and excavations it appears that the original nucleus of the building consisted of a rectangular nave which continued into a wide presbytery, separated from the nave by three arches borne on two columns and terminating on the east in an apse curved internally and polygonal externally. On either side, with access from the presbytery, were two rectangular funerary chapels. The walls had pilaster buttresses at the corners. The two columns, identified as two now in the crypt of Canterbury Cathedral, are formed of drums, with cubiform capitals suggestive of some Romanesque types but divided into three bands above a wide necking. The windows were splayed only internally. In a second phase (in the eighth century, according to Peers) three chapels were built which provided the nave with a bracket-shaped ambulatory and enclosed the atrium, as at St. Peter and St. Paul, Canterbury.

Another very early southern English church is that of Bradwell-on-Sea,

Reculver
FIG. 69

Bradwell

Gold buckle from Sutton Hoo. 7th century. *British Museum. Cf. p. 163.*

which is probably that recorded as having been built at Ythancester by St. Cedd in 653. This has a simple rectangular plan with three 'portici', one on the front and one on either side. The apse was apparently curved and separated from the nave by three arches, of which traces remain attached to the side walls. Much of the façade and lateral walls still exists, with buttresses reaching halfway up the walls.

These churches correspond in their arrangement to the almost contemporary church of S. Arcangelo in Romagna, the work of Byzantine masons, in the rectangular nave and external supports. Another characteristic which may be of southern origin is the separation of the presbytery by a triple arcade on pillars (as at Bradwell). Three similar arches were built in S. Stefano, Verona, after the early stage, perhaps at the end of the sixth century.

The skill of the goldsmiths of southern England is demonstrated in the wonderful collection of the royal burial mound at Sutton Hoo. This treasure was the product of a pagan and not a Christian civilization, so that even a cursory examination of it does not properly belong to our subject; it is not irrelevant, however, to point out that the site of the discovery is opposite the Belgian coast, far from Ireland, and that accordingly the presumed Irish provenance of some of the enamel work, the millefiori escutcheons of the great Hanging Bowl, for instance, is hypothetical. *Metalwork: Sutton Hoo*

The orfèvrerie in general is of cloisonné enamel, but some pieces have zoomorphic motifs engraved and embossed. Of great importance is the great gold buckle with ribbon interlace decorated with niello dots and serpent heads. The design is dynamic but irregular with knots of great complexity, and thus cannot be attributed to the Insular designs in which the strands have regular breaks and joins. The close links with the original Scandinavian sources of Germanic art is obvious, and the similarity with certain articles at Fétigny and Castel Trosino, for example, probably derives from the direct dependence of both upon northern influence rather than from reciprocal influences. PLATE P. 162

The kingdom of Northumbria was founded at the beginning of the seventh century. King Edwin, who was converted to Christianity in 626, undertook to spread his religion throughout Northumbria and East Anglia. He contrived to impose in his large dominion a degree of orderliness which had hitherto been lacking, but in 633 he was defeated and killed by the pagan Penda. The struggle between the leaders of pagan reaction and the Christians continued until 655, when Penda was crushingly defeated at the battle of Winwaedfield, and wars with neighbouring kingdoms continued after this. In 679, however, Mercia achieved a position of firm supremacy. Northumbria continued to display lively spiritual activity throughout the seventh and early eighth centuries, assisted by the proximity of Ireland, with which it had close links. This movement, whose creativity was certainly *Northumbria*

163

CODICIBVS SACRIS HOSTILI CLADE PERVSTIS
ESDRA DO FERVENS HOC REPARAVIT OPVS

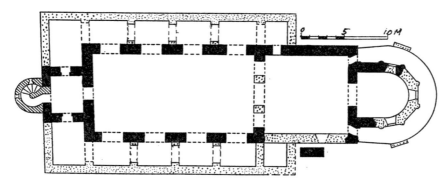

FIG. 70 – *Church, Brixworth: plan*

no less than that of Ireland, was quite independent of continental Europe.

A passage in Bede tells us that the church of St. Peter, Monkwearmouth, was built by Benedict Biscop, the first abbot of Monkwearmouth and Jarrow (*c*. 675). The front and the south side of the nave remain; it is very long and narrow (65 by 19 metres) and is preceded by a two-storey tower, but the presbytery is missing. (A door in the front of the upper storey of the tower seems to indicate that the buildings were contemporary.) The heavy arch at the entrance to the porch is supported by the famous stone columns, squat cylindrical shafts with rings, turned on a lathe. As a base for these supports there is a block of stone carved with a ribbon interlace and two bird heads with crossed beaks.

According to Gilbert the nave and the walls which join it to the chancel date from the time of Benedict Biscop, as does the lower storey of the tower. The upper storey is attributed to the period between 710 and 735, the three arches of the porch and the ornamentation to *c*. 800. Fisher however dates the arches to *c*. 675, which seems more probable. The church of Brixworth in Northamptonshire is perhaps the most important surviving late seventh-century building in the British Isles and belongs to the same very early group of Christian buildings as those of Kent. It was a basilica with three naves and a square presbytery; the latter was divided in the middle by means of the usual three

Monkwearmouth, St. Peter

Codex Amiatinus: the Prophet Esdras. *Circa 700. Biblioteca Laurenziana, Florence. Cf. p. 168.*

165

Echternach Gospel-book: beginning of Gospel according to St. Mark. *Bibliothèque Nationale, Paris (Cod. Lat. 9389, fol. 75 v.). 25.7 × 19.3 cm. Cf. p. 168.*

IMAGO hOMINIS

Echternach Gospel-book: Imago hominis. *Bibliothèque Nationale, Paris (Cod. Lat. 9389).* *25.7 × 19.3 cm. Cf. p. 168.*

arcades and terminated in an apse. The side aisles have been destroyed, but the porch and the tower of the façade have survived.

The building was constructed of rough stone but the archivolts of the arches, in two concentric circles, are of brick.

Northumbria attained its cultural zenith during the reigns of Egfrith (671–85) and Aldfrith (685–701). Cuthbert was called to Melrose and later became one of the most famous abbots of Lindisfarne; Wilfred visited Italy and on his return rebuilt the church at York, building *Benedict Biscop* new ones also at Ripon and Hexham. Benedict Biscop, abbot of Jarrow and Wearmouth, visited Italy no less than five times, and Bede tells us that he purchased there and brought home relics, embroideries, paintings and, above all, books; he also called to his monastery master-masons from France and skilful workers in glass.

Among the collections of books brought from Italy was part of the library assembled by Cassiodorus in the monastery of Vivarium, near Squillace. He had copies of these codices made in England in order to spread them, one of which is the Codex Amiatinus. Benedict intended to present this magnificent Bible to the Pope, but he died on the journey (716) and the book remained in the monastery of Monte Amiata, passing thence to Florence (Biblioteca Laurenziana, Amiat. 1).

Codex Amiatinus The scene with the prophet Esdras which occupies one page seems to
PLATE P. 164 have been inspired by an original in the library of Cassiodorus (*ob.* 580). Not only is the figure of the scribe similar to sixth-century models, but the books are arranged in the *armarium* according to Cassiodorus' system. Another page shows Christ in Majesty between two angels on a celestial globe surrounded by the four Evangelists and their symbols, in the Byzantine manner.

Echternach Gospels A probable masterpiece of Northumbrian illumination is the Echter-
PLATES PP. 166, 167 nach Gospel-book (Paris, Bibliothèque Nationale, Lat. 9389), which takes its name from the Belgian abbey founded by the Northumbrian missionary St. Willibrord, who was transferred to Utrecht in about 680. The Insular origin of the work is beyond doubt, and is confirmed by the characteristics of the script, an elegant miniscule with traces of uncial and with capitals sometimes surrounded with red dots. Large full-page miniatures preface the Gospels, with the symbols of the lion, the eagle and the ox, expressed with extraordinary refinement of line and variety of colour, unrivalled as heraldic figures. The Evangelist 'Imago hominis' is transformed by the artist into a figure transcending human reality.

A particular sensitivity to the potentialities of multi-colour ribbon

fragmentu quatuor euangelier̃ Hic Liber olim imp is
a Gregorio pp ad augustini archiep̄; sed nuper sit mutilatus
1778

imago aquilae·

Imago aquilae. *Corpus Christi College, Cambridge (Cod. 19, fol. 246). Cf. p. 170.*

interlacing, and a lack of zoomorphic decorative elements seem to confirm Frankish influence. The Celtic elements (such as spirals) are absent; the interlace patterns are not varied and irregular as in some examples of Germanic taste, but are carefully organized, according to the scrupulous Insular regard for order, into designs which are only occasionally interrupted by breaks and joins.

The prototype character of this work is evident. As in the Books of Durrow and Lichfield, the Evangelist appears as an isolated figure *(Homo)*; the phrase 'Liber generationis . . .' which opens the Gospel according to St. Matthew is written in small characters on the book held by the 'imago hominis' and appears also on fo. 19, a monumental calligraphic page on which the letters L I B, interwoven according to Insular practice, do not dominate the composition as they do in later miniatures. This moderation, and the elegance and detail of the interlace decoration, suggest attribution to the more refined style of Northumbria rather than to Ireland, where the tendency is toward a more 'popular' expressiveness.

Corpus Christi
MS 19
PLATE P. 169

Another elegant manuscript with similar characteristics is the fragment of a Gospel-book, MS. 19 at Corpus Christi College, Cambridge. The 'imago aquilae' miniature shows the symbol executed in a variety of colours within an impressive frame of green ribbons which extend to form crosses internally at the corners. Some of the angular projections recall those of the Ashburnham Pentateuch. There are tenuous connections between the oldest original Anglo-Saxon illuminations and the art of the Mediterranean world as well as with that of the neighbouring Franks.

V. THE END OF BYZANTINE TRADITIONS AND ART IN ITALY. THE CREATION OF A NEW POLITICAL, ECONOMIC AND CULTURAL ENTITY IN EUROPE (700–800)

The eighth century was a time of political and economic crisis in Europe. The 'Roman' Emperors had always been regarded as the *de iure* masters of the Mediterranean lands. The Popes had recognized them, first at Rome and later at Constantinople, as leaders, while the Pope for his part was under normal circumstances accepted as the first patriarch of the Empire. Towards the middle of the eighth century, however, there occurred a papal *volte-face:* after sounding opinion at Rome through one of the new German bishops, Burchard, Pepin deposed the last Merovingian king and three years later Stephen II officially crowned Charles king. Twenty years after this, Charlemagne made a triumphal entry into Rome and was crowned Emperor there on Christmas Day 800, with the *acclamatio* and the usual Byzantine formulae.

This radical political revolution coincided with very substantial economic changes. The economy of the early Middle Ages, up to the seventh century, was a continuation of that of Rome and the ancient world, based on maritime trade within the 'mare nostrum'. In the course of the eighth century trade declined and land became the sole source of wealth. The maritime cities of the south, which had once been the wealthiest cities of Gaul, now became impoverished. Pirenne writes: 'Whereas before the impulse had come from the south, now it was the north which gave its character to the age.' Meanwhile new road routes were opened up and new Alpine passes facilitated land communications. In Italy the same phenomenon occurred. Inland centres gained new life: Milan, Pavia, Brescia, Cividale, Spoleto and Benevento became centres of culture.

The main causes of this drying-up of commerce were the destruction of most of the maritime cities of Greece and Asia Minor and the blockade of the Arab littoral by the Byzantine fleet rather than any action of the Islamic fleet. If trade was affected by religious movements – for such essentially was the advance of Islam – politics underwent the same influence to an even greater extent. The main factor which drove the Popes into conflict with the Byzantine Emperors was the question of iconoclasm. Byzantine legislation against images, which began in 726, was to some extent the product of the political need to

deprive Islam of a useful instrument of propaganda, but its principal cause was the deeply-rooted conviction of a group of extremist theologians and moralists.

From the sixth century onwards icons had become the object of ever-increasing devotion, and images of the Saviour and the Virgin and of saints and angels had taken the place of the previous symbolic iconography. The 'crucifix', at first an idealized image, became increasingly realistic in its sorrowfulness and its humanity. A valuable document which marks the dividing-line between old and new is the famous eleventh canon of the Council of Constantinople of 692 ('in Trullo'): 'Certain pictures and sacred images portray the Precursor pointing with his finger to the Lamb. We have adopted this portrayal as an image of grace; it was the shadow of this Lamb, Christ our God, as shown to us by the Law. So after first accepting these figures as signs and emblems we now prefer to them grace and truth, that is, the fulness of the Law. Hence in order that perfection may be revealed to the eyes of all through painting as well as by other means, Christ our God shall be portrayed in human form instead of as a Lamb as formerly. We must be able to contemplate the full sublimity of the Word through His humility. The painter must bring us, as though taking us by the hand, to the memory of Jesus living in the flesh, suffering and dying for our salvation, to obtain redemption in the world.'
Cult of icons

As is well known, these decisions served to aggravate the disputes between the Iconoclasts and their opponents. The latter developed a fanatical devotion to sacred images, while the strict zeal of the former insisted on the maintenance of the traditional portrayals, in particular the jewelled cross as the symbol of the divine sacrifice. Leo III's laws of 726 and 730 divided the population of the Empire into two hostile parties and open warfare between these continued until 843.
Iconoclasm in the East

Feeling in Italy was at first in favour of the traditional symbols and Pope Sergius, who was in any case hostile to the Council of 692 on account of its failure to recognize the supremacy of Rome, introduced the *Agnus Dei* into the Mass. In the course of time, the opinions of theologians and of the faithful in the West became firmly hostile to the rigid position of the Iconoclasts. Pope Gregory II, a Roman by origin, who followed a succession of seven Greek and Syrian Popes, issued a bull of protest against the iconoclast laws and later wrote an
Reaction in Italy

Virgin. Detail of mosaic from Oratory of Pope John VII, Rome. *Museo di S. Marco, Florence. Cf. p. 184.*

insolent letter to Leo the Isaurian, rejecting the Emperor's threat to destroy the 'statue of St. Peter' at Rome, which seems to have been regarded at Constantinople as the principal idol of the West. The next Pope, Gregory III, though of eastern origin, maintained the same position. In the year of his election, 731, he convoked a Council which rejected iconoclasm but sought to remain on friendly terms with the Byzantines, with sufficient success for the Exarch Eutichius to present the Pope with six columns of onyx. In 733 the Emperor Leo III made an attempt to regain authority in Italy but this ended in failure when his fleet was wrecked. The Byzantines now took up a more courageous position. The quarrel became more bitter after the accession of Constantine V Copronymus, a fanatical Iconoclast who drove hosts of monks into exile. The presence at Rome of thousands of these embittered religious refugees further poisoned relations between the Church and the Empire, and soon afterwards Paul I (757–67) invited the 'truly orthodox' Pepin to oppose the threatened attack on Ravenna by the 'most wicked Greeks'.

Cult of the Saviour Probably the hostility of the West towards the Iconoclasts was due less to the local icons of the Virgin and saints than to the now common portrayal of the Saviour, His sufferings on earth and His triumph in heaven. Religious foundations of the Dark Ages dedicated to the Saviour are numerous and important: mention has already been made of the cathedral at Canterbury (Christ Church) founded by St. Augustine and of S. Salvatore at Spoleto, and reference will be made to another S. Salvatore, at Brescia. This phenomenon was widespread throughout Europe. Heitz has published a surprisingly long list of great churches and monasteries with this dedication in Germany, the Rhineland, Austria, Belgium, Holland, Switzerland and France: to these may be added such Italian foundations as Farfa and Monte Amiata. Nearly all these buildings date from the eighth century and many of their founders were rulers anxious to emphasize the divine derivation of their own power.

Yet the cult of the Saviour as experienced by the great mass of the faithful had little to do with politics; it was as old as the Christian religion itself and in the primitive spirituality of Christianity the Resurrection and the Holy Places of Jerusalem were of great significance. With the adoption of their new religion the early Christians had passed from anxiety to the certainty of liberation from death. The Resurrection of the Saviour on Easter Saturday was the anticipation of eternal life for all, and the article of faith concerning the rebirth of the flesh was a consolation to those who could not separate the idea

Fresco of saints. S. Maria Antiqua, Rome. *Cf. pp. 184.*

of spiritual immortality from corporal existence. Thus the Anastasis and the Holy Sepulchre were at the heart of the serene life of the early Christians, and they were commemorated in the act of Christian initiation, in the primitive ceremony of baptism by the descent into the piscina and the return into the Church, symbolizing death and the subsequent ascent into the eternal dwelling-place of the blessed. This piece of symbolism was clear to all adult converts, but in time it disappeared owing to the conversion of entire peoples and the consequent administration of baptism to infants by aspersion. Baptisteries thus came to lose their original liturgical function and were now built as a single unit, without annexes for the instruction of catechumens, dressing-rooms and so on. Even so, the elaborateness of the baptisteries of the sixth and seventh centuries seems rather at variance with the considerably simplified purpose they served. The dimensions of those at Classe and Marseilles could be due to the importance of the two cities, but it is not so easy to justify a large rotunda such as that at Nocera dei Pagani as the baptistery for a small population centre. It is possible, therefore, that buildings erected for baptismal purposes after the sixth century were used also for services celebrating the Anastasis.

The centre of the cult of the Anastasis from the earliest times was naturally the round church of the Holy Sepulchre in Jerusalem. Etheria, the rich and devout lady who made a pilgrimage to the sanctuaries of the East at the end of the fourth century, makes particular mention of it and describes the impressive procession which left the church of the Ascension and reached it late in the evening of Palm Sunday, with a great display of lights.

But the title of Anastasis was not given only to the rotunda at Jerusalem: many very early churches and cathedrals in both East and West were called 'church of the Resurrection'. The *Notitia* of Constantinople in the time of Theodosius II names one in the Seventh district ('ecclesias tres, Irenen, Anastasiam et S. Pauli', i.e. of Peace, of the Resurrection, of St. Paul), and the cathedral of Ursus and that of the Arians at Ravenna were both Anastasis, according to Agnellus.

In many cathedrals the early title, which we think was probably widely used, must have been changed at a later period to that of St. Mary, and in the case of churches to particular saints or St. Anastasia, and the cult of the Anastasis was perhaps then transferred to the baptistery, already implicitly the site of a symbolic resurrection and no longer used for mass immersion, or to rotundas built for the purpose (S. Sepolcro), often situated at the east end of the atrium—as indeed in many cases (Aquileia, Parenzo, Pula) were fifth- and sixth-century baptisteries themselves.

As the centre of the cult of the Holy Sepulchre the atrium acquired a new character and became a kind of liturgical image of Paradise. It was natural that this should also include the places devoted to the cult of the archangels. During the first centuries of Christianity, the 'Heavenly Jerusalem' had not been represented in actual buildings erected for religious purposes but only in mosaics, as a city with walls, towers and buildings of gold and precious stones. From the seventh century onwards it was symbolized in the buildings of the atrium, to which the name 'paradise' was given (Fr. *parvis*). Du Cange lists many references of the seventh century and later in which atria at Rome and Benevento, in France and Germany, are named 'paradisus'. The Greek word means 'garden', but it occurs frequently in the New Testament as a synonym for the kingdom of Heaven.

Changing character of atrium

But beyond a generic name no precise description can be given: the form of the 'paradise' of churches and the buildings of which they consisted varied from one place to another. In some cases there was a quadriporticus with cult centres for the Anastasis and for the archangels, but in the cathedral of Milan, for example, according to a drawing published by Giulini, there were separate chapels for the archangels, those for Gabriel and Raphael on one side, for Michael and Raguel on the other. In the large majority of cases, however, if our reasoning is correct, the 'paradise' of churches consisted only of altars and pictures which constituted the stations of the great processions which formed part of the rites of Holy Week.

At the present time, on the days during which the Divine Sacrifice is celebrated, the preliminary services of Palm Sunday are followed by the funereal liturgy of the Triduum and finally by the celebration of Easter. Up to the eighth century this was evidently not so: the Holy Week liturgy was an addition to the celebration of the Resurrection. The earlier attitude corresponded to a tradition which is still followed by the Orthodox Church. For the Greeks the Resurrection is the dominating theme throughout the liturgy: every Saturday and Sunday the *Anastasima* are chanted, emphasizing the comforting resurrection of the dead, and even in Holy Week the services of mourning conclude with the assurance that at Easter Christ will rise again. It is well known that for the Orthodox Church Easter is by far the most important feast of the year, and emphasis is laid on the story of the three holy women, the empty sepulchre, the soldiers – standing for the forces of evil – overthrown and bewildered by the Resurrection that has taken

Introduction of Holy Week liturgy

place. These scenes appear on the Munich ivory, some of the silver flasks from Monza, and so on. In the second half of the eighth century, as has been said, the sorrowful liturgy of the Passion and the Burial took the place of that of the triumphant Resurrection, and to correspond with these dramatic and mournful prayers there were displayed everywhere, as aids to devotion, crucifixes which showed Christ suffering in pain and anguish.

But in the West popular sentiment was directed not only to lamenting the sufferings of the Saviour on the Cross but also to the wide horizons of hope and divine justice, and to meditation on the Apocalypse. The prophetic final book of the New Testament had enormous popularity in the Dark Ages; the Council of Toledo in 633 actually threatened with excommunication whomever did not read it publicly in Holy Week. The promise of 'Judgement' in the Apocalypse, assuring the restoration of order and a just retribution, and the visions and symbols it contains, made the story attractive and significant to the early Christians. The Revelation of St. John was concerned with spiritual history, and it was a source of hope because it conveyed on a universal scale what the Passion had demonstrated in an earthly context. The images relating to the Apocalypse were accordingly often concentrated in those buildings which represented the 'Heavenly Jerusalem' (Heitz). The liturgy had a great influence on the architecture of the Dark Ages also because of the multiplication of cults and of altars. Whereas in the early Christian period there had been a single altar in each church, from the mid-sixth century onwards there were often three apses and three altars, and in the ninth century each church was to have many altars. European church architecture in the eighth century was therefore affected by new requirements of the liturgy (where the arrangement was concerned): form was determined by tradition and particular circumstances.

In theory the artistic ideal of decoration had not changed substantially since the late Roman period, and when possible churches were built with interiors covered with marble, stucco and glittering mosaics, and with the nave borne on gleaming columns; but the means of achieving this were no longer what they had been; the Byzantine Emperors no longer sent marble and mosaic tesserae as a matter of course. With increasing frequency, therefore, the walls were covered with frescoes, since it was by now very difficult to procure even used material. We know that marble was sought far afield: Charlemagne looked for marble for his palace at Aachen in Rome and Ravenna. Sometimes voyages were undertaken for this purpose: a passage in the *Henrici*

178

S. Salvatore, Brescia: interior. *Cf. p. 190.*

miracula S. Germani about the reconstruction of the church of St. Germain at Auxerre (mid-ninth century) tells us that 'since there was a shortage of marble in the province' some of the brothers undertook a perilous expedition through 'the great gorges of the Rhône', journeying to Arles and Marseilles. There, 'with boldness and cunning they overcame the many dangers, and tearing down the ruins of ancient buildings they obtained great abundance of precious marble by means of money as well as with permission, and loading their ships with the booty they achieved a memorable triumph: this was brought about with divine favour, overcoming fear of the threatening waves and of the infidel peoples' (*Henr. Mir. S. G.* ed. Duru, II, 162–4).

The employment of the meagre amount of marble thus recovered, lacking uniformity of colour or dimension, conditioned the forms of proto-Carolingian and Carolingian architecture. The use of these materials precluded the achievement of classical proportion and imposed the adoption of a decorative technique suited to the use of spoils.

Decline of Byzantine power in Italy

Eighth-century Italy was no longer dominated by local struggles between Byzantines and Lombards; the important factors were now papal and Frankish intervention and the progressive decline of Byzantine power, which was challenged in the East by the Arabs. The first quarrels between the Popes and the population of Rome on the one hand and the Byzantine Emperors on the other occurred after the death of John VII. The Emperors could no longer use force, as they had in Martin I's time, but had to come to terms, deriving what credit they could from the assistance they had rendered in the crisis of the Lombard threat. At times the Lombard kings also attempted to ally themselves with the papacy. Liutprand (712–14) ruled over a kingdom entirely Catholic, founded churches and monastic houses, and was obsequiously obedient to Church law and the Roman juridicial tradition. The reign of Aistulf (749–56) was the swan-song of Lombard warrior traditions. Raised to the throne by national elements, he reorganized the Lombard army, won control over the duchies of Spoleto and Benevento and eventually occupied the exarchate of Ravenna itself (751), forcing the Byzantines to make a final withdrawal. But this achievement of expansion at the expense of the Greeks earned him the enmity of the Papacy. Stephen II called in the Franks, who brought about the failure of Aistulf's schemes. King Pepin's two brief Italian campaigns (754–6) forced Aistulf to give up the territory he had captured from the Byzantines and to yield rule over it to the local population.

Lombard occupation of Ravenna

Fresco on south wall of S. Procul, Naturns (S. Tirol). *Cf. p. 202.*

The last years of the Lombard kingdom saw the collapse of the authority of Desiderius (756–74), an energetic administrator and proud fighter whose means were inadequate to combat papal hostility and Frankish power. Papal threats caused him to abandon the campaign against Rome which he launched late in 773. Adrian I then called in Charlemagne, who inflicted a heavy defeat on Desiderius in a pass near Susa, and besieged him in Pavia while his son Adelchis attempted to defend Verona. After the fall of these two strongholds, Desiderius was held as a prisoner in the monastery of Corbie, Adelchis fled to Constantinople, and Charlemagne assumed the title of King of the Lombards.

Not all the political and religious vicissitudes of eighth-century Italy are reflected in the art of this period. The dividing-line between the two cultural traditions remained clear, Rome and Ravenna maintaining the link with Byzantine taste while the area occupied by the Lombards gave birth to a special kind of art which grafted Germanic motifs

Desiderius

Charlemagne

BYZANTINE AND
LOMBARD ART

181

on to a Byzantine-Mediterranean trunk. But after 774, the year of Charlemagne's visit to Rome, Byzantine culture and art disappeared rapidly from the Italian scene, to be replaced by very different local and European influences.

Art in Ravenna

At Ravenna in the eighth century, in the atmosphere of withdrawal and imminent departure, the Byzantines had no thought for the erection of new buildings, and left only very modest examples of sculpture. The

Sarcophagi

sarcophagus of Archbishop Felix (*ob*. 723) bears motifs that are still symbolic, but the sense of significance which was typical of fifth- and sixth-century work has been lost. On the front are three cramped arches, of which one encloses a cross, two pendant crowns, two rather horse-like lambs, two small crosses, two candlesticks with lighted candles and finally two small pillars. On the cover there are discs bearing two crosses with α and ω, and a large cross.

'Iconoclast'
sarcophagi

APPX. PL. 13

Two other sarcophagi, those of Bishop John (*ob*. 748) and Bishop Gratiosus (*ob*. 788), have three crosses with curling ends separated by shields on the front, and more crosses on the cover. The obsessive repetition of the cross motif shows that this is an 'iconoclast' type. Very similar examples can be seen in the temple of Augustus, later a church, at Ankara.

Basilicas at Rome

No great churches were built in Rome during the eighth century and the only significant characteristic of the basilicas of this date are the three apses. This is true at S. Paolo (later S. Angelo in Pescheria), which was built by Theodotus, uncle of Pope Adrian I, in the ruins of the portico of Octavia (757–67); and also at S. Maria in Cosmedin, rebuilt in 771–95 by Adrian I himself. Of this, the 'bene ornata' church of the Greeks, the upper part of the nave, and the three apses remain; from beneath the roof the old walls pierced by small windows are visible, adorned with frescoes of the time of Adrian I (*clipei* of prophets between the windows, large panels below).

St. Peter's: oratory
of John VII

A work of considerably greater artistic interest was the oratory built by John VII, a friend of the Greeks (705–7), in the Vatican basilica, with interior walls covered with mosaic. It was destroyed in 1606 and only the drawings of a certain Grimaldi and a few fragments of tessellated pavement provide evidence of the richness of its decoration. Following a Byzantine practice, the chapel was dedicated to the Theotokos ('Domus Dei Genetricis Mariae'): the nave walls were decorated with scenes relating to St. Peter and St. Paul, and in the apse was the Virgin with the Pope kneeling and scenes from the life of Mary and of Christ in three registers. The Theotokos cycle from the Annunciation to the Presentation in the Temple was depicted according to Byzantine

Gateway of the monastery at Lorsch. *Cf. p. 211.*

iconography, which has been discussed with reference to Castelseprio, and the penultimate episode, the Crucifixion, was presented in its most complete form, with Christ between the spear-bearer and the sponge-bearer, the Madonna and St. John, the sun and moon.

PLATE P. 172 One of the mosaic fragments, now preserved in Florence, shows the central figure, the Virgin with her arms raised in prayer, standing on a pedestal, crowned and richly dressed in a robe of imperial purple with a strange fold at the hem, a large collar and border of pearls, and embroidered with precious stones on the shoulders. The similarity of some of the details with the figures at Cividale is evident, and this figure, isolated in a golden sky, has a powerful and magnetic spirituality of feeling. It is not rash to suppose that it is the creation of Greek masters, using tesserae probably sent by Justinian II.

Rome, S. Maria Antiqua Eighth-century painting in Rome is represented principally in S. Maria Antiqua. John VII (705–7), whom we have already mentioned as a good friend to the Greeks, was responsible for important work here also. He was the son of Plato, a *curator palatii*, whose epitaph in S. Anastasia nearby records repairs carried out by this imperial official to a staircase of the old palace, which was thus evidently in good working order in the seventh century. On his election to the Papacy John VII took up residence in the Palatine, where he had an 'episcopium' and he made S. Maria Antiqua his chapel. The work carried out on his orders included the present Schola Cantorum and many frescoes. Excavation has brought to light the interesting presbytery complex in the centre of the nave, with a large enclosure for the cantors and the clergy and a central ambo in the Byzantine fashion. The lower step of this ambo has the name of the Pope carved in Latin and Greek.

The frescoes executed on his orders are on the end and side walls. For this work John VII made use of a Greek artist, who set himself the task of expressing, adapted to the curve of the vault, the new iconography prescribed by the Council of 692: Christ on the cross 'suffering in the flesh', but in a heavenly setting, accompanied by four seraphs and two ranks of angels arranged on either side. In the zone below is an acclaiming crowd of human beings, perhaps representing the Resurrection. The seraphs are spiritual beings, with beautiful features and graceful attitudes; the lower zone includes four Popes, shown frontally, among whom is the donor with a square nimbus (unfortunately the inscription naming him is lost), and further below are medallions showing Fathers of the Church. On the side walls are scenes from the life of Christ and other medallions showing the Apostles, impressive for their line and colour. This group of paintings, which is probably

PLATE P. 175

the work of a fresco-painter sent by Justinian II, is the swan-song of Byzantine painting in Italy. Later frescoes bear witness to the general crisis and the break between Byzantium and the Papacy; master painters no longer came from Constantinople – and indeed after 726 their work was profoundly disturbed by the iconoclast controversy – but the work was executed by artisans employed by Popes who endeavoured to win popularity among the local Greeks by adorning their church with new paintings. The iconography and the figures are still Byzantine in type but the spirit animating the figures is different: instead of the elegant freedom of the Byzantine tradition they are heavy, almost devoid of any emotive value.

During the papacy of Zacharias (741–52) a certain Theodotus, '*primericius* of the defenders', or chief of the consistorial advocates, was responsible for the arrangement and decoration of the chapel to the left of the presbytery; he had the side walls painted with panels showing the martyrdom of St. Quiricus and St. Julitta. The donor is represented and named three times, and his family is also shown. On the end wall is a complex Crucifixion surrounded by four large symbols of the Evangelists; below is the Virgin as queen of heaven between St. Zacharias and St. Theodotus. The scenes of martyrdom are mediocre, those of the end wall a little better. The inscriptions are in Latin.

In the principal apse Paul I (757–67) had painted a large standing Christ in the act of benediction, among angels in a 'celestial region', with the Virgin and the donor. In addition he had frescoes painted on the side wall of the left aisle: above are scenes from the Old Testament with explanatory captions in Latin, and below Christ is a long line of twenty saints, with heavy, full-face figures and large hands, bearing volumes or occasionally a cross or a crown. The names beneath these saints are written in Greek.

The rather nobler frescoes executed on the order of Adrian I (772–95) – the Pope who received Charlemagne in Rome – are also Byzantine, perhaps the work of a painter from Byzantium. Adrian himself is shown as an old man in priestly attire with a large nimbus, flanked by dignified figures of saints clad in the rich materials of court costume, in the act of offering crowns.

No outstanding work of decorative carving datable to this era remains *Carving in Rome* in Rome. A sketch of a *pluteus* inspired by those of S. Clemente (532–5), with panels of intersecting squares and lozenges, shows large 'iconoclast' crosses like those of the tomb of Bishop John at Ravenna, but the fragments that remain are all ninth-century copies (Palazzo del

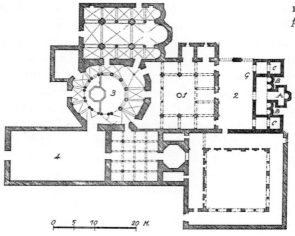

FIG. 71 – *S. Stefano, Bologna:*
plan

Governo Vecchio, S. Sabina, S. Prassede, S. Cecilia etc.). Only those
in the Museo Petriano appear to be of the eighth century: these are
two fragments carved with crosses between lozenges decorated with
lilies, and a slab with rosettes and a panel of intersecting squares.

Bologna, S. Stefano
FIG. 71

More important examples of architecture and art are found in north
Italy. The complex of churches now known as S. Stefano at Bologna
is of great value as evidence of the liturgy of the Anastasis. It arose on
the site of an ancient cemetery, as the tradition suggests which con-
nects its origin with St. Petronius; already by the eighth century it
had become a 'New Jerusalem', a group of buildings commemorating
the sanctuaries of the Holy City in Palestine, which since 637 had
been in Moslem hands. The evidence for this leaves no room for doubt:
on a sixteenth-century pedestal in the central atrium is a large stone
basin with an inscription of 735–43 ('. . . receive O Lord the prayers
of our humble lords kings Liutprand and Hilprand and of Bishop
Barbatus. They offered privileges to Jerusalem that this basin might
be filled with the supper of the Lord'). A diploma of 887 expressly
names the church as 'Sancta Hierusalem'.

What remains above ground of the existing buildings is of the twelfth
century and later, but these often follow older foundations and show
the earlier disposition of the buildings. Excavations carried out in 1914

Sacramentary of Gellone: illuminated text. *Bibliothèque Nationale, Paris (Cod. Lat. 12048). 29 × 17 cm.*
Cf. p. 215.

INCP DNI NRI IH̄V XP̄I INCP LIB' SACRAMTR

In uigil̄ nativt̄. d̄ni hora
nona · ad scā maria;
qui nos redemptionis
n̄r̄e · annua expecta
tione letificas · presta
ut unigenitū tuum · quē redēpto
rē

revealed the original foundations of the group of buildings to the east of the 'courtyard of Pilate'.

In the middle of a group of seven chambers or absidioles arranged parallel to each other was a cruciform *sacellum* (A) with a curved apse flanked by two pairs of horseshoe-shaped absidioles (B) and at the end on either side two square chapels (C) preceded by vestibules independent of the central area. The only certain remaining part of the entrances consisted in the shoulder of an arch (G): the two other openings appear to have been reconstructed. This complex of niches and little chapels, rather than a place for worship, was perhaps a place for burial, a cemetery attached to a church which may have occupied the site of the present 'courtyard of Pilate'. There were similar arrangements in the choir at Corvey (882) and again at Concordia Sagittaria, in a chamber with lobed niches attached to the presbytery of the church, or in the Carolingian crypts of St. Germain at Auxerre.

The western part of the central nucleus of the S. Stefano complex is no less important than the eastern. Here is the 'rotunda of the Holy Sepulchre' as it must already have existed in the eighth century, a domed chamber on 12 pillars with an ambulatory. It was the custom on Palm Sunday for the procession which left from the chapel 'in Monte Oliveto', on a small hill nearby, to move towards this Anastasis, repeating the Jerusalem liturgy. The present edifice of S. Sepolcro is Romanesque and so are the sculptures of its central aedicule, but it is nevertheless of great importance by way of confirmation of all that has just been said. Externally the church has facings of coloured brick and stone in patterns of checks and stars. It was therefore an 'Image of the Heavenly Jerusalem' in which the beauties of Paradise were represented concretely not by gold and precious stones, as in mosaics, but by rich polychrome masonry unique in the architecture of Emilia, even bearing in mind the atrium of Pomposa.

According to a certain Bianconi, writing in 1772, there were paintings in the dome: the Eternal Father with a Lamb in His arms surrounded by the Elders of the Apocalypse and the symbols of the Evangelists and below, in a circle, various scenes from Genesis. This is confirmed by Lanzi who says, however, that the episodes depicted were from the Gospels: the Nativity, Epiphany, the Disputation in the Temple . . . These frescoes were destroyed eight years after Lanzi had described them. A few fragments of the New Testament scenes were rescued and are now in the Museo di S. Stefano.

There can be little doubt that the earlier, eighth-century building was also centrally planned with an ambulatory, polychrome masonry and

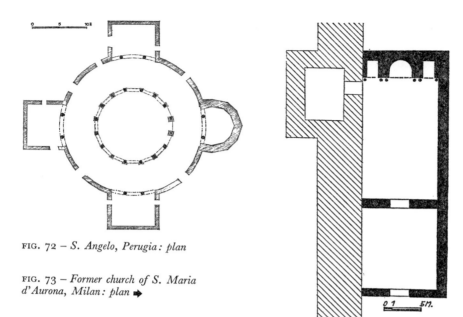

FIG. 72 – *S. Angelo, Perugia: plan*

FIG. 73 – *Former church of S. Maria d'Aurona, Milan: plan* ➡

Apocalyptic frescoes in the dome, so that the rotunda is valuable evidence of both the liturgy and the art of the Dark Ages. Unfortunately it is not possible to correlate all the surviving architectural elements of the ancient sanctuary in order to form a clear idea of its original form and what analogies there actually were with the buildings of Jerusalem; here a large Constantinian basilica led to a courtyard where the chapel of the Crucifixion stood a little to the left ('golgothān ecclā,' according to the plan made by Arculf now at Vienna, cod. 458 f.4v), and finally the rotunda. At Bologna, the Gothic church of the Crucifixion, thought to be built on eighth-century foundations to the left of S. Sepolcro, is now relatively large; instead of the grandiose 'Constantinian' basilica, however, there is a porticoed courtyard, and on the east the presbytery complex of parallel chapels, and not an entrance atrium.

Another building which may have been built in imitation of the Holy Sepulchre at Jerusalem is S. Angelo, outside the ancient walls of Perugia. This is a polygonal church with an ambulatory in an almost perfect state of preservation. From the central core project four small arms, three rectangular and one octagonal, and the presbytery is curved. In the interior, the rectangular chapels are each separated by a triforium with the central arch wider than the side ones, on two

Perugia, S. Angelo
FIG. 72

columns. The inner ring consists of columns of spoils supporting arches on rough pulvins. The drum, circular internally and sixteen-sided externally, has small windows and must have been crowned by a light timber-frame dome. Entrance was by means of doors in the perimeter wall and there were also two smaller doors to each of the chapels, one each side, of a postern type. The masonry is of brick, and the archivolts of the windows are traced in brick. The technique offers no assistance for a precise dating; the building could equally well be from the seventh or eighth century, or from the end of the sixth.

The title of S. Angelo obviously points to a date later than 550, but to nothing more precise. Perugia remained in Byzantine hands for a long time, except for some years at the end of the sixth century. The shape, which is very close to that of the Anastasis of Jerusalem (annular with four apses), suggests a copying of that church (De Angelis) rather than a 'Heavenly Jerusalem' like that in Bologna. In the three small rectangular chapels there must have been altars to the three archangels, which would justify the present rather generic title and the existence of a central structure reminiscent of the aedicule at Jerusalem.

Milan, S. Maria d'Aurona **FIG. 73** The church of S. Maria d'Aurona, Milan, was of a completely different type. According to accounts in medieval chronicles the monastery to which it was attached was founded in 735, and is ascribed to Bishop Theodorus, who was buried there with his sister Aurona. The plan of this church is known from an old drawing: it had a hall-nave (18.80 by 10.2 metres) whose side lay against the turreted walls of the city, and terminated in three apses within the thick walls, one semicircular and two rather longer rectangular ones. The nave side of the façade was decorated with six small columns, as is the chapel of Malles (*c.* 800). A kind of atrium or ante-church preceded the nave, equal in breadth to it but rather shorter in length.

Brescia, S. Salvatore The most important eighth-century buildings in north Italy are, however, S. Salvatore at Brescia and the Tempietto at Cividale. The monastery to which the church of S. Salvatore belonged was founded by King Desiderius and Queen Ansa in 753, as we learn from many ancient documents, and is referred to in others of the ninth century as 'monasterium novum'. During recent excavations (1956–60) foundations of an earlier church were discovered beneath the present building, with a single nave flanked by two long and narrow chapels at the east end. The three chambers terminated in three horseshoe-shaped apses, and a portico on two columns preceded the nave. The evidence of pottery and a fibula found here suggests that this building goes back to the seventh century. The crypt of the central apse, with four supports, has also been attributed by the excavators to this phase of the building, but this is still an open question.

At a later stage the church was rebuilt on a larger scale with a colonnaded nave and two aisles. Six bays are still preserved, but originally there were eleven arches on either side supported on ten columns (Panazza). The masonry is of large bricks, and the arches of the doorways have two concentric archivolts; the windows are arched, with a narrow span (c. 80 centimetres), and their axes do not correspond with the elliptical arches. The exterior of the building is decorated with blind arcading, recently restored: at the lower level the blind arches are close together, concentric with the windows, with narrow pilaster strips between then. Above the roofs of the aisles, at clerestory level, however, the arches are much smaller, enclosing small windows. Internally, the surviving columns all have re-used capitals, some Corinthian, with flat caulicoles (as in the old cathedral at Verona), while others are inverted pyramids with fifth-century decoration of arabesques and small acanthus leaves of sixth-century Byzantine type; one is of stucco. Traces of narrative frescoes are preserved in the nave, but in present circumstances it is impossible to determine their iconography and artistic value.

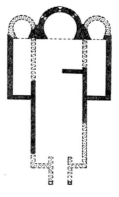

The discoveries of stucco work made in the course of these excavations are of great, even of sensational, importance. The intradoses of two of the arches have been found to retain their ornamental reliefs; the others have only faint traces remaining, or supporting nails still in place, but many fragments, some of them capable of reconstruction, have been dug from the floor or found among masonry. One of the soffits still in place has an interlace pattern of double strands, which at first seems Constantinian in type but on closer inspection reveals the breaks typical of northern work. The second soffit has a double rinceau of large stylized acanthus leaves and small grape clusters, and a third bore panels with quatrefoil rosettes having three lanceolate leaves at each corner and simple leaves arranged axially. Some of the archivolts of these interior arches had motifs almost identical with those found in the Tempietto at Cividale: a plain band with inset coloured glass vials (green and yellow) and outside this a wreath of triple acanthus leaves alternating with longer curling leaves (motifs D and D' of Peroni's publication); or simpler versions of this pattern (A,A',E); or leaves within intersecting circles (B,B'), spirals (F) or

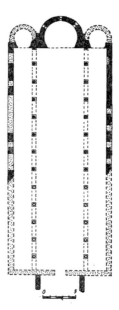

FIG. 74 – S. Salvatore, Brescia: phase I (above), phase II (below)

191

FIG. 75 – *Baptistery, Cividale: arch*

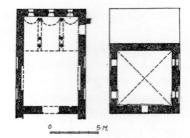

FIG. 76 – '*Tempietto*', *Cividale: plans*

plaits (C,C′), all open-work. The execution is, however, perhaps a little cruder than that of the Cividale chapel.

Cividale   The town of Forum Iulii acquired special importance in the history of the Veneto in the Dark Ages by succeeding to the political and administrative functions of Aquileia. At Cividale the Lombards established a stronghold for their government from which they could control the region, and the Byzantines had to establish new centres among the lagoons, first at Grado and then in Venice.

The period of greatest glory for Cividale was the eighth century; it became the seat of the Patriarchate of Aquileia in 730, and was considered by Paul the Deacon as the capital of Venetia, a local supremacy which it maintained until the Carolingian age. Other evidence for its importance in the eighth century, in addition to some

Cividale, Tempietto   fine carving, is provided by the so-called Tempietto, a building of

FIG. 76   great beauty. This famous little church, still almost intact, stands near S. Giovanni. It consists of an almost square chamber and three rectangular absidioles within a single low, projecting structure; the narthex has disappeared; the windows are framed by blind arches. The principal chamber has a cross-vault with rounded groins, and the corbels are decorated with small stucco leaves. The three presbytery areas are barrel-vaulted upon two internal stone architraves, each supported by a pillar and two columns.

The rich interior decoration is still organized according to Byzantine tradition: the lower part of the walls has polychrome marble revetments, the upper part stucco and frescoes, and mosaics covered the presbytery vaults. The doorway has an architrave decorated with a

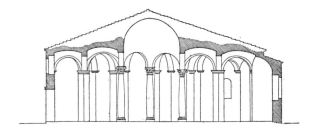
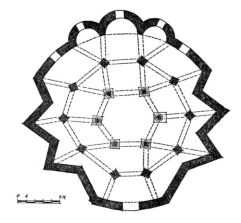

FIG. 77 – *S. Sofia, Benevento: section and (right) plan*

confronted-S pattern in stucco and fragments of capitals apparently resting on corbels. Above this the lunette contains a fresco with busts of Christ and the Archangels Michael and Gabriel. Around this is an archivolt of rich stucco work comprising two borders of rosettes containing glass of different colours between reel-moulding, and between these borders is a wide open-work band containing a vine scroll: this has a thin undulating stem, from which a leaf and a grape cluster grow within each curve, and a single leaf in each triangular space. This graceful foliage decoration is free-standing, and so is the outer border of the archivolt, of crescents and tongues.

Above this, an upper zone of ornament has two horizontal bands of florets with glass centres, between which stand six large nimbed figures of female saints, three on each side of a window which is also decorated. The two inner saints of the group are in the attitude of prayer, holding out their hands, and they are modestly dressed as religious, with tunic, cloak and veil. The other four wear royal dress, rich with embroidery and gems, and bear a crown in one hand and a cross in the other; in the outer pair the hand holding the crown is veiled. The window has two columns and an archivolt outlined by a band of northern-type knotwork and by open-work foliage, Byzantine in style – five-pointed acanthus leaves separated by spirals and other longer three-pointed leaves. The columns of another window have recently been found. In the spaces below the lower floret border are paintings of saints against a background of the Heavenly Jerusalem; they are nimbed, each bearing a crown, and the architectural elements are in perspective: piazzas or porticoed streets, the columns with dadoes and covered with precious stones, the upper storeys with ornamental cornices and arched windows. A fresco with the Virgin between two angels has recently been discovered in the lunette over the north door, very well painted in an astonishing style of Byzantine character.

Benevento, S. Sofia
APPX. PL. 9
FIG. 77

Lombard architecture in south Italy is exemplified by a building of great importance and originality, S. Sofia in Benevento.

In the eighth century the small duchy of Benevento acquired a special significance by surviving the collapse of the kingdom of Desiderius. After being forced to submit by Charlemagne in 786, Duke Arichis succeeded in winning the confidence of the Byzantines, who nominated him their representative in Italy, and he was able to resist a succession of expeditions sent against him by Charlemagne between 791 and 802. Arichis was on very close terms with Byzantium. Paul the Deacon taught Greek to Princess Adelperga, and Arichis boasted of receiving from the East silk and purple stuffs, cups of gold and engraved silver, and goods from India, Arabia and Ethiopia. It was he who was responsible for the construction of S. Sofia. According to a *Chronicon . . . Sanctae Sophiae* the church was consecrated in 762 and Erchempert, writing at the end of the ninth century, asserted that this was an imitation of the famous church of the same name; but, as we shall see, both as regards form and dimensions the similarity is only relative. After the reconstruction of 1696 the building appeared as a rotunda with two internal rings of columns. Research and excavations carried out between 1947 and 1957 have revealed the curious original plan, enabling us, with the help of some elements of the elevation now engulfed by the Baroque structure, to envisage the early building: the eighth-century structure can still be recognized in the building as it stands (Rusconi).

It is a centrally-planned arcaded hexagon with one ambulatory with ten supports (eight brick pillars and two columns) and a second ambulatory with a star-shaped perimeter and apses. This external wall is slightly curved towards the entrance; the three apses are curved both internally and externally. The masonry is of alternate bands of brick (usually two courses, less often three, occasionally four and five) and of tufa. The vaulting of the ambulatories was high, and part of the brick arches of the original structure has been preserved; the central area was covered by a dome of which a few courses remain.

Sa cramentary of Gellone: illuminated text. *Bibliothèque Nationale, Paris (Cod. Lat. 12048, fol. 1 v.)* *29 × 17 cm. Cf. p. 215.*

penitur noxiur prxcentorx cnminū liberneti rerudi
gruetiar pħmi dō repperant remp et bneđicheant
nom ei; rem inrela relorx pōnim nrm iłim xpm qu uxu
rū iudicare. unior. Item· SUP FEMINAS· xxx

S habrax dš isahac dš iacob dš
qui tribį irxt monuisti ocxuranna de
fxlxocnmen liberxsti. texupplix depeor
dne. ut liberer & har famolax tuar &pđu
cerx ecer dignerx adgnetiā baptirmatui;
Ergo mxledicte. SUp· mascolus· dicex
xon x xrote inmunde ħr innomine patrir
& fili & xpš rei ut exiar & xxredar ab hur
famulxrdi. ipre enim tibi imperxt male
dicte damnate quipedibį supmarxam
bo l auit ex pxtrx mxxenre dexterampomex
Ergo maledicte. Item· SUP FEMINAS· xxxx

xor exxote inmunde ħr ppatrem & filium & xpū
xcō ut exiar & xxre dar ab har famolardi
ipxernim tibi imperxt mxledicte damnate
x qui exro nato hoc ulxraperuit & quatxdua
num· lazarx demonomxntu rurcitauit· Ergo

Deinde dxt prbt oħ inposita manum·
Sup capita infantū his uerbis· xx

ternahac iurtirtima piwxtem tuā dxpeor
dne. rce pax ompr· & nedr luminir & ue
nxatir famulor & famulax tuar ut digx
nxhr cor inluminare. lumxn intelligen
xxe tue; mundax cor & rxxpifica. dx eir rxxrnxā
uxxe ut dignixxpiciant accedere adgnetiā

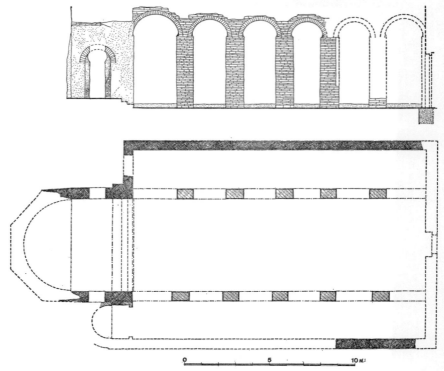

FIG. 78 – *S. Massimo, Collegno: phase III (reconstruction), section and plan*
FIG. 79 (below) – *Church, Isola Comacina*

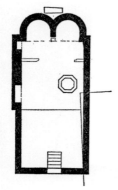

The double-ring plan of S. Sofia is reminiscent of the almost contemporary Umayyad building, the large and splendid Qubbat-as-Sakhra at Jerusalem. Both buildings clearly derive from Byzantine models, but the star-shaped perimeter combined with the three curved apses of the church at Benevento seems to be an original conception of Lombard architects.

These late Lombard buildings also mark an essential stage in the evolution of a new sensitivity in the treatment of space. It has already been observed with reference to the churches at Spoleto that in a second phase of pre-medieval taste the passion for spacious, noble, well-lit interiors gave way to a preference for more restricted areas, with masses of masonry enlivened by a play of contrast between light and darkness. Some eighth-century churches, especially the more original ones such as those at Cividale and Benevento, represent a further stage in the elaboration of contrast. Space is broken up, and large and small columns are used together in relatively large numbers so as to obtain startling effects of rays of light striking walls and columns in a diffused penombra, which inspire a sense of strangeness and mystery.

Externally, the simple, compact mass is replaced by a variety of forms and volumes in varied arrangements which assert the newly acceptable values. This elaboration is synthesized in the towered façades of early Carolingian buildings which, added to the basilican church with a domed transept, prepare the way for the noblest examples of medieval monumental architecture.

Besides these luxury buildings, churches of less intrinsic importance were built in the eighth century which are nevertheless of great value in view of our present state of ignorance. It was probably in the eighth century that the nave of the church at Collegno, near Turin, was rebuilt, with masonry pillars taking the place of columns to support horseshoe arches, which are to be seen today.

Minor churches of north Italy

A small church was built in the castle of the Isola Comacina, at that time of considerable military importance, with a nave and twin absidioles on a horseshoe-shaped plan. A simple mosaic floor decorated the chapel.

There are many fine examples of north Italian relief carving. In these pieces, which are mostly church furniture, there are rarely any figures; the altar of Duke Ratchis (later king from 744–9) at Cividale has on the principal face Christ between two seraphs in a mandorla held by four flying angels, and on the sides the Visitation and the Adoration of the Magi. The sculptor was not interested in representing the human figure, for essentially he was a mediocre craftsman, incapable of achieving artistic value with his primitive skills.

Lombard ornamental carving

Other examples of decorative sculpture are found in the urban centres of Lombard Italy, the seats of kings and dukes, and are of great interest. The chronology of these is fairly certain, depending largely on inscriptions.

S. Giorgio di Valpolicella has four arches on squat columns for a ciborium, c. 722, roughly carved, and dated by an inscription naming King Liutprand (712–43) and Bishop Dominicus (ob. 712). The decoration of the archivolts has a simple scroll pattern and that of the cornice S-shaped volutes.

S. Giorgio di Valpolicella

The sarcophagus of Theodota (ob. 720) at Pavia has borders with a delicate 'paired leaf and grape-cluster' motif; one face has two confronted peacocks with a vase between, and the other has two chimaerae facing a 'tree of life'; at the head is a crucifer Lamb.

Pavia, sarcophagus of Theodota

At Cividale the arches of the ciborium over the baptismal font (712–43) were executed on the order of Patriarch Callistus in the reign of King Liutprand, according to the inscription which runs round the top. The columns have capitals similar to those of the Tempietto; on the curved archivolts are rinceaux containing a variety of motifs within the curves of the scroll: two have a sinuous vine scroll with single grape clusters, leaves or various flowers. Three others have a 'trumpet pattern' stem: in the first the curves contain paired leaves, in the second leaves and grape clusters, in the third alternately single leaves and grape clusters. The sixth archivolt has an interlace consisting partly of four-stranded ribbon, partly of dotted ribbon. Similar dotted interlacing decorates the edges of the tympana, which also have a variety of decorative motifs.

Milan, S. Maria d'Aurona The eighth-century carvings of S. Maria d'Aurona, now in the Museo Civico, dating from *circa* 735, came to light in 1868 in the course of excavations and demolitions carried out on the site of the monastery, together with fragments of sixth-century capitals and some fine pilaster capitals of the late eleventh century. The capital of one thick pilaster, with a jewelled cross and scrolls of trumpet pattern belongs to *circa* 735, together with pillars from an iconostasis which are decorated with two symmetrically curving stems enclosing large paired leaves or grape clusters with spirals, and some smaller fragments. In spite of their lack of intrinsic importance these are nevertheless of interest for the decorative motifs: heart-shaped leaves, sinuous ribbons with pellets, and abstract compositions of spirals, darts and grape clusters.

Modena Cathedral The surviving fragment of the inscription of Bishop Lopicenus (*ob.* 750) in Modena Cathedral has patterns of confronted S and small grape clusters similar to those of the Cividale Tempietto. In the Cathedral Museum there are also some other large stone slabs with rather roughly carved but interesting designs, one with a border of foliage scrolls enclosing a panel carved with a cross and various animals: four deer, two lions and two peacocks. Another has a rinceau border of cornucopia and leaves and alternating panels with rosettes or animals.

Brescia, S. Salvatore Of the reliefs from S. Salvatore at Brescia, now in the Museo Cristiano, and dating from *circa* 735 we may note the well-known tympanum with a peacock between scrolls which end in lobed leaves and grape clusters, and a band of dynamic interlace in an Irish pattern of concentric circles. Other fragments have simple intersecting circles.

Cividale The marble carvings of Cividale were re-used in the font, and the inscription indicates that they were carved on the order of Sigvald, Patriarch from 764 to 786. One is still complete and shows a variety

Ashburnham Pentateuch: Jacob and Esau. *Bibliothèque Nationale, Paris (Nouv. Acq. Lat. 2334, fol. 25).*
37 × 32 cm. Cf. p. 215.

199

of motifs: the symbols of the Evangelists framed by rings of heart-shaped leaves, a cross between two candlesticks, and two griffins facing a 'tree of life'. A second is composed of two fragments, one with a stylized rosette and the other with the symbols of two Evangelists, and part of two other panels with the 'tree of life' below these. It seems probable that originally this pluteus was made up of eight sections separated by interlacing. The upper band is a dynamic interlace, Germanic in style.

An examination of Lombard carving of the eighth century reveals two chief sources of inspiration. First of all, naturally, Byzantium: many elements are inherited from the sixth-century repertory of decoration and symbol whose prototypes are to be seen at Ravenna – confronted S (Orthodox baptistery mosaics), vases, crosses, Chi-Rho, animals. It should be remembered that many ornamental and mystic animals other than doves and peacocks and deer are found on Byzantine ambos of the sixth century. But the ancestry of the liveliest motif, the rinceau or scroll of fine double stems enclosing a leaf and a grape cluster in each curve, is not so ancient, and is found in Umayyad art of the eighth century, well-known to be of Byzantine descent (engraved bronze plaques on beams in Qubbat-as-Sakhra, Jerusalem; stuccoes in the palace of Khirbet-el-Mafjar; eighth-century wooden Mimbar at Kairouan). When our knowledge of Byzantine art of the eighth century is more exact than at present, significant examples will no doubt be found in Greece and Asia Minor. The minute attention to detail in the finest work, such as the sarcophagus of Theodota, the archivolts of Cividale and the open stucco-work rinceau of the Tempietto, must have been inspired by Byzantine art of this century. Even the 'trumpet' type of scroll so common in the west is to be found in the Byzantine world, for example in the Panagia in Antalya.

Byzantine provenance of Lombard carving

From Germanic art derive the vigorous representation of animals designedly ferocious in appearance, sometimes strange and mythical, sometimes 'naturalistic' (lions, reptiles, dragons), and woven patterns of the northern type – continuous interlace of dotted strands, which is certainly Germano-Scandinavian in origin – and dynamic interlace such as that of the Sigvald panel at Cividale and the peacock panel at Brescia. From the evidence of the dynamic interlace in stucco of the Lombard Tempietto and those of the archivolts of S. Salvatore at

Germanic influence

Sacramentary of Godescalc: Fons vitae. *Bibliothèque Nationale, Paris (Nouv. Acq. Lat. 1203, fol. 3). 30.5 × 21 cm. Cf. p. 217.*

Brescia, it is evident that in the course of the eighth century the motifs of popular Germanic art were transferred from small articles of personal adornment to the monumental art of Lombard Italy.

But the most important innovation is that in the ornamental fields there are inserted realistic and expressive animals, fairly faithful to their actual form. Some of them are symbolic and are in the style of Byzantine tradition (peacocks drinking from a goblet, deer, doves, evangelical symbols); others have a purely decorative function (birds pecking a grape, wild beasts such as lions, snakes and dragons); the latter display their ferocious natural characteristics, in accordance with Germanic or Scandinavian practice, and constitute prototypes or forerunners of the ornamental wild beasts of Romanesque art.

Lombard painting: Naturns, St. Procul

The small single-nave church of St. Procul at Naturns has fragments of rather unusual painting. On the end wall, on either side of the arch of the apse, is an angel in a white paludament with black stripes, holding a long-stemmed cross, an iconographical subject that is

PLATE P. 181

Byzantine in origin. On the south wall are three fragments of which only the centre one is identifiable; this shows St. Paul escaping from Damascus by a rope let down from the city wall (Acts, IX, 25). The unusual style has suggested affinities with Irish art and especially with the Cuthbrecht Gospels (*c.* 800) for its line and colour – broad outlines and almost flat colours for both flesh and architecture, coloured lines for drapery folds. The perspective presentation of Damascus merits a special note, with a roof projected against the background and a strange window-frame, a yellow cornice with black dots ending in 'sofa-arm' volutes. The intrados of the triumphal arch has traces of praying angels similar to those of a band of relief at Ventimiglia of *circa* 800.

The customary dating (to *c.* 800) and the stylistic analysis are not in fact certain: the decorative band below, of coloured-strand key pattern in perspective, has parallels in the Romanesque period, and on the other hand the dilation of the eyes suggests seventh- and eighth-century Byzantine influence. It may well be an example of popular art of the Ottonian or even of the early Romanesque period, and the relatively sophisticated treatment of some of the drapery (the neck of the third figure on the left in the group of women) adds to the element of doubt. The decorative band above, with a chequer pattern where plaited strands cross, is popular in taste and of late date.

Münster, St. Johann

The frescoes at Münster (Müstair), in the Grisons, are very different in character and are more characteristic of this period, having been executed towards 800. Chronologically they lie outside the scope of

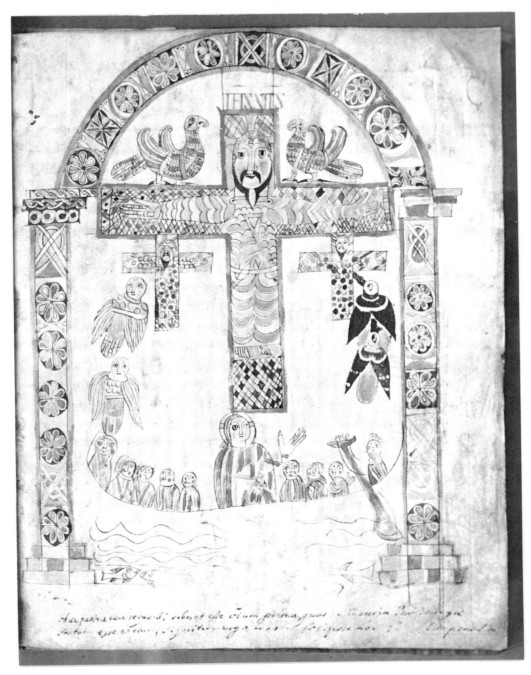

Crucifixion. *Universitätsbibliothek, Würzburg (Mp. Th. fol. 69 [fol. 7 r.]). 22.5 × 28.5 cm. Cf. p. 219.*

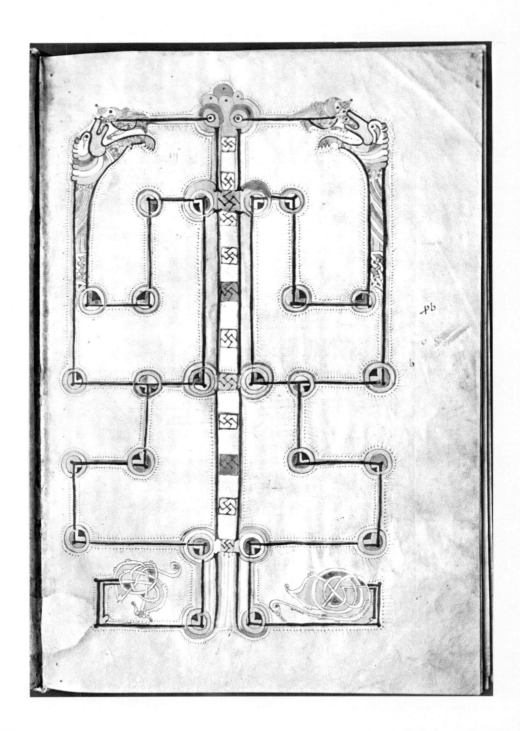

204

this study, but it is surely legitimate not only to mention them but to point out their affinity as compositions with those of Castelseprio (a Byzantine work of the sixth century in Lombardy), and the typically Carolingian character of the iconography.

The eighth century in Gaul saw the rise and triumph of the Carolingian dynasty. Originally, these descendants of Arnulf of Metz and Pepin of Landen were great landowners in the Ardennes and Brabant; two of their properties, Landen and Herstal, provided names for the family. They came to the fore in 687 when Pepin II led the Austrasian Franks to victory over the Neustrians. Now mayor of the palace without any potential rival, Pepin undertook the royal task of defending Francia against external attack. Among other actions, he drove the Frisians from Utrecht, installing there as a missionary named Willibrord, an Englishman, whose Evangeliarium we have already admired.

After Pepin's death in 714 power passed to his illegitimate son Charles Martel, who gave his name to the dynasty and completed his father's work by extending the frontier beyond the Rhine, assisted by the missionary work of another Englishman, St. Boniface.

Martel was to be remembered in history for his martial vigour: although the battle that he fought and won outside Poitiers in 732 may have been exaggerated by the chroniclers, and the Moslems whom he defeated may have been no more than a raiding band, the event had important local consequences and was seen as a significant achievement in Charles' defence of south-western France against the Moors. The Islamic threat hung over all western Christendom and hence Charles Martel's successes contributed enormously to his prestige. When in 751 Pepin the Short overthrew the Merovingian dynasty he encountered no opposition.

From Dagobert onwards all the Merovingian rulers had been weak in spirit and physically degenerate; between 690 and 715 no king had achieved adulthood. Hence they had lost much of their authority, and in the absence of royal power some provinces had assumed virtual independence; Aquitaine, for example, had become a separate duchy from about 675–80. Hence it was not difficult for Pepin the Short to dispossess the last ruler, Childeric III, and to send him and his son as prisoners, their hair ignominiously shorn, to the abbey of St. Bertin. The rise of the Carolingian dynasty continued unchecked with the

GAUL
Carolingian dynasty

Charles Martel

Decline of Merovingians

Ornamental page. *Universitätsbibliothek, Würzburg (Mp. Th.fol. 67 [fol. 2 r.]). 21.5 × 32 cm. Cf. p. 219.*

Multiple image of the Four Evangelists, by the scribe Thomas. *Cathedral Treasury, Trier (Cod. 61, fol. 5 v.). 26 × 23 cm. Cf. p. 219.*

victorious campaigns of Charlemagne against Saxons and Lombards, and he visited Rome in triumph in 774. On Christmas Day, 800 Charlemagne received the imperial crown in St. Peter's with the same formulae that had been used in the coronation of the Byzantine Emperors. Meanwhile the unification of their state kept pace with their growing prestige. Aquitaine was reconquered by Pepin the Short in a series of campaigns between 760 and 768, after which its administration was reorganized by the capitulary of Saintes. Saxon Germany was forced to submit to Charlemagne between 778 and 804. Carolingian legislation was varied and complex, since each of the subject peoples possessed its own law; it was promulgated in the constantly revised 'capitularies'. *Coronation of Charlemagne*

No really great monumental work of the eighth century remains in France or western Germany. The last important buildings raised in the final decades of the century have been demolished and the only remaining evidence for them is to be found in excavations, written descriptions and a few unreliable drawings. *Architecture*

The famous abbey church at St. Denis was built by King Dagobert I in *circa* 630 and was rebuilt by Pepin the Short in *circa* 750, following the plan of the original church, with colonnaded nave and aisles, an apse and a wide transept. A narrow portico or narthex, less than 3 metres wide, adjoined the façade. Externally, it seems there was a tower, which was imprudently heightened (or rebuilt) by William the Conqueror, and collapsed. *St. Denis*

The columns rested on heavy carved bases. One of these, found by Viollet-le-Duc, had large leaves and grape clusters; another, found by MacCrosby, had flat petalled quatrefoil rosettes. A capital excavated by Formigé was bell-shaped with large low-relief leaves at the corners, two wide flat volutes and circular rosettes with intersecting florets. *Grenoble, St. Laurent*

The 'crypt' of St. Laurent, Grenoble, was probably a funerary chapel; in the surrounding area finds of fifth- and sixth-century tombs have been made. The building is still in a good state of preservation, but restorations of 1848–54 removed valuable details which are shown in the old reliefs of the architect P. Manguin. These were stucco rinceaux laid on a base that had been ridged for better adhesion.

The plan is rectangular with four projecting niches which give it a Latin cross shape. Access was by two lateral doors, now approached by steps. It has a barrel-vault on columns, twenty in number but of

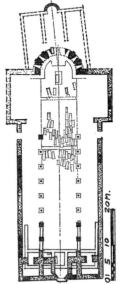

FIG. 80 – *Abbey church, St. Denis: plan*

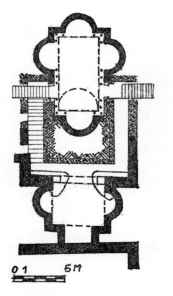

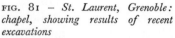

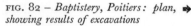

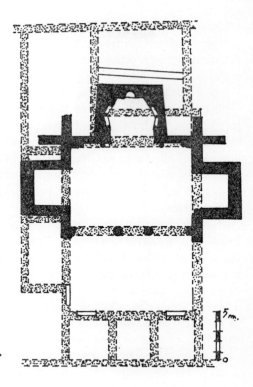

FIG. 81 – *St. Laurent, Grenoble: chapel, showing results of recent excavations*

FIG. 82 – *Baptistery, Poitiers: plan,* ➡ *showing results of excavations*

small dimensions, and these were the dominating element of the composition. In order to show them off the architect provided them with massive pulvins above the capitals, with horizontal stone slabs running above these, and with breaks corresponding to the apse and door openings. The principal apse and the barrel-vault were supported at a higher level on a low pedestal; this is decorated in front of the presbytery by two small columns, which constitute a second row. The apses have vaults of a complex and rare kind, which demonstrates the skill of the builders; during construction they were supported by centering, the marks of which are still visible. The capitals have leaves with gentle folds and undulating edges, short caulicoles sharply tapered, and rosettes in high relief. The pulvins are decorated with lambs, doves, crosses ending in curls and rinceaux (somewhat similar to the Lombard 'trumpet' type) rising from pod-shaped vases with handles. The whole repertory of decoration indicates on the one hand the eighth-century liking for Byzantine and symbolic elements (doves, vases, crosses, rinceaux etc.) and the still rather soft treatment of foliage and rosettes, but on the other hand it contains elements that are already clearly Carolingian, such as the short, thick caulicoles and various details that differ very little from those of the church of Germigny-des-Prés (c. 800). The original clustering of columns and of vaults also corresponds to proto-Carolingian taste, and the most probable dating is to the last quarter of the eighth century, as Hubert has already suggested. Recent excavations have brought to light the traces of another *memoria,* older and larger, with a trilobate presbytery, to the west of the present building.

Another French building that I am inclined to attribute to the eighth *Poitiers, Baptistery* century is the most interesting part of the baptistery at Poitiers. The present building was preceded by one dating back to earliest Christian times, revealed by excavations in 1890–7. A kind of pronaos divided into three chambers was found; in the present building the lower part of the walls of the room containing the font are clearly those of the primitive structure. In the first phase of building the baptismal FIG. 82 chamber was preceded by another, evidently an annexe for the catechumens. The original basin for immersion was discovered in 1803 and can still be seen.

The building which belongs to the Dark Ages consisted only of a room containing the font, two lateral absidioles (perhaps originally rectangular, now rebuilt in semicircular form), an eastern apse, polygonal internally and trapezoidal externally, and buttressed corners. The upper part of the structure was heightened and elaborately APPX. PL. 12 decorated. This masonry is of considerable refinement: on the east and west fronts, at the level of the windows, rows of tiles are interpolated into the courses of limestone, the cornice has a pattern of half-circles of stone with four-lobed brickwork filling the spaces between, and there are other decorative areas of brick. This ornamental masonry also includes detailed chiselled reliefs. At window level are short pilaster strips surmounted by a cornice with alternating triangular and semicircular tympana. On the east and west faces there are other triangular tympana and a kind of aedicule, all decorated.

Internally, the arrangement is Carolingian, similar to that of Germigny-des-Prés, (c. 800), with a free play of blind arcading, arched openings, arches and apses, enriched with columns of spoils and bands of moulding differently articulated according to the height of the columns. The interior of the apse is also decorated with blind arches on columns. APPX. PL. 1 In the upper part the arched windows are joined by a fascia at impost level, and between each pair of window openings is a triangular tympanum, alternating in agreement with the decoration of the exterior.

Evangelistary of Cuthbrecht: St. Mark. *Österreichische Nationalbibliothek, Vienna*
(Cod. 1224, fol. 71 v.). 31 × 23.8 cm. Cf. p. 221.

Apart from the re-used capitals, which are Roman or later, there are others which match and were evidently carved for this building; these belong to the upper arches of the interior, and resemble some of the stucco capitals of Germigny-des-Prés. These have broad leaves at the corners with indented edges and surfaces in low relief, and thin Corinthian caulicoles. The abacus has a decoration of vertical tongues. The marble capitals in the corners of the small hall and those on either side of the main apse have similar elements, with spiral composite-type volutes. The architectural elements of decoration herald the repertory of the *renovatio carolingia:* much use is made of ornamental corbels in the cornices of the main structure and that of the two side chapels, in the semicircular tympanum at the centre of the blind galleries of the east and west fronts; there is bead-and-reel moulding in the triangular tympana of the same galleries and in the limestone capitals of the upper arches of the interior. These motifs derived from Roman usage are accompanied by others that are clearly Carolingian ones – multifoil florets within discs (six-spoked wheels of intersecting circles) with trilobate leaves at the corners. Similar types of ornament to these can be seen in stucco fragments from Malles, Disentis and Germigny-des-Prés. These elements, together with some indications of zoomorphic motifs, suggest a mid-eighth-century dating. The unusual richness of the external decoration, together with the addition of three absidioles, may suggest that the building had been adapted in the eighth century to a 'Heavenly Jerusalem' pattern with altars for the three archangels. The present Romanesque frescoes may reproduce other earlier ones relating to the Apocalypse, with Christ among the Angels, the Elders and the Four Horsemen. Other early Romanesque frescoes with apocalyptic scenes have recently been found in the baptistery at Novara.

The foundation of the first monastery at Lorsch was the work of Count Cancor in 763; it comprised a hall-type church with a rectangular presbytery and a cloister surrounded by rooms for the monks. The second foundation, rich and important, was accompanied by large donations in 772–3, at the behest of Charlemagne. The new church was built about 600 metres from the old and was consecrated in 774. From 784 to 804 Abbot Richbod built the cloister, the perimeter wall of the monastery and the 'ecclesia triplex'. In 876–82 was built the mausoleum behind the apse in which Louis the German was buried. In 951–72 Abbot Gerbod covered the 'paradisum totum' with lead and built the 'pulpits' in front of the doors of 'paradise'. Some traces remain today of the church, the westwork and the antechurch, which

Lorsch Monastery
PLATE P. 183
FIGS. 83, 84

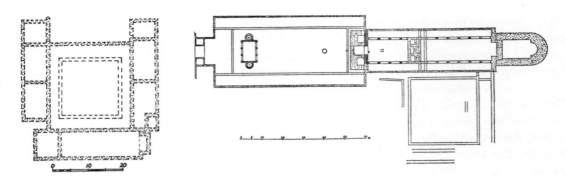

FIGS. 83, 84 – *Monastery, Lorsch: plan of original church, founded 763 (left); present plan as excavated (right)*

also had towers, but both dating and arrangement are uncertain, except that the presbytery of the church was similar to that of the monastery of 763.

The chief claim upon the interest of the student is the chapel of St. Michael within the long arched building that stood before the monastery. The lower floor was originally open with three large arches each side so as to form a triple passage. On the upper floor is a rectangular hall entered by two spiral staircases at the ends. The exterior decoration is of great beauty. On a background of stone carefully laid in patterns of two colours are two registers of architectural ornament: the lower consists of half-columns with composite capitals, the foliage treated similarly to that of the pedestals at St. Denis, and above, instead of trabeation, runs a band of leaves similar in design to those of the Carolingian flabellum in the Carrand Collection, Florence. The upper register consists of nine triangular arches on each front, on pilasters with fluting broken half-way up and Ionic capitals with two rows of flat ovoli. In the upper chapel there were originally architectural frescoes, pilaster strips on a high plinth, and a high entablature with fasciae.

The extreme elegance of the external decoration suggests a building intended to represent the Heavenly Jerusalem and in particular a chapel dedicated to the cult of angels, which the title of St. Michael and the position of the oratory on the upper floor also indicate. It is well known, and has already been mentioned in this work, that since the heavens were deemed to be the abode of angels, the places dedicated to their cult were on mountains or, in the absence of natural heights, on the upper storeys of buildings. We do not know exactly

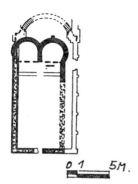
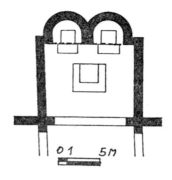
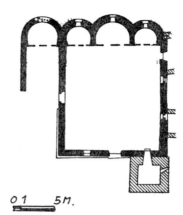

FIG. 85 *(left) – S. Martino, Mendrisio: plan*
FIG. 86 *(centre) – Church, Mittelzell, Reichenau I.*
FIG. 87 *(right) – St. Peter, Müstail*

the liturgical significance of the room between the long porticoes of the 'paradise': it may have been a representation of the Heavenly Jerusalem, or of the gate guarded by St. Michael, or it may have been merely a chapel in a raised position dedicated to this particular archangel or to all three. The artistic and liturgical characteristics of the building concur, in any case, to attribute the building to the last quarter of the eighth century.

The final development of this cult complex in the West took place at the beginning of the ninth century, when the altars dedicated to the archangels were removed to a towered building in front of the church. The plan of St. Gall (*c.* 820) shows altars to the archangels at the top of the towers of the façade, as defenders of a spiritual fortress; the *translatio S. Adelphi* provides evidence that shortly before 899 the 'sacellum et altare arcangeli Michaelis' at Remiremont was moved from outside the church to the interior. Finally, the inscription at Corvey proves that in the ninth century the whole west-work there was considered as a 'Heavenly Jerusalem' *(civitatem)* protected by angels. In this building a fragment of painting has been found which represents the Apocalypse (Heitz).

Origin and development of the westwork

In the area which is now French-speaking Switzerland the type of simple apsed hall with two side chambers was common. The first church at Romainmôtier was of this kind, but the front part of the apse was screened by two stretches of wall and an arch, as at S. Maria at Castelseprio and the first reconstruction of the presbytery in Milan Cathedral. Probably this first building goes back to the monastery founded by Duke Chramnelène in about 636 with monks brought from Luxeuil. Another building, on the same plan but larger, excavated

Romainmôtier

213

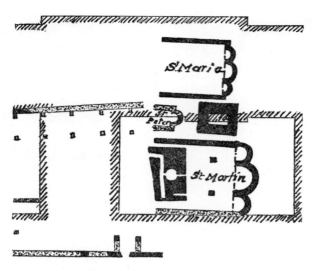

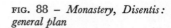

FIG. 88 – *Monastery, Disentis: general plan*

together with that already mentioned beneath the present church by A. Naef, must be the one consecrated by Pope Stephen II in 753 when he visited Pepin the Short. An ambo panel found in the building, carved with an elaborate cross (upright, decorated with acanthus pattern, arms of interlace with pellets, terminal spirals) with two tufts of acanthus at its foot and a border of irregular plaited work is in mid-eighth-century style.

FIG. 85   The typical eighth-century arrangement was however a hall with two or three apses. The small church excavated beneath S. Martino at Mendrisio had projecting twin apses of horseshoe shape whose depth shows that they held both clergy and cantors, like the projecting presbyteries of the sixth century. The angular position of these apses may well explain the form of those at S. Salvatore, Brescia, which

FIG. 86   excavations have failed to elucidate. Another twin-apsed hall anterior to 799 was excavated at Mittelzell, Reichenau.

Three-apsed halls   Many churches, some of which still survive, had three apses, the most important being St. Johann at Münster, of *circa* 800, which has an external decoration of blind arcading. This important building falls outside the chronological limits of this study, but it is probable that

FIG. 87   other similar churches come within it, such as St. Peter, Müstail and the 'Ecclesia Resurrectionis', Schaffhausen.

Disentis   The complex of buildings at Disentis certainly belongs to the eighth century; this consisted of two three-apsed churches, Ste. Marie and

St. Martin, and a small chapel, St. Pierre. All three are named in a donation of 766 of Bishop Tellus: 'tres ecclesias sancte Mariae . . . seu Sancti Martini . . . seu Sancti Petri . . . constructas in loco qui dicitur Desertina . . .'. The three buildings were revealed by excavation in 1906, and beneath St. Martin were found remains of an earlier church FIG. 88 (622–70) with traces of a centrally planned crypt (in which the martyr Placidus was probably buried) and many fragments of stucco. These pieces of stucco work found beneath the floor were collected and are kept in boxes in a room of the convent: they include more that seventy heads, many hands, and pieces of archivolt, painted with triple acanthus buds, *peltae* and saw-tooth pattern. Parts of the body, too, are painted; on the heads the hair and lips are painted and not modelled. Carolingian illumination of manuscripts, a characteristic product of *ILLUMINATED* the luxury of the Court, does not come within the field of this study, *MANUSCRIPTS* which will therefore be confined to an examination of the currents which contributed to the style, and to a single early Carolingian manuscript, the Godescalc Sacramentary.

The Gellone Sacramentary (Bibl. Nat. Lat. 12048) takes its name from *Gellone Sacramentary* the monastery to which it once belonged, but the abbey of Rebais (in the diocese of Meaux, Seine-et-Marne) is mentioned several times in the text, and it is now believed that this is most likely to be the place of origin of the manuscript. The semi-uncial and minuscule lettering (late eighth century) in which the text is written differ from the more sinuous hand of Luxeuil and of the 'oratio dominica' of the Gelasian Sacramentary, but the decoration, which is confined to the initials, is a development of it. Here also are birds and fish, long-necked storks, rabbits, ducks and wild boar, drawn in red and green on a yellow ground. Sometimes these have polychrome bodies of the 'oriental carpet' kind, but with a degree of sensitive naturalism and a humour which are highly individual: dogs leap, black eagles soar with a lamb in their talons or a snake in their beaks, and a cock struts or pecks at corn. Sometimes fish are arranged to form letters; sometimes a single fish is shown caught on a hook and line held in a hand. Among zoomorphic subjects are some small sacred figures – angels, Mary at the Cross, and with the box of spices, crucifixes with Christ wearing a loin-cloth, and the Evangelists. Other elements seem to derive from Anglo-Irish art: Mary's robe is decorated with a key pattern, and some initials are outlined by red dots. But substantially the work is an original one, and can be dated to the period between 750 and 790.

The so-called Ashburnham Pentateuch (Bibl. Nat. N.A. 2334), which *Ashburnham* until 1842 was in the library of Tours, presents a problem which *Pentateuch*

216

deserves a study to itself. It is generally attributed to a Spanish or North African scriptorium and no significance is usually attached to its appearance in northern France. The nineteen full-page illuminations show either a single episode, such as two of the Flood on fol. 9, or cycles of episodes, such as those on fol. 6, from Adam and Eve to the killing of Abel; Jacob and Esau, on fol. 25; the life of Joseph, on fols. 40–44, and so on. The strongest colours are used, flat, for the backgrounds – red, green, purple – with architectural elements in white; the figures are lively and seem already fully medieval; the disposition of the scenes is not organized and neither the action nor the identity of the figures is immediately obvious. The figures have not the flow and rhythm of Byzantine work deriving from Hellenistic art, nor the strength and mass typical of Roman Africa. Some of the cyclical compositions and some colonnaded buildings in perspective recall the miniatures of the Utrecht Psalter, and the reasonable theory has been advanced that, like the Psalter, the Tours Pentateuch derives from an archetype of some antiquity, possibly Hebrew. This is suggested by comparisons of the rubrics with those of the Mitraschim, by parallels with the paintings in the Dura synagogue, and by details of clothing such as the high coiffures of the women, which resemble those of Palmyra. The execution however is western and seems to belong to the late seventh or early eighth century. The terminal heart-shaped leaves at the corners of the frames have parallels in early Carolingian and (in more complex forms) in Anglo-Irish manuscripts; the palaeography of the rubrics is a combination of majuscules and miniscules of a type near to Carolingian.

PLATE P. 199

The Godescalc Sacramentary, dated to 781, is sufficient to demonstrate the new cultural and artistic spirit at the court of Charlemagne. At the beginning of the codex is a Christ enthroned in the act of blessing. The scene of the 'Fons vitae', which derives from Byzantine prototypes, shows animals copied from nature and depicted in vivid colours around the well, which glows with gold. This scene is contained within a frame of golden arabesques which adds nobility and richness. On the page opposite, the writing occupies the whole area within a frame of narrow gold interlace. Insular influence is evident in the large letters of fine interlacing and scroll work, but here there is a new restraint, a new nobility; the letters are not strangely shaped but reproduce

Godescalc Sacramentary

PLATE P. 200

Evangelistary from Kremsmünster: evangelical symbol. *Kremsmünster Abbey (Cim. 1, fol. 110 r.). 30 × 20 cm. Cf. p. 221.*

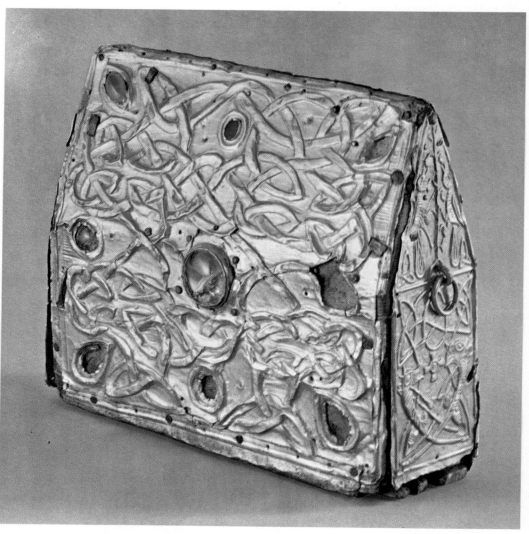

Reliquary from Chur. *Cathedral Treasury, Chur. Cf. p. 222.*

Roman capitals; the colours are not bright and contrasted but shaded with some delicacy: brown and gold stand out against a ground of purple.

GERMANY
St. Boniface

Western Germany, which had been the theatre of widespread missionary activity in the course of the seventh century, was definitively converted to Christianity by St. Boniface, a native of Devonshire, who had joined St. Willibrord in Frisia in 716 and was an active and successful champion of the Roman Church until his death in 754. His letters show that he sought books both religious and profane to help in the propagation of the faith and of culture, and that he was helped by other missionaries from the British Isles.

The Irish Kilian (689) and the Anglo-Saxon Burchard (called by St. Boniface in 743) founded monasteries at Würzburg which were to have a long existence, in the course of which many codices were collected; some of them are preserved in the library of the university in that city, catalogued as 'scottice scripti'. The miniatures which they contain are not Anglo-Irish in style, as might be expected. In the most famous of these manuscripts, the Epistles of St. Paul (Mp. Th. f. 69), the Crucifixion bears every sign of originality, and if any influences are to be traced in it they are Frankish. The iconography is strange: within an arch is Christ crucified, wearing the long garment, the *colobium*; on either side are smaller figures of the two thieves, depicted without any attempt at realism; at the foot of the cross is the Church, represented as a ship from which rise in flight the souls of the elect and, with black wings, those of the damned. The composition of the arch, with rosettes, and the two birds on the arms of the cross, have antecedents in the Gelasian Sacramentary (seventh century); it has patterns of continuous interlace or simple knots in the Frankish manner. The work is popular in style but the colours, which are subtly shaded from yellow to brown, bear witness to an ingenuous strong artistic drive ('Kunstwollen').

Still more impressive, and further removed from Insular designs, is the page of abstract ornament of Codex Mp. Th. f. 67, which probably comes from the monastery of the Saviour. Germanic and Frankish elements predominate here, such as the animals at the upper corners and the capricious contortions of the lower angles, which terminate in small curling acanthus leaves. The predominance of yellow tones resembles the colouring of the Crucifixion already described.

The effects of transplanting Anglo-Irish taste to Germanic territory, and the origins of Carolingian illumination are well shown in the Trier Evangelistary, written around 750 in the scriptorium at Echternach, the monastery founded by St. Willibrord. On the famous page which the scribe has signed ('Thomas scripsit') the four symbols of the Evangelists are combined into a single monstrous figure, which is not fashioned from pure abstract lines, as in seventh-century Insular examples, but equally makes no attempt to achieve effects of modelling or perspective. The frame of dynamic or zoomorphic interlacing, al-

Würzburg

Epistles of St. Paul
PLATE P. 203

Codex Mp.Th.f. 67
PLATE P. 205

Trier Evangelistary

Tassilo chalice from Kremsmünster. Copper and silver. Circa 777 (?).
Kremsmünster Abbey. Height 27 cm. Cf. p. 224.

though it derives from Insular examples, has neither the grace nor the balanced symmetry which characterize them. For the canon tables another artist has copied Mediterranean models, transforming architectural elements, such as the bases of columns, with scroll work and spirals, and the mystic birds beside the capitals are accompanied by cocks. These same elements are to be found in Carolingian manuscripts of the Ada group. The initials are both of the Insular type, with spirals, dots and animal interlace, and of the continental type, with curling leaves, animals and fish in the Merovingian manner.

Other codices influenced by Anglo-Irish art are found in Austria. The Evangelistary of Cuthbrecht was probably executed at Salzburg during the episcopate of the Irish Bishop Vergilius (743–84) or, if it is later, is due to the influence of the cultural centre which he founded and which spread later into Styria and Carinthia. This work shows many motifs taken from the Insular repertory, especially that of dynamic ribbon interlace (independent or as background), but in general animal subjects are expressed with a naturalism which is in strong contrast to the typical Insular stylization. Sometimes the bodies are elongated, but they are also depicted realistically and with a certain humour which seems to owe more to Merovingian inspiration. Rabbits, goats and good-natured dragons are shown in this way. The Evangelists, each with his symbol, within an arch decorated with scrolls or in a frame decorated in a variety of ways, make a rather grotesque impression, albeit unintentionally.

Evangelistary of Cuthbrecht

PLATE P. 210

The Kremsmünster Evangelistary was executed in the neighbourhood of Salzburg several decades later, and shows a different taste, typically western. Here the artist, exemplifying recognizably Carolingian characteristics, takes a fresh view of his material: St. Mark's lion, well drawn, leaps fiercely within an arch covered with evenly spaced regular knots. The colouring, however, is of deep contrasting tones and differs from that of typically Carolingian artists who painted lavishly with gold and silver on noble grounds of purple.

Kremsmünster Evangelistary

PLATE P. 216

Eighth-century sculpture also has original features; the best known example is the Hornhausen stele group (sometimes attributed to the seventh century), which shows a knight armed with a lance and shield, and below this an interlace of long-beaked animals.

Hornhausen stele

The stele discovered in the castle of Gondorf, on the Moselle, probably belongs to the second half of the eighth century. This represents a bearded figure, without a nimbus, holding a book; on either side of the head, within a circle, are two doves, and this *clipeus* is enclosed within a frame decorated with a stylized bead-and-spindle pattern, with the

Gondorf stele

busts of four animals and the head and claws of a wolf but a curved beak, Anglo-Irish in taste, at each corner. The central figure, the beaded frame and the cross-shaped triple acanthus rosette above the head derive from Byzantine motifs which have been transformed by Carolingian *renovatio*.

METALWORK Following Germanic tradition, orfèvrerie in Frankish territory and in the British Isles developed considerably during the eighth century, but the finest and most valuable works of this kind have almost all disappeared, victims of human cupidity, and the examples that remain are often of relatively slight value as far as the metal is concerned.

Chur reliquary
PLATE P. 218 In the cathedral at Chur is a reliquary of gilded copper in the shape of a small steeply pitched sarcophagus. On one of the principal faces is a ribbon interlace enclosing nine coloured stones *en cabochon*; on the opposite side a border of similar interlace encloses a space on which

S. Comba de Bande, Galicia. *Cf. p. 224.*

S. Comba de Bande, Galicia: interior. *Cf. p. 224.*

four semicircles of granulated ribbon ending in serpent heads intersect a circle of similar ribbon. Above this is nailed a strip of Byzantine-type acanthus which came from another reliquary. On the sides is more ribbon interlacing, terminating in stylized animal heads and bodies; two roughly shaped peacocks cover the tympanum. The dynamic interlace has the chaotic capriciousness of Germanic taste rather than the regularity of the Irish style, and the work can be dated to about 750.

Tassilo chalice
PLATE P. 220

The chalice which, according to an inscription on its base, was presented to the abbey of Kremsmünster by Tassilo III, Duke of Bavaria, and the Duchess Liutpirc (777–88) is a more elegant piece of work. It is of cast bronze, engraved and gilded, with nielloed silver decorations representing the Saviour, in the act of blessing, and the four Evangelists on the cup and four saints on the base. The bands framing the figures are of dynamic interlace, Insular in type; the triangular spaces between them have zoomorphic ornament; the design and 'chip-carving' technique of these animal patterns is related to Scandinavian practice; the motifs of the cup have been compared to those of the Danish silver Fejø cup. A 'dog' body can be identified, with paws, tail and tongue, repeated in various ways, a fantasy of form and line which is typical of Germanic rather than Insular art.

SPAIN

It will be remembered that from 711 onwards the Iberian peninsula was occupied by the armies of Islam, and although the north was spared from invasion it was overrun by swarms of refugees and armed soldiers, so that the arts of peace had little chance to flourish.

A king, Pelagius, was elected, who installed his court at Cangas de Onis in 735, where a small cruciform church was built on a dolmen. The capital remained here until 805 but thereafter was transferred to Pravia and then to Oviedo. Alfonso II (791–842), who founded the new city, endowed it with a royal palace, built baths and defensive walls around the church, and supplied it with water by aqueducts.

Architecture

St. Comba de Bande
PLATES PP. 222, 223

No buildings in Spain can be dated for certain to the eighth century, and some churches presumed to have been built at that time now appear to be of later date. The church of S. Comba de Bande, in Galicia, seems to be of the late ninth century. It is cruciform, with barrel-vaulting and a cupola at the crossing, and with horseshoe arches. The date of building seems clear from a document of 982 which reveals that in 872 Alfonso II, king of Léon, had granted certain

Book of Kells: illuminated initial. *Circa* 700. *Trinity College Library, Dublin (fol. 29 r.). Cf. p. 233.*

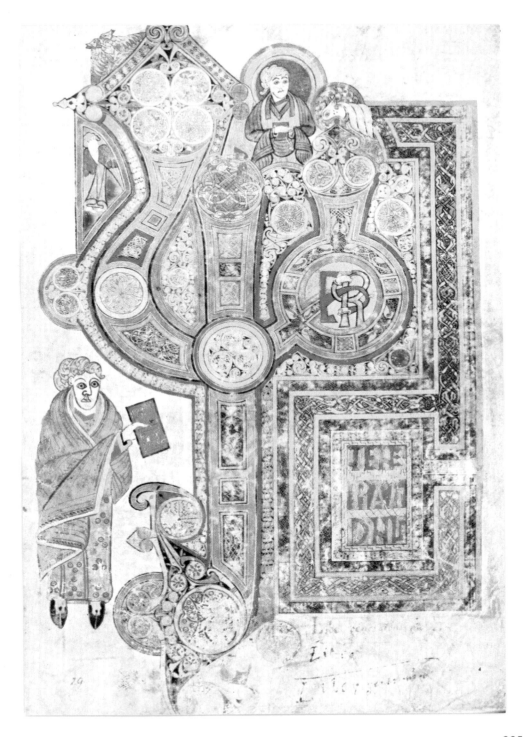

lands and buildings to one Oduarius, 'digno bellatori', with the obligation to keep them in good repair. This Don Odoario in his turn divided part of this property with others and allotted to a cousin, the deacon Odoynus, a villa near the river Limia with the obligation to rebuild two churches which had fallen into disrepair. One of these, dedicated to the martyr St. Comba, is the church with which we are concerned, a building in many respects similar to S. Zeno at Bardolino, on Lake Garda, which is from the second half of the ninth century.

Quintanilla de las Viñas The little church of Quintanilla de las Viñas is from the beginning of the tenth century. It was a basilica with a nave and two aisles, vaulted, but only the transept now remains. On the exterior the walls, of 'grand appareil', have decorative bands with intersecting stars, stylized plants and animals in relief. In the triumphal arch are incorporated the now famous figural carvings, one of which has a sun and a votive inscription from the modest and pious foundress 'Flammola'. Father Pérez de Urbel has identified her as the wife of Gonzales Telles, who is mentioned in donations of 912, 915 and 929. The church may certainly be dated to this period, and some carved monograms help to confirm this.

IRELAND The eighth century saw a great monastic movement in Ireland, but religious faith and artistic inspiration were not accompanied by political and governmental achievements. Many independent 'tuatha' existed within the island and the so-called 'high king' had no real authority. Hence it was easy for the Danes and other Vikings to ravage the island and to settle there after 790. In the eighth century the population was still divided into distinct orders, each with its own privileges and duties: there were nobles (landowners), serfs and 'aes-dana', the intellectual class which has already been mentioned. The economy corresponded to this division, being based on pastoral farming centred on the 'rath' or farmhouse. In these lived the owners ('boaire'), who were themselves divided into six different categories according to the size of their flocks.

Architecture The extremely primitive nature of Irish architecture in the seventh and eighth centuries is thus comprehensible. Both raths and monasteries consisted of groups of huts within a circular enclosure which might itself be enclosed by a larger concentric circle. Each enclosure had a boundary formed by stones, earthworks and a ditch; some had an outer palisade. This defence was intended to secure the occupants

Book of Kells: St. Luke. *Circa 700. Trinity College Library, Dublin (fol. 32 v.). Cf. p. 233.*

227

FIG. 89 – *Irish church.*
From the Book of Kells

against robbers and wild animals, not against organized military assault. Many of these dwelling-sites were situated amid lakes or marshes, often on natural or artificial islands.

The churches, from what remains of them, seem to have been extremely simple in plan—small halls with no internal supports, measuring 6, 10 or 12 metres in length. These were sometimes wooden structures, probably painted. An idea of what they may have looked like is perhaps given by the picture of the Temple on the 'Temptation of Christ' page of the Book of Kells: this shows a high pitched roof perhaps ornamented with painting, perhaps carved; the beams at the ridge and gables terminate in erect animal heads which cross each other (or perhaps are joined by wooden pegs) and which recall similar ornaments on Etruscan huts. A band of key pattern runs below the ridge, and a second band of rich zoomorphic decoration follows the eaves. The wall has polychrome decoration imitating curtain hangings.

The rectangular stone churches often had an overhanging roof like those of the primitive 'navetas' of the Balearic Islands. They were built without mortar, and the walls continued the line of the vaulting, sloping outwards. In other churches constructed with mortar the walls were vertical and less thick, and were usually supported by buttresses at the corners: the roof was very steep.

Monastic communities were frequently established on islands. The complex excavated at Nendrum, near Downpatrick, was apparently founded in the middle of the seventh century, and continued until 974 when Abbot Sedna O'Deman was 'burnt in his own house'. The monastery consisted of two concentric enclosures, and there are traces

Wooden churches
FIG. 89

Stone churches

Monastery of Nendrum
FIG. 90

228

FIG. 90 – *Monastery,*
Nendrum: plan

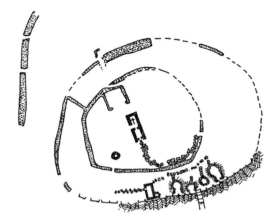

of a third, considerably wider, circle. In the centre was a church with
two rectangular chambers (possibly a narthex and a hall for services)
and a round tower. Within the perimeter wall were the foundations
of four round huts, in one of which were traces of bronze and a mould
for casting pins. Another rectangular building of stone and clay mortar
was assumed to be a school, and here were found slate tablets with
sketches of patterns and of letter-shapes, a piece of a compass and
several iron styli, one of which was of a type used for writing on wax
tablets. Fragments of charred wood show that the building was destroyed by fire.

Other islands had similar monastic complexes. Off the coast of Sligo *Inishmurray*
there was one on the island of Inishmurray, which was enclosed by
a drystone wall about 5 metres thick, surrounding an area of some
45 to 58 metres in diameter. Remains of stone huts and churches
have been found here and many stelae carved with a variety of designs,
including simple crosses and others with curling ends and interlace
patterns. The monastery of Inchcleraun, to the north of Clonmacnoise,
was on an island in a lake, surrounded by an enormous circular wall.
A typical group of monastic buildings is preserved on Skellig Michael *Skellig Michael*
(Kerry), on a high crag in the sea. There are five huts standing,
covered by corbelled domes of rough stone; they are comparatively
large (5 to 8 metres in diameter) and their height, which reaches
6 metres, makes it possible that they were divided by a floor into two
storeys. The church is in the shape of an upturned boat and beside
it is a stone cross: there is another very small oratory at the edge of the
cliff. The almost inaccessible site of the ancient monastery explains

its preservation and the dedication to St. Michael. These huts, almost isolated beneath the sky, might symbolize the mystic spirit of the early monks, akin to the Greek monks of the Meteora in their fondness for infinite space.

In large monastic establishments there seems to have been a great number of these cells, occupied by two or three persons, which thus formed a complex comparable to the large villages of primitive peoples, both ancient and contemporary, but archaeological evidence for this is unfortunately lacking in the case of the most important monasteries. At Armagh only the layout of the streets of the city indicates the line of the walls of the enclosure; at Glendalough, founded by St. Kevin at the end of the sixth century, parts of the wall still stand, and there *Iona* are ruins of churches of various periods. Of the monasteries of Iona, where the life of St. Columba was written and perhaps the Book of Kells begun, only a few traces of huts have been found, and some crosses excavated, which are no longer *in situ*.

Little or nothing remains of the non-monastic churches of the eighth century: Françoise Henry gives as an example the cathedral of Glendalough (Wicklow). It is probable that this was originally built at the end of the century and then enlarged, and possibly raised on its perimeter walls during the Romanesque period. Parts of the west and north walls belong to the original structure. The building is rectangular and fairly large (950 by 16 metres). The lower part of the original walls is of large slabs of dressed stone set in courses; the jambs of the door overhang; two buttresses at the corners of the front also overhang and are not bonded to the masonry between them.

Other forms of Irish art The relative modesty of Irish architectural remains of the eighth century cannot be taken as a yardstick of general accomplishment: the spirit of the country was alien to the production of monumental works of architecture, as it was to ambition for power and material conquest; but the artistic impulse and Christian spirit of the people of the Emerald Isle were strong and were to have a profound influence throughout the whole continent of Europe. Examples of the arts of manuscript illumination, sculpture and metalwork in Ireland before the ninth century are of remarkable beauty.

Illumination The beginnings of Irish manuscript decoration, and the Durrow Book, have already been discussed, and the Book of Kells, the most splendid and famous of Irish manuscripts, will be examined shortly; but for the intervening period it is hard to make safe assertions, since in many important cases the problem arises as to their possible English provenance.

Book of Kells: cross with abstract ornament. *Circa* 700. *Trinity College Library, Dublin (fol. 33 r.). Cf. p. 233.*

This uncertainty arises even in the case of the St. Gall Gospel-book (MS. 51), although it is known that the monastery founded by Gall, the disciple of Columbanus, kept its links with Ireland over a long period, and in spite of the fact that the miniatures which illustrate the codex abound in the spiral decorations favoured by Irish artists. In this manuscript the most famous pages are those depicting the Crucifixion, with oriental iconography including Christ wearing the *colobium*, two angels and the figures bearing the sponge and the lance; the Last Judgement; and the 'surrealist' Evangelist portrayed between panels of interlace and spiral decoration and symbols of the Evangelists. The proportions of the large Chi-Rho monogram (half-way between Lindisfarne and Kells) suggest a dating in the middle of the eighth century. To the same period would seem to belong the book of MacRegol, with pages of large script, and a smaller work, the Book of Dimma. *St. Gall Gospel-book*

The Book of Kells is an imposing volume (35 by 27 centimetres) and the execution of its 339 folios of thick parchment must have been the work of many years. It is thought to have been begun in the late eighth century at Iona (the monastery founded in 563) and after the destruction of that community by the Vikings (802 or 805) taken by Abbot Cellach to Kells, where it was completed. *Book of Kells* PLATES PP. 225, 227, 231

The script is a majuscule of great beauty but not very clear, and the lettering is badly spaced. The text is full of errors and incoherences, but the work is overwhelmingly impressive because the artistic effort is directed towards achieving a majestic overall impression rather than towards textual accuracy. Illuminated letters follow one another in the lines of script in disconcerting variety, and even the corrections provide a pretext for ornament. It is impossible to differentiate between the hands of the various artists: the presence of a master and of lesser craftsmen is evident, but the work as a whole has a unity which extends to consistent elegance.

There are many whole-page illuminations and these include not only the conventionally decorated leaves (canon tables, crosses of abstract ornament, portraits of the Evangelists, and their symbols, within a wide variety of frames) but also illustrations which are foreign to Insular tradition: the Virgin and Child between four angels, the Temptation of Christ, or His arrest. The initial pages of the Gospels

Irish carved cross. *Clonmacnoise Monastery. Cf. p. 236.*

moreover are filled by large letters with such rich decoration that they constitute a kind of independent calligraphic composition: one of these pages contains the verse from Matthew, xxvii, 38, relative to the Crucifixion.

The enrichment of the iconographic repertory is undoubtedly due to influence from both Mediterranean and Frankish art: the Virgin with four attendant angels derives from Byzantine examples; the inclusion of human elements in the interlacing and the bands of zoomorphic decoration show a new interest in anthropomorphic motifs; the rich pages of single letters within large frames seem to owe something to the work of the Carolingian Palace school which was making itself felt at the end of the eighth century. However, the work remains a typical product of the Anglo-Irish manner, and shows that Ireland preserved throughout the eighth century its own, Celtic, creative spirit. Some pages, it is true, have an almost Baroque exuberance of ornament, but others retain the mathematical inspiration and preciseness of execution of the earliest Irish work – for example, the page with the cross covered with delicate arabesques of spirals and zoomorphic motifs.

Stone crosses Carved stone crosses are characteristic of the period. Large numbers of them were erected in monasteries, of which we have evidence in the plan of the monastery shown in the Book of Mulling. This miniature shows a circular enclosure with eight crosses outside it, at the four points of the compass, dedicated to the four Evangelists and four prophets, and other crosses within the enclosure bearing symbols of Christ, the Apostles and some angels; one cross for the Holy Spirit is marked on the wall itself. Fragments of religious writings quoted by Françoise Henry mention the 'pious cloister' of Disert-Bethech 'behind a circle of crosses', the monastery of Clonenagh 'of many crosses', and Cormac, 'a devout city with a hundred crosses'.

Not many Irish crosses remain from the earliest times and those that do remain are on the east coast facing England, or in the centre of the island; there are none on the Atlantic coast. Generally they are between 3.5 and 4 metres high. The early ones have simple projecting arms, but as a rule the arms are connected by a characteristic circle. Their origin has been sought in the stone slabs with crosses of various forms engraved on them which marked tombs; but the large decorated and articulated crosses rising from a base had a ceremonial rather than a funerary function and their prototypes should be sought in the symbolic crosses common to the whole of early Christendom. It has already been shown that gold and jewelled crosses were used in the

Crucifixion from Athlone. Bronze. St. John's near Athlone. Mid-7th century. *National Museum of Ireland, Dublin. Cf. p. 239.*

fifth and sixth centuries to symbolize the triumph of the Divine Sacrifice; in the seventh century the representation of Christ on the Cross was encouraged by the sanction of the Trullan Council of 692, but the reaction of the rigorists in the iconoclast period had restored to favour the cross on its own, without figural representation.

Decorated crosses
The Irish crosses probably reproduced ancient crosses made with gold and gems which, unlike the Byzantine crosses, did not have a smooth surface with coloured stones inset, but were covered with enamel and filigree in interlacing, spiral, and key patterns, and occasionally had zoomorphic subjects. In general, eighth-century Irish crosses are of this kind: Duvillaun (Mayo), Gallen (Offaly), Iona (Scotland), Kilrea (Kilkenny), Kilkeeran (Kilkenny), Ahenny (Tipperary) and so on. Maire and Liam de Paor have shown that on the crosses of Ahenny there are imitations of bronze bosses used to cover nail heads and of mouldings which covered the joints of sheets of metal. Many of them have projecting hemispheres of a particular kind which seem to derive from enamelled studs, and it is also possible that in some cases the stone was coloured.

Some crosses have figural representations as well as abstract or zoomorphic decoration. The scenes are divided in panels covering the base and continuing on to the cross itself. Some have figured panels only.

Moone cross
The cross at Moone (Kildare), apparently of the eighth century, displays a fairly complex iconography in the number and variety of the episodes depicted: scenes of the Crucifixion and the Flight into Egypt are accompanied by subjects familiar in Coptic Egypt: the hermits St. Paul and St. Anthony, and the Temptation of St. Anthony. All these figures are presented schematically, squat and wide, and carved very simply in low relief. On the base the Twelve Apostles are shown in three identical rows one above the other, like the 96 little figures which surround the ninth-century Turin miniature of the Last Judgement.

PLATE P. 232
The full development of the Irish carved cross, with regard both to shape and to iconography, sometimes representing Irish saints, comes somewhat later: on the Cross of the Scriptures at Clonmacnoise, King Flann's Cross (*ob.* 913), are depicted, within the circle, the Last Judgement on one side and the Crucifixion on the other.

Naturalistic portrayals of Christ in correct proportion to the cross itself do not seem to have existed in the earliest period; the stele at Duvillaun (Mayo) bears a naked Christ crucified, but it is very roughly cut and probably of late date.

Lindisfarne Gospels: illuminated page. *Circa 700. British Museum. Cf. p. 240.*

Lindisfarne Gospels: illuminated page (fol. 26 v.). *Circa 700. British Museum. Cf. p. 240.*

The strong artistic urge of the Irish finds full expression also in orfèvrerie. Two works of the early eighth century are famous, the Ardagh chalice and the so-called Tara brooch. The cup of the chalice is of beaten silver, enriched by bands of elegant gold ornament, fine dynamic ribbon and animal interlace in filigree, enamel bosses and plaques of a type peculiar to Ireland. The incomparable workmanship makes it a masterpiece. Equally fine is the Tara brooch, a bronze ring about 10 centimetres in diameter with a long pin. In the cast bronze are cells containing little panels of gold filigree with spirals and animal interlace; bird heads of primitive Germanic taste project along the edge of the ring. On the reverse side the bronze is decorated with zoomorphic subjects executed in 'chip-carving'. Enamel studs in the customary colours of blue and green enliven the work, which is of great beauty and delicacy. *Metalwork*

Ardagh chalice

Tara brooch

The Athlone Crucifixion shows Christ wearing the *colobium*, and the usual figures of Mediterranean iconography, but translated into the 'Irish idiom': spirals and key pattern cover the bodies and garments with an abstract geometric design similar to that used in the Book of Kells and on some of the crosses. *Athlone Crucifixion* PLATE P. 235

It would be wrong to omit from a discussion of Irish art the observation that certain of its characteristics, and in particular the dynamic interlace, have been considered, since the publication of Clédat's work on the interlace of the frescoes at Bawît, to owe something to Coptic art. Undoubtedly there were connections between monasticism in Ireland and in the East, as indeed there were commercial relations between Egypt and the British Isles, but the claim for the influence of eastern knotwork is another matter, and might well be made the other way round: the dating of Bawît as of other monuments is still *sub iudice*. This being so, it is astonishing that some scholars can continue to attribute to Egyptian influence the invention of motifs which are inspired by a spirit quite alien to the Byzantine idiom and which are in fact the proud accomplishment of northern inventive genius and in particular of Anglo-Irish artists. *Connections with* *Coptic art*

Relations between the kingdoms of Anglo-Saxon England were chaotic, frontiers changed frequently and larger states absorbed smaller ones. Yet one kingdom after another seems to have enjoyed for a time a position of political and spiritual supremacy: first Kent, then in the seventh century Northumbria, and in the eighth century Mercia. Mercian ascendancy began with Aethelred's victories over Kent, Wessex and Northumbria (675–710), then suffered a brief eclipse under his successors, but was consolidated by Aethelbald (716– ENGLAND *Mercian supremacy*

57) and Offa (758–96). Aethelred's successors were assisted by the work of Theodore of Tarsus, whom Pope Vitalianus had appointed to the see of Canterbury. Theodore assessed correctly the future greatness of Mercia, gave the kingdom his support and founded new dioceses there. Aethelbald inflicted defeats on Northumbria and for a time reduced Wessex to subjection, styling himself 'King of the Mercians and the South Angles'. Offa then consolidated and increased this power with such success that Popes wrote to him as 'king of the English'.

Lack of architectural remains The architecture of this period has left no certain or significant remains in Mercia or Northumberland. To obtain some idea of the artistic attainment in the larger of the British Isles we must turn to the art of manuscript decoration and to the great carved crosses.

Lindisfarne Gospels
PLATES PP. 237,
238, 242 The Gospel-book of Lindisfarne, a monastery in Northumbria, is dated by a tenth-century colophon which refers to Bishop Eadfrith (698–721). The luxurious, almost complete manuscript contains pages of monumental calligraphy on which initials of a size half-way between those of the Durrow Book and those of the Book of Kells are richly decorated with spiral patterns, elaborate dynamic interlace and stylized animals. Other pages, inappropriately called 'carpet pages', are filled by a large cross, which can easily be recognized bearing in mind the many types of lobed and carved crosses on Insular tombstones. The ornamentation of the panels of the cross and of the background is finely detailed, with complex polychrome dynamic and animal interlace. The construction of the zoomorphic pattern is remarkable: the animal shapes are repeated and reversed symmetrically in successive panels following a preliminary tracing (identified on the manuscript by R. Bruce-Mitford FIG. 91 as arcs and grids). The backgrounds are decorated with a scroll pattern composed of claws, tails and necks. The apparent variety does not exclude a fundamental naturalism: the animals are of two species only, cormorants in profile for the birds (n. 559) and dogs if they are quadrupeds (n. 499).

The adherence to nature and the humour with which the animal world is conveyed seem to show Frankish influence, but other artistic forces are present in the miniatures of this wonderful codex. The portraits of the Evangelists are drawn with perspective and foreshortening in spite of the flat colouring, which betrays their Mediterranean and Byzantine derivation: St. John, with the eagle *(imago aquilae)* above him, bears an inscription in Greek (O AGIOS IOHANNES). The source for this presentation must be an unknown archetype—according to Bruce-Mitford, a source common to that of the Copenhagen Evangelistary of *circa* 980.

FIG. 91 – *Page from the Lindisfarne Gospels: scheme of drawing (R. Bruce-Mitford)*

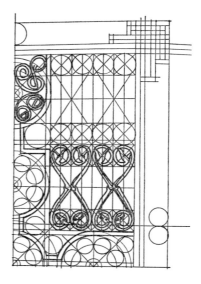

Another manuscript of English origin is the Codex Aureus of the Royal Library, Stockholm, of the late eighth century, which shows still more clearly signs of continental influence. It was written in Canterbury – which had been the see of the Roman bishops – and contains portraits of the Evangelists which clearly follow Mediterranean examples, with figures within arches on marble columns with curtains, and with naturalistic representation of the appropriate symbols. Insular elements, on the other hand, are well in evidence, both in the canon tables and in the Evangelist portraits. There are decorative discs at the imposts of the arches which destroy their architectural function, and the pilasters and archivolts are covered with a rich pattern of interlace and spirals. Carolingian influence alternates with Insular elements and can be seen in the foliage and in the composition of the full-page illustrations.

Codex Aureus
PLATE P. 243

The Lichfield Gospels (*c.* 740) are of unkown provenance and in a fragmentary state, but have ornamental cross-pages which are similar in quality and design to those of the Book of Lindisfarne, but have a more developed form. The Evangelist portraits and their symbols are stylized, as in the oldest Anglo-Irish manuscripts.

Lichfield Gospels

Figural elements featured alongside pure ornament also in Anglo-Saxon carving, and the remaining fragments of the wooden sarcophagus of St. Cuthbert (*ob.* 698) have justly been compared to the sarcophagus in the *hypogeum* at Poitiers for the simple outline figures of angels which both have on the sides, and those of Christ and the Evangelists on the

Sculpture: sarcophagus of St. Cuthbert

241

Lindisfarne Gospels: St. John with Imago aquilae. *Circa* 700. *British Museum. Cf. p. 240.*

Codex Aureus: St. Matthew. Canterbury, *circa* 750. *Royal Library, Stockholm (A 135, fol. 9 v.).*
39.4 × 31.8 cm. Cf. p. 241.

covers. Another characteristic piece is the embossed silver portable altar of St. Cuthbert: this has no figures but a central disc bearing a close dynamic interlace pattern surrounded by the letters of an enigmatic inscription; at the four corners are roughly shaped volutes. These elements are all in accordance with eighth-century Insular taste; so also is a type of 'trumpet pattern' foliage scroll which is found on the piers of some arches in the church of Britford (Wiltshire), reminiscent of Lombard-Byzantine taste, and in a more rudimentary form on the foot of the cross at Bakewell (Derbyshire).

Figured crosses The large Anglo-Saxon figured crosses, on the other hand, lie outside the tradition of continental and Irish sculpture of the eighth century. Their chronology is probably that proposed by Collingwood in 1927, who attributed the oldest to the second quarter of the century, but this attribution must remain hypothetical in the absence of any comparable carvings in Europe either at that time or in the seventh century.

Bewcastle cross The most famous of these crosses are at Bewcastle (Cumberland) and Ruthwell (Dumfriesshire). The Bewcastle cross has a simple arrangement: on the principal face are three sunk panels, like niches, containing St. John the Baptist with the Lamb, Christ blessing and trampling on two beasts, and St. John the Evangelist (or perhaps Columcille) with the eagle. The figured niches recall those of one of the ambo fragments at Ravenna which has already been illustrated; Christ blessing with the scroll of the Law recalls the prophets of S. Apollinare Nuovo, and the Agnus Dei belongs to the iconography of a period that was already remote. On the sides are panels with, alternately, the characteristic motifs of the Anglo-Irish repertory, dynamic interlace and knotwork, and chequer and foliage ornament. The latter consist either of common eighth-century designs (sinuous stems with grape clusters in symmetrical pairs) or of free stylizations of tree and leaf forms. The back has a simple vine scroll inhabited by birds: the stem is reminiscent of the 'trumpet pattern' stylization. The runic inscription on the principal face has been given various interpretations. Those which connected the carving with Alcfrid (654–64) have been shown to be untenable by R. I. Page and F. Henry, who, in agreement with Collingwood, have attributed the cross to a period between 750 and 850. Corroborative evidence for this, as Baldwin Brown suggested, may be afforded by the cross of Acca, bishop of Hexham, who was buried in 740; this has a motif of double tendrils and grape clusters similar to that at Bewcastle.

Ruthwell cross The fragment of Acca's cross has analogies with that at Ruthwell, in the actual form of the cross, which is different at Bewcastle. The Ruthwell cross has a rich iconographic repertory: the figured panels cover two faces and there are episodes from the Theotokos cycle (Annunciation, Visitation, Flight into Egypt, perhaps the Nativity, in a very damaged panel), and with these are scenes from the Gospels, Christ with two beasts, as at Bewcastle, the healing of the blind man, a kneeling Magdalene, the Crucifixion with the sun and moon and the bearers of the lance and sponge, and also the meeting of St. Paul and St. Anthony in the desert, and St. John the Evangelist.

At Moone, as we have said, the figures are disproportionate and seem to be roughly carved sketches, but at Ruthwell they are life-like, in calm, dignified attitudes. Here too one is reminded of the Ravenna ambo fragment which has a figure in a rectangular panel. The same harmony of the Byzantine models is conveyed in the figures of these two famous Anglo-Saxon crosses, but a medieval and European spirit informs them which foreshadows Romanesque monumentality in figure carving. The rinceaux of the lateral faces, with small animals interspersed in a variety of attitudes within the curves and counter-curves of the tendrils, also have more in common with Romanesque and Gothic scrolls than with the calm convolutions of classical art.

The Ruthwell cross is close in date to that at Bewcastle, and indeed their locations are not far distant. The greater iconographic richness and plastic accomplishment of that of Ruthwell are indicated by some as evidence of the stronger creative force to be expected in a prototype, whereas others find it indicative of a later development of the style; it is difficult to decide between these views.

These two examples, together with fragments of other figured crosses from Reculver (Kent), Easby (Yorks), Rothbury (Northumberland), are evidence of the advanced spiritual and artistic standard of Britain in the seventh and eighth centuries, and make it clear that the favoured positions held by Alcuin and other 'Angli' at the court of Charlemagne were well justified by the vigorous spirit of their motherland. On the other hand, Anglo-Saxon art was influenced by Carolingian taste, as shown in the little silver Ormside bowl of *circa* 800, with its delicate reliefs of foliage and birds.

Thus the art of the countries of the north exchanged and developed influences and set an example for the whole of Europe as it entered upon a flourishing period of independent artistic life.

GLOSSARY

abacus: flat top of the capital of a column.

absidiole: small apse.

aedicule: decorative frame of architectural elements, such as pillars or columns supporting a gable or arch.

ambo: pulpit.

ambulatory: the aisles surrounding the central area of a church, which may include a passage behind the altar.

apse: semicircular or polygonal termination to the nave, aisles or presbytery of a church.

architrave: the lowest part of an entablature; by extension, a stone or timber lintel carried on the top of columns or pillars.

archivolt: a moulding or architrave following the line of an arch, door or window.

ashlar: masonry of cut stone, as distinct from rubble or unhewn stone from the quarry.

atrium: forecourt, often surrounded by porticoes.

basilica: hall for assembly, usually rectangular, with two rows of columns, originally for secular purposes, later adapted for Christian churches.

bow fibula: brooch, which in its original form consisted of a piece of wire twisted in the middle to form a spring and at one end to catch the other, pointed, end. In its elaborated form it has a head, which is an elaboration of the spring, and a foot which conceals a catch for the pin, joined by a bow, curved to hold folds of the garment on which it was used, all susceptible of decoration.

caulicole: small volutes representing the acanthus stalks in a Corinthian capital.

champlevé: form of inlay in which cells dug out of metal are filled with enamel, paste or jewels.

Chi-Rho: sacred monogram formed from the Greek letters χ and ρ, the first two letters of Christos, χριστός, used as decoration in early Christian art ('Chrismon').

ciborium: canopied structure over an altar or font or piscina.

clipeus: medallion containing a bust-portrait, derived from the ceremonial shields which bore portraits of heroes.

cloisonné: decorative inlay in cells made by soldering strips of metal or wire to a base, which are then filled with enamel, glass paste or garnets.

conch: a semi-dome surmounting a semicircular niche or apse.

corbel: a projection of stone, brick or timber to support a superimposed weight. A corbel table is a row of corbels often used as a cornice.

cornice: uppermost part of an entablature, or any crowning projection.

crossing: in a cruciform church, the area of intersection of the nave and transepts.

dentils: a moulding resembling a row of teeth, used ornamentally in cornices.

diapering: pattern of small motifs, such as squares or lozenges, repeated continuously over a surface.

dome: concave ceiling or hemispherical roof covering a circular, square or polygonal area.

drum: circular or polygonal upright structure which carries a dome.

dynamic interlace: a complicated interlace with no loose ends or plain loops but with centres of interest to interrupt an effect of textile uniformity.

entablature: in classical architecture, the structure which lies horizontally upon the tops of the columns, consisting of architrave, frieze and cornice.

extrados: upper surface curve of an arch.

hypogeum: any subterranean structure, but particularly applied to tombs.

hypostyle: hall with its roof supported by columns.

iconostasis: screen separating nave from presbytery.

impost: horizontal moulding or capital on top of a pillar, or the upper course of masonry or brickwork, from which an arch springs.

intrados: soffit or under surface of an arch.

lunette: a semicircular or crescent-shaped space in a vaulted or domed ceiling or over a lintel.

martyrium: church containing the relics of a martyr or on the site of a martyrdom.

narthex: vestibule or porch across the entrance to a basilica, either inside or outside the façade.

niello work: inlay of silver sulphide in a design cut in metal.

opus alexandrinum: paving of various coloured marble slabs in conjunction with mosaic.

opus sectile: paving or wall-covering of marble slabs in a variety of shapes, predominantly geometric.

ovolo: convex moulding used in classical architecture, semicircular or oval in section.

pelta: shield-shaped motif.

pendentive: spherical triangle between each pair of supporting arches used in the construction of a dome resting on a square base.

pilaster strip: flat vertical band against the face of a wall, usually built into it but projecting slightly, with shallow arcading at the head of the wall, a decorative rather than a structural feature.

pluteus: closure slab, or carved panel used in various ways to enclose an area within a church; *cf. transenna.*

podium: continuous base or platform.

presbytery: part of a church reserved for the clergy, usually the eastern part of the chancel, or the chancel itself.

propylaeum: structure erected in front of an entrance gateway.

pulvin (= dosseret): a block of stone, usually carved, placed on top of the capital of columns in an arcade in Byzantine architecture to support the arch.

rinceau: decorative scroll-like pattern predominantly of stems and foliage.

scallop niche: niche whose semi-dome has the form of a scallop shell.

soffit: ceiling or underside of any architectural member.

solea: raised passage from presbytery to ambo.

stele: upright block of stone or marble carved in low relief, usually employed as a tombstone.

synthronos: bench or benches for clergy in an apse or presbytery, sometimes stepped.

transenna: open-work screen or lattice, generally of marble, cf. *pluteus.*

tribune: semicircular or polygonal apse of a basilican church.

trichora: small church consisting of three semicircular apses.

triclinium: room in which Romans ate, normally having couches on three of its four sides.

tympanum: triangular space between the horizontal and sloping cornices of a pediment, or between a lintel and the top of an arch.

volute: scroll or spiral ending, a distinctive feature of an Ionic capital.

westwork: elaborate west front typical of Carolingian churches, usually containing a raised chapel between two raised towers.

CAPTIONS TO APPENDIX OF PLATES

1 – Baptistery, Poitiers: interior. 8th century. Archives Photographiques, Caisse Nationale des Monuments Historiques, Paris. *Cf. p. 209.*

2 – S. Salvatore, Spoleto: interior. 6th-7th century. Gabinetto Fotografico Nazionale, Rome. *Cf. pp. 123 f.*

3 – St. Laurent, Grenoble: interior. 8th century. Archives Photographiques, Caisse Nationale des Monuments Historiques, Paris. *Cf. p. 207.*

4 – Tomb of Mellobaudès, Poitiers. 8th century. Archives Photographiques, Caisse Nationale des Monuments Historiques, Paris. *Cf. pp. 138 f.*

5 – S. Salvatore, Brescia: stucco decoration of arch soffits. 8th century. Photo: A. Luisa, Brescia. *Cf. p. 191.*

6 – S. Sabina, Rome. 5th century. Photo: Anderson, Rome. *Cf. p. 22.*

7 – S. Agnese fuori le mura, Rome. 7th century. Photo: Anderson, Rome. *Cf. p. 116.*

8 – S. Lorenzo fuori le mura, Rome. 7th century. Photo: Anderson, Rome. *Cf. p. 116.*

9 – S. Sophia, Benevento. 8th century. Sopraintendenza dei Monumenti, Naples. *Cf. p. 194.*

10 – 'Basse-Oeuvre', Beauvais. 5th century. Photo: P. Verzone. *Cf. p. 43.*

11 – S. Giovanni Evangelista, Ravenna. 5th century. Photo: Anderson, Rome. *Cf. p. 19.*

12 – Baptistery, Poitiers. 8th century. Archives Photographiques, Caisse Nationale des Monuments Historiques, Paris. *Cf. p. 209.*

13 – Sarcophagus of Bishop John. 7th century. Photo: Istituto d'Arte Ravennate e Bizantine. *Cf. p. 182.*

14, 15 – Fragments of an ambo, Ravenna. 8th century. Museo Nazionale, Ravenna. *Cf. p. 122.*

16 – Cenotaph, St. Dizier. 7th century. Photo: J. Hubert. *Cf. p. 142.*

17 – Sarcophagus of St. Angilberta, Jouarre. 7th century. Photo: De Bernardi. *Cf. p. 140.*

18 – Sarcophagus, St. Dizier. 7th century. Photo: J. Hubert. *Cf. p. 142.*

19 – Fragment of an altar, 5th or 6th century, found in church of St. Germain, Geneva. Musée d'Art et d'Histoire, Geneva. *Cf. p. 104.*

20 – Sarcophagus of St. Theodechild, crypt of St. Paul, Jouarre. 7th century. Photo: De Bernardi. *Cf. pp. 137, 140.*

21 – Reconstruction of the altar of St. Germain, Geneva. Stucco. Musée d'Art et d'Histoire, Geneva. *Cf. p. 104.*

5

6

7

8

9

10

12

+HIC TVMV
LVS CLA SVM
SERVAT COR
PVS ·DN̄

IOHANNIS
SC̄ISSIMI
ACTERBE
ATISSARCHIEP

13

14 15 16

17

18

19

20

21

CHRONOLOGICAL TABLE

ITALY	GAUL AND RHENISH PROVINCES	SPAIN	BRITISH ISLES
425–57 Byzantine hegemony under energetic rule of Theodosian dynasty	425–60 Rhine *limes* gradually given up under pressure from Germanic invaders	425–70 Spain devastated by campaigns; living conditions rendered difficult	425–60 Ireland partially christianized; England gradually evacuated by Romans
458–76 Decline of Western Empire under weak Byzantine rule	460–520 Gaul gradually occupied by Germanic peoples and old-established upper class loses power	470 First Visigothic invasion of Spain	460–520 Final withdrawal of Romans from England; landing of Teutonic tribes
476–88 Military rule by Odoacer, a tolerant Arian			
488–526 Theodoric in Italy: Arian Goths erect churches in Ravenna and other important towns; Catholics hindered from building churches	520–600 Strengthening of Merovingian power and of episcopal influence in numerous abandoned towns	507 Visigoths abandon Septimania and move to Spain in large numbers	520–600 St. Columba founds various monasteries in Ireland and Iona (563). St. Columbanus goes to the continent, where he founds other important monasteries (Jouarre, St. Gall, Bobbio); dies 615. Influx of Germanic peoples continues, esp. in southern England
526–35 Amalasuntha favours Byzantines and Catholics; propaganda by Byzantine churchmen			
535–54 War and occupation of country by Byzantines		550 Byzantines occupy southern Spain	
554–68 Byzantines consolidate political power and cultural influence			
568–700 Lombard invasion; Byzantine navy defends some ports and towns on lagoons, also Rome, and their environs; these towns become 'Byzantine islands'	600–700 Various cultural centres in northern Gaul and Aquitaine	600–714 Muslims inundate Spain (714); Christians flee to north of Iberian peninsula	600–700 Mission of St. Augustine in Kent (597); population of England and Scotland converted to Christianity. A still 'primitive' culture survives in Ireland. In kingdom of Northumbria (from 626), cultural and artistic efflorescence (to 8th cent.)

CHRONOLOGICAL TABLE

ITALY	GAUL AND RHENISH PROVINCES	SPAIN	BRITISH ISLES
700–800 Partly owing to conflicts engendered by Iconoclasm, the Popes gradually break off relations with Emperors of the Eastern Empire and align themselves with the Franks. Lombards succeed in occupying Ravenna (751) but are driven out by Charlemagne (774) 800 Coronation of Charlemagne in Rome; birth of Carolingian Empire, the new centre of political power and culture in Europe	700–800 Carolingians acquire power, overthrow Merovingian dynasty (751) and then unify the state; Charles Martel crowned king (754). Europe begins to develop along independent lines, with interior routes of communication displacing Mediterranean ports. By end of 8th cent. political and economic life are established on new basis		700–800 Political and economic conditions in Ireland remain primitive. England in period of efflorescence, esp. in Northumbria and Mercia

BIBLIOGRAPHY

ARCHITECTURE

Brusin, G. and Zovatto, P. L.: Monumenti paleocristiani di Aquileia e di Grado. Udine, 1957.

Clapham, A. W.: English Romanesque Architecture before the Conquest. Oxford, 1930.

De Angelis d'Ossat, G.: Studi ravennati: problemi di architettura paleocristiana. Ravenna, 1962.

Egger, R.: Frühchristliche Kirchenbauten im südlichen Norikum. Vienna, 1916.

Fisher, E. A.: The Greater Anglo-Saxon Churches. London, 1962.

Krautheimer, R.: Corpus Basilicarum Christianarum Romae, vol. i, nos. 1–4, The Early Christian Basilicas of Rome (ivth-ixth Cent.). Vatican City, 1937–.

Krautheimer, R. with Frankl, W. and Corbett, S.: Corpus Basilicarum Christianarum Romae, vol. ii, nos. 1–2, The Early Christian Basilicas of Rome (ivth–ixth Cent.). Vatican City, 1959–.

Krautheimer, R.: Early Christian and Byzantine Architecture. Harmondsworth, 1965.

Lehmann, E.: Der frühe deutsche Kirchenbau: die Entwicklung seiner Raumordnung bis 1080. Berlin, 1950.

Oswald, F., Schaefer, L. and Sennhauser, H. R.: Vorromanischer Kirchenbau, vol. i. Munich, 1966.

Taylor, H. M. and J.: Anglo-Saxon Architecture. Cambridge, 1965.

Verzone, P.: L'architettura religiosa dell'alto medio evo nell'Italia settentrionale. Milan, 1942.

PAINTING, MOSAIC, ICONOGRAPHY

Bovini, G.: Mosaici di Ravenna. Milan, 1956. Ravenna Mosaics. Translated by G. Scaglia. Greenwich, Conn., 1956.

Grabar, A.: Martyrium: recherches sur le culte des reliques et l'art chrétien antique. 2 vols. (Paris), 1946.

Heitz, C.: Recherches sur les rapports entre architecture et liturgie à l'époque carolingienne. Paris, 1963.

Morey, C. R.: Early Christian Art. Princeton, 1953.

Ricci, C.: Tavole storiche dei mosaici di Ravenna. 4 vols. Rome, 1930–7.

Wilpert, J.: Die römischen Mosaiken und Malereien der kirchlichen Bauten vom 4.–13. Jahrhundert. 4 vols. Freiburg, 1916–.

ILLUMINATION

Grabar, A. and Nordenfalk, C.: Le haut moyen âge du 4e au 11e siècle. Geneva, 1957. Early Medieval Painting from the 4th to the 11th Centuries. Translated by S. Gilbert. Lausanne, 1957.

Micheli, L. G.: L'enluminure du haut moyen âge et les influences irlandaises. Brussels, 1939.

Zimmerman, E. H. (ed.): Vorkarolingische Miniaturen. Berlin, 1916.

METALWORK AND GERMANIC ART

Allen, J. Romilly: Celtic Art in Pagan and Christian Times. London, 1904.

Bain, G.: Celtic Art. Glasgow, 1944.

Baum, J.: La sculpture figurale en Europe à l'époque mérovingienne. Paris, 1937.

Fuchs, S.: Die langobardischen Goldblattkreuze aus der Zone südwärts der Alpen. Berlin, 1938.

Fuchs, S. and Werner, J.: Die langobardischen Fibeln aus Italien. Berlin, 1950.

Jessup, R.: Anglo-Saxon Jewellery. London, 1950.

Salin, B.: Die altgermanische Tierornamentik. Stockholm, 1904. New ed. Stockholm, 1935.

Van Scheltema, F. A.: Die altnordische Kunst: Grundprobleme vorhistorischer Kunstentwicklung. Berlin, 1923.

Werner, J.: Münzdatierte austrasische Grabfunde. Berlin–Leipzig, 1939.

Zeiss, H.: Die Grabfunde aus dem spanischen Westgothenreich. Berlin–Leipzig, 1934.

HISTORICAL AND GENERAL WORKS

Åberg, N.: Corsi di cultura sull'arte ravennate bizantina. Ravenna, 1955–.

Åberg, N.: The Occident and the Orient in the Art of the Seventh Century. 3 vols. Stockholm, 1943–7.

Atti dei congressi internazionali sull'alto medioevo. 1948–.

Cabrol, F. and Leclercq, H.: Dictionnaire d'archéologie chrétienne et de liturgie. 15 vols. Paris, 1903–53.

Cahiers archéologiques. Fin de l'antiquité et moyen âge. Paris, 1945–.

Congressi internazionali di archeologia cristiana. Rome, 1900–.

Elbern, V. H. (ed.): Das erste Jahrtausend. 3 vols. Düsseldorf, 1962.

Enciclopedia universale dell'arte Venice – Rome, 1958–.

Gerke, F.: Spätantike und frühes Christentum. Baden-Baden, 1967.

Germania. Berlin, 1917–.

Guyer, S.: Grundlagen mittelalterlicher abendländischer Baukunst. Beiträge zu der vom antiken Tempel zur kreuzförmigen Basilika des abendländischen Mittelalters führenden Entwicklung. Einsiedeln, 1950.

Hodgkin, T.: Italy and her Invaders. 2nd ed. Oxford, 1931.

Pirenne, H.: Mahomet et Charlemagne. 1st ed. Brussels, 1935. Mahommed and Charlemagne. Translated by B. Miall from the French of the 10th Edition. London, 1939.

Rivista di archeologia cristiana. Rome, 1924–.

Smith, E. B.: The Dome: a Study in the History of Ideas. Princeton, 1950.

Van der Meer, F.: Atlas de l'antiquité chrétienne. Paris – Brussels, 1960.

ITALY

Åberg, N.: Die Goten und Langobarden in Italien. Uppsala, 1923.

Haseloff, A.: La scultura preromanica in Italia. Munich – Bologna, 1930. Pre-Romanesque Sculpture in Italy. Translated by R. Boothroyd. Florence – Paris, 1930.

Schaffran, E.: Die Kunst der Langobarden in Italien. Jena, 1941.

Verzone, P.: L'arte preromanica in Liguria ed i rilievi decorativi dei secoli barbari. Turin, 1945.

GAUL, SWITZERLAND AND THE RHINELAND

Åberg, N.: Die Franken und Westgoten in der Völkerwanderungszeit. Uppsala, 1922.

Garntner, J.: Histoire de l'art en Suisse. Neuchâtel, 1941.

Hubert, J.: L'art pré-roman. Paris, 1938.

Hubert, J.: Les origines de l'art français. Paris, 1947.

Mâle, E.: La fin du paganisme en Gaule et les plus anciennes basiliques chrétiennes. Paris, 1950.

SPAIN

Ars Hispaniae, vol. 2. Madrid, 1947.

Menéndez Pidal, R. (ed.): Historia de España, vol. 3. Madrid, 1940.

Puig y Cadafalch, J.: L'art visigothique et ses survivances. Paris, 1961.

BRITISH ISLES

Åberg, N.: The Anglo-Saxons in England during the Early Centuries after the Invasion. Translated by J. Charleston. Uppsala, 1926.

Brown, G. Baldwin: The Arts in Early England. 2nd ed. London, 1925–.

De Paor, M. and L.: Early Christian Ireland. London, 1958.

Henry, F.: Irish Art in the Early Christian Period (to 800 A.D.). Completely revised ed. London, 1965.

Kendrick, T. D.: Anglo-Saxon Art to A.D. 900 ... London, 1938.

Nash-Williams, V. E.: The Early Christian Monuments of Wales. Cardiff, 1950.

Porter, A. Kingsley: The Crosses and Culture of Ireland. New Haven, 1931.

INDEX

The numerals in italics refer to the plates and figures. The letter (G) indicates the Glossary.

103, 109, 182, 194, 215; Marian iconography
39, 103; cf. cult

mask	69
Massacre of the Innocents	61
matroneus	75, 116
Matthiae, G.	22
Maurice, Emperor	107

mausoleum 26, *57*, 58f., 65, 110, 140, 211; cf.
Ravenna

Maximian	75, 78, 84, 91, 97, 117
Mayen	18
Mayo	236
Mazulevitch, L.	95
Meaux	215

medallions 23, 184; cf. *clipeus*

Medina Sidonia	72
Melchizedek	118

Mellobaudès: cf. Poitiers

Melrose	168
Mendrisio: S. Martino	*213*, 214
Mengen	104

Merced, La: cf. Barcelona

Mercia	163, 239f.

Merovingian: architecture 103; art 113;
Franks 145; history 101f., 136, 171, 205;
manuscripts 145f., 157, 221; sculpture
140f., 248, *255*

metalwork 68f., 71, 104ff., 122f., 130f,. 146,
155, 163, 222, 230, 239

Meteora	230

Metz 140, 205; St. Pierre 44, *45*, 142

Michael	88, 103, 110, 177, 193

Milan 19ff., 31, 37, 39, 53, 61, 73, 75, 107, 198;
Cathedral 85, 177, 213; Cathedral Treasury
61, 70; Palatium 26; S. Ambrogio 65, 71, 104,
133; chapel of S. Vittore 65, 104; S. Lorenzo
23f., *24–5*, 26, 34, 36, 39, 65; chapel of S.
Aquilino 26, 34, 36, 39; of S. Ippolito 26;
of S. Sisto 26; S. Maria d'Aurona *189*, *190*,
198; S. Nazaro 36; S. Simpliciano 36

Mimbar	201
Mirabella-Roberti, M.	80

miracle 56; cf. Cana

missionary	136, 155f., 219
Mitraschim	217
Mittelzell	*213*, 214
Modena: Cathedral	198
Moissac	*143*, 144

monastery 61, 128, 135ff., 145, 156, 181, 190,
198, 211ff., *212*, *214*, 215, 226, 228ff., *229*,
233

Monceau	70
monk	61, 63, 155f., 229
Monkwearmouth: St. Peter	165
Monothelites	122

Monza: ampullae *110*, 110, 121, *132*, 134;
Cathedral 111, 130; Cathedral Treasury
130ff., *131–4*, 133f.; cross of Agilulf 131,
132; crown *133*, 134; diptych 68; flask 178;
hen statue 132, *134*; Theudelinda Gospel
130, *131*, 132, 154

Moone, cross at	236, 245
Moors	205
Moracchini, Mme.	68
Morey, C. R.	29
mortar	43

mosaic 13f., 20f., 39, 53, 62f., 68, 77, 82, 86,
90, 95, 116, 120, 137, 177f., 182, 184, 201;
apse 19, 40, *41*, 87f., 92, 114, 118, *119*, *121*,
121; dome *30*, 53f.; floor 29, 32, 35, 37, 45,
60, 66, 80, 103, 114f., 144, 159, 197; gable
78; inscription 22f., 34, 52, 66, 117; narthex
26, 117; nave 54, *55*, 67, 92f.; revetment 23,
40; triumphal arch 116, 118; vault 101, 192

Moselle	221
Moses	91
mosque	122
mother-of-pearl	78, 132

motifs: anthropomorphic 234; arabesque
191, 217, 234; checker 159, 202, 244; circle
60, 66, 70, 78, 100, 115, 131, 149, 151, 191,
198, 211; 'cornucopia' 144; disc 78, 130,
139, 211, 244; dot 142, 157, 221; 'dynamic
interlace' (G), 112, *113*, 135, 142, 159, 198,
201, 219, 221, 224, 239ff., 244; floral 121,
139, 146, 168, 198; heart-shaped 139, 142,
151, 154, 198, 201, 217; interlace 142, 146f.,
163, 165, 170, 198, 201, 213, 219, 221f., 224,
229, 233; key 215, 236, 239; knotwork 142,
219, 221, 244; lace-like 136; leaf 139f., 142,
154, 191, 193, 197f., 201, 212, 217, 221, 244;
lotus flower 142; lozenge 66, 77f., 115, 120,
129f., 137, 140, 151, 157, 186; palmette 124,
142, 151, 154; plant 226; rectangle 66;
ribbon 122, 142, 147, 149, 198; rinceau (G),
21, 27, 32, 39, 80, 101, 120, 124, 127, 135,
140, 142, 144, 191, 198, 201, 207f., 245;
rosette 67, 77, 106, 117, 186, 191, 193, 198,
201, 207, 209, 219, 222; S-shaped 193, 197f.,
201; scallop shell 26, 58, 117, 140; scroll 63,
80, 84f., 104, 144, 154, 197f., 201, 217, 221,
240, 244; spiral 70, 157, 159, 191, 193, 198,
221, 233f., 236, 239f.; triangle 69f.; zigzag
117, 130, 135, 142, 154; zoomorphic 111,
135, 139, 145ff., 163, 215, 219, 224, 228,
234, 236, 238

Mulling, Book of	234
Mungersdorf	18
Munich	178

Münster 96; St. Johann 202, 214

271

273